Praise for

Workshops for Siblings of Children with Special Needs
REVISED EDITION

"Don Meyer has been the leading voice in our profession in recognizing the special needs of brothers and sisters who have siblings with disabilities. His work with siblings has received international acclaim as being straightforward, fun, and effective with siblings of all ages. For the past two decades, *Sibshops* has been used extensively as the premier guide for professionals designing and implementing interactive workshops to help siblings confront the special issues they face. Now he and Dr. Pat Vadasy have revised this fundamental text to include new activities aimed at a new generation of brothers and sisters. This new edition is a must for professionals who aim to assist the whole family as they deal with the complexity of disability.

Anything that Don Meyer does is done with style and unique insight. This new edition will be a tremendous resource for the profession."

Thomas H. Powell, Ed.D.
President
Mount St. Mary's University

"A most valuable book! Parents, prepare to gain insights that will help you forever. Facilitators, learn not just the hows of running Sibshops, but also the whys. And typical sibs, get ready for the camaraderie you've always craved but never thought you'd find."

Rachel Simon
Author, *Riding the Bus with My Sister*

"This book convinced us of one thing: Every agency working with families with disability should be running Sibshops. Are they hard to run? Not if you've got a copy of *Sibshops*. Don Meyer and Patricia Vadasy have been there and back—and they've worked out the logistics and invented terrific programming that you can tailor to fit your audience. Run a Sibshop. Make a difference."

Paul and Judy Karasik
Authors, *The Ride Together: A Brother and Sister's Memoir of Autism in the Family*

"I use *Sibshops* constantly. It is *the* resource for sibling support. It is a professional resource with reliability, and I refer to it for every workshop."

Christina Rogers, B.S.W
Strong Families Manager
Riley Hospital for Children
Indiana University School of Medicine

"Essential reading for anyone thinking of starting a Sibshop for the brothers and sisters of children with special needs . . . The authors have not left out anything that would be useful in starting one of these highly effective play and discussion groups. Written in a lively, informal, easy-to-understand way, this book is excellent."

Mary McHugh
Author, *Special Siblings: Growing up with Someone with a Disability*

"I gratefully acknowledge and thank Don Meyer for identifying the importance of meeting the needs of some very significant family members. I have thoroughly enjoyed my time as one of the facilitators of our sibling support group and eagerly anticipate the next evening that will be spent with this great group of children."

Jane Wysman, B.A.
Respite Supports Manager
Sibshops Facilitator

"Despite the fact that I will be advocating for my adult son until the day I die, I am increasingly aware that he and his sisters will most likely have the longest family relationship. They deserve to have their needs met for their own sakes, as well as for the sake of family relationships over time. One of the greatest gifts I can give my son is to raise his sisters in a way that they will feel unconditional love for him. I highly recommend this book as a valued resource to enhance sibling quality of life and overall family quality of life—now and for the future."

Ann Turnbull, Ed.D.
Codirector, Beach Center on Disability
Ross and Marianna Beach Distinguished Professor
The University of Kansas

"Sibshops are an innovative strategy for supporting families that has stood the test of time. This newly revised volume provides clear, practical guidelines for implementing Sibshops in a way that is likely to meet the needs of siblings of children with disabilities and their families."

Ann P. Kaiser, Ph.D.
Susan W. Gray Professor of Education and Human Development
Department of Special Education
Vanderbilt University

Sibshops

Workshops for
Siblings of Children
with Special Needs

REVISED EDITION

by

Don Meyer, M.Ed.
Director
Sibling Support Project
Seattle

and

Patricia Vadasy, Ph.D.
Senior Researcher
Washington Research Institute
Seattle

·P·A·U·L·H·
BROOKES
PUBLISHING CO.®

Baltimore • London • Sydney

Paul H. Brookes Publishing Co.
Post Office Box 10624
Baltimore, Maryland 21285-0624
USA

www.brookespublishing.com

Typeset by Maryland Composition, Inc., Laurel, Maryland.
Manufactured in the United States of America by Versa Press, Inc., East Peoria, Illinois.

Preparation of this book was supported, in part, by Project #MCJ-535077-01-0 from the Maternal and Child Health Program (Title V, Social Security Act), Health Resources and Services Administration, U.S. Department of Health and Human Services.

The illustrations appearing on the cover and inside this book are the original work of Cary Pillo Lassen.

The vignettes and personal stories appearing in this book are drawn from published sources, personal communications with the authors, or statements posted by SibNet participants. Full names have not been used to protect confidentiality.

Library of Congress Cataloging-in-Publication Data

Meyer, Donald J. (Donald Joseph), 1951–
    Sibshops : workshops for siblings of children with special needs / by Don Meyer and Patricia Vadasy.—Rev. ed.
        p.   cm.
    Includes bibliographical references and index.
    ISBN 978-1-55766-783-0 (alk. paper)
    1. Children with disabilities—Family relationships. 2. Children with disabilities—Home care. 3. Brothers and sisters. I. Vadasy, Patricia F. II. Title. III. Title: Workshops for siblings of children with special needs.

    HV888.M495 2008
    362.4'043083—dc22   2007042037

British Library Cataloguing in Publication data are available from the British Library.

Contents

*Denotes a new activity or game

About the Authors

Don Meyer, M.Ed., Director, Sibling Support Project, 6512 23rd Avenue NW, Seattle, Washington 98117

Don Meyer is the director of the Sibling Support Project, a Seattle-based national project dedicated to the lifelong concerns of brothers and sisters of people with special health, developmental, and mental health concerns. A sought-after speaker, Don has conducted workshops on sibling issues and trainings on the Sibshop model in all 50 states and in seven countries. He is the editor of *The Sibling Slam Book: What It's Really Like to Have a Brother or Sister with Special Needs* (Woodbine House, 2005), *Views from Our Shoes: Growing Up with a Brother or Sister with Special Needs* (Woodbine House, 1997), and *Uncommon Fathers: Reflections on Raising a Child with a Disability* (Woodbine House, 1995). With Patricia Vadasy, Mr. Meyer wrote *Living with a Brother or Sister with Special Needs* (University of Washington Press, 1996). His work has been featured on ABC News and National Public Radio and in *Newsweek, The New York Times*, and *The Washington Post*. Don is married to Terry DeLeonardis, a special education preschool teacher and consultant. They have four children.

Patricia Vadasy, Ph.D., Senior Researcher, Washington Research Institute, 150 Nickerson Street, Seattle, Washington 98109

Patricia Vadasy is currently senior researcher at Washington Research Institute in Seattle, where she conducts research on early reading instruction. She is most interested in research that may help children at risk for reading disabilities and children who are English language learners. Patricia and her colleagues have developed programs that paraeducator tutors can effectively use to supplement reading instruction for beginning readers.

Foreword

Over the past 40 years, professionals have been trying to describe the sibling experience. The literature has portrayed brothers and sisters of people with disabilities as everything from emotional misfits to healthy, happy, well-adjusted individuals. Studies have examined the various nuances of the sibling experience, attempting to characterize the relationship from the perspective of birth order, sex, family size, severity of disability, and responsibility for the sibling. People have been working hard to tell us whether having a sibling with a disability is a "good" or a "bad" thing.

Not Don Meyer. Don recognized the unique concerns and strengths of siblings and decided to do something to support them. Siblings benefit, he says, from getting to know other siblings, taking in some information, being able to ask questions, and sharing the experience—good, bad, or indifferent. Don is a pioneer in the sibling movement; he has been at its forefront for more than 25 years. Although this book represents the revised edition of *Sibshops*, this model will likely continue to flourish for years to come. That's because we really have just begun to realize all that siblings need and have to contribute.

Sibshops offers a model intervention for sibling support, learning, and fun. The book is prescriptive yet leaves plenty of room for leader and member creativity. The Sibshops model recognizes and reinforces a strengths-based approach. It also promotes relationship building between sibs through a variety of games and activities. Sibshops are all about giving siblings some lifelong tools—not about identifying pathology or suggesting that siblings might be maladjusted because of their family experiences. The *Sibshops* book is also committed to offering a wide array of resources and references for parents, professionals, and sibs themselves. If parents can have support, information, and advocacy networks, then why can't their children?

For more than 20 years, my graduate students at The Ohio State University have been running sibling support groups, a somewhat modified version of Sibshops. I always provide them with a copy of *Sibshops*, but I explain that I just want them to use the book as a resource and guide, since our groups only last 8 weeks and we cannot strictly follow the Sibshops format. Nonetheless, I always spot my students with their copy of *Sibshops* in hand, exclaiming what a wonderful tool it has been both for them and the families with whom they work. Every time I threaten to take the book away from them because they might be relying on it too much, they become petrified. Sibshops activities are so well-structured that student facilitators may readily implement them in support groups. My students absolutely love their experience leading sibling groups, and thanks to Don and Pat, they have a guide that helps them to help the sibs in their groups.

Just like chicken soup, Sibshops are good for the soul. They enrich the lives of group leaders, sibling members, and families as a whole. They heighten public awareness that sibs matter and should not be an afterthought when it comes to supporting families of people with disabilities.

Tom Fish, Ph.D.
Director, Social Work and Family Support Services
The Ohio State University Nisonger Center

Preface

The fact that you are holding this book suggests that you already have an interest in the well-being of brothers and sisters of children with special health, mental health, and developmental needs. Perhaps you are a parent of a child with special needs who wants to create peer support and educational programs for brothers and sisters in your community. Or, maybe you are an adult sib who wishes that there had been programs like Sibshops when you were younger and would like to share your experiences as a Sibshop facilitator. Or, perhaps you are a human services professional who realizes that there is much more to serving families of children with special needs than just meeting with children's parents. Regardless, this book is for you.

It is our hope that this book will be somewhat different from other books you have read. Here are our goals for *Sibshops*:

1. *To increase the number of programs, services, and considerations for brothers and sisters of individuals with special health, mental health, and developmental needs.* With this book, we hope to give you the rationale, tools, inspiration, permission, and encouragement to make community-based programs for siblings as available as Parent-to-Parent programs are for parents of children with special needs. As important as these programs are, however, they are not enough. We hope to provide you with information that will allow you to challenge current practices to ensure that siblings' issues are addressed. We seek fundamental change in the way schools, clinics, agencies, and organizations "do business" with respect to brothers and sisters. As a friend puts it, we hope to subvert the dominant paradigm!

2. *To increase the reader's understanding of specific issues experienced by brothers and sisters of individuals with special needs.* To be an effective Sibshop facilitator, you will need to be conversant about sibs' lifelong and ever-changing issues. The first part of the book provides an overview of the unusual concerns and opportunities experienced by siblings as reported in the clinical and research literature and by siblings themselves.

3. *To provide specific information for local agencies and parent groups to create programs for siblings of individuals with special needs.* The second part of this book is devoted to the Sibshop model, a lively peer support, educational, and recreational program for school-age brothers and sisters. In this section, we present activities that can be adapted for different disabilities and illnesses as well as for different ages.

Throughout, we have tried to write this book in a style that is accessible and even enjoyable to read. We know that most people who wish to create services and programs for brothers and sisters are not academicians. We also know that most readers, even academicians, seem to enjoy and learn more from books that don't appear to be designed to induce sleep. And we know that there is much good news to share about siblings of people with special needs. Our intent is to present the information that follows with the grace, vitality, and insight we frequently see in brothers and sisters of people with special needs.

We hope you will let us know if we have accomplished our goals.

Acknowledgments

We are fortunate to have many friends who share our commitment to providing services for brothers and sisters of people with special needs. Many of the people listed below have pioneered programs for siblings in their communities; others have provided us with support, advice, and encouragement over the years and as we prepared this volume. Although their contributions are varied, each shares the belief that brothers and sisters deserve our time, effort, and consideration. We are grateful to them all: Sandy Ardnt, Yasuko Arima, Marianne Barnes, Addison Beck, Patty Belmonte, Tamara Besser, Hanna Bjornsdottir, Gail Cervarich, Sherry Charlot, Raphielle (Raye) Chynoweth, Ann Cirimele, Terry DeLeonardis, Rosanne Feder, Tom Fish, Margaret Fox-Hawthorne, Stephanie Gantt, Carolyn Graff, Anne Guthrie, Nora Fox Handler, Cathy Harrison, Kris Higginson, Amanda Johnson, Judy Karasik, Tara Kosieniak, Toni LaMonica, Stacy Levin, Victoria Liska, Mary Marin, Doug McJannet, Nancy Micca, Nanci Morris, Charley Moskowitz, Catherine O'Connor, Michelle O'Connor-Teklinski, Debbie Parkman, Kameron Partridge, Tina Prochaska, Kristine Rasmussen, Harriet Redman, Carol Robbins, Margaret Roberts, Marguerite Roberts, Christina Rogers, Suzanne Salmo, Andrea Sanchez, Susan Sandall, Barbara Sapharas, Greg Schell, Robin Sowl, Erin Spaulding, Jo Ann Spencer, Lenore Stern, Sheila Swann-Guerrero, Kiko Van Zandt, Pat Walsh, Jennifer Weisman, and Maryjane Westra.

We would also like to thank Mimi Siegel and the staff of the Kindering Center, the Sibling Support Project's parent organization. Having offered Sibshops and programs for fathers of children with special needs for more than 20 years, the staff of the Kindering Center have been pioneers in providing family-centered services that acknowledge the contributions of *all* family members.

Finally, a special acknowledgement is reserved for the George A. and Marion M. Wilson Foundation. Without the Wilson family's commitment to our work, you would not be holding this book and there would be far, far fewer Sibshops worldwide.

Sibshop facilitators are amazing people. They invariably offer Sibshops in addition to a million other things they are supposed to be doing for their "day jobs." They somehow find time in their busy schedules and give up weekends and evenings because they care deeply about young brothers and sisters and their concerns. It is with gratitude that we dedicate this book to them.

Chapter 1

What Are Sibshops?

For the adults who plan them and the agencies that sponsor them, Sibshops[SM] are best described as opportunities for brothers and sisters of children with special health, mental health, and developmental needs to obtain peer support and education within a recreational context. They can reflect an agency's commitment to the well-being of the family member most likely to have the longest-lasting relationship with the person who has special needs.

However, for the young people who attend them and the energetic people who run them, Sibshops are best described as *events*. Sibshops are lively, pedal-to-the-metal celebrations of the many contributions made by brothers and sisters of kids with special needs. Sibshops acknowledge that being the brother or sister of a person with special needs is for some a good thing, for others a not-so-good thing, and for many something in between. They reflect a belief that brothers and sisters have much to offer one another—if they are given a chance. The Sibshop[SM] model intersperses information and discussion activities with new games (designed to be unique, offbeat, and appealing to a wide ability range), cooking and craft activities, and special guests who may teach participants mime, how to juggle, or, in the case of one guest artist who has cerebral palsy, how to paint by holding a toothbrush in your mouth. Sibshops are as fun and rewarding for the people who host them as they are for the participants.

Sibshops seek to provide siblings with opportunities for peer support. Because Sibshops are designed for school-age children, peer support is provided within a lively, recreational context that emphasizes a kids'-eye view.

Sibshops are *not* therapy, group or otherwise, although their effect may be therapeutic for some children. Sibshops acknowledge that most brothers and sisters of people with special needs, like their parents, are doing well, despite the challenges posed by a family member's illness or disability. Consequently, although Sibshop facilitators always keep an eye open for participants who may need additional services, the Sibshop model takes a wellness approach.

The goals of the model that guide Sibshop activities are discussed below.

WHO ATTENDS SIBSHOPS?

Originally developed for 8- to 13-year-old siblings of children with developmental disabilities, the Sibshop model is easily adapted for slightly younger sibs and teens. It has been adapted for brothers and sisters of children with other special needs, including cancer and other health impairments, hearing loss, and mental health concerns. It has even been adapted for children of parents who have special health, mental health, or developmental concerns. Children who attend Sibshops come from diverse backgrounds including suburban communities (e.g., Bellevue, Washington; Northbrook, Illinois), urban communities (e.g., New York City, St. Louis), rural areas (e.g., Wyoming, Wisconsin), and areas with unique cultural heritages (e.g., Alaska, Hawaii, South Central Los Angeles).

WHO SPONSORS SIBSHOPS?

Any agency serving families of children with special needs can sponsor a Sibshop, provided it can offer financial support, properly staff the program, and attract sufficient numbers of participants. We strongly recommend, however, that agencies consider working together to cosponsor a local Sibshop for all the brothers and sisters in a given community. (This important topic is further discussed in Chapter 5.) Among the agencies collaborating to host Sibshops in their communities are autism societies, chapters of The Arc, United Cerebral Palsy affiliates, children's hospitals, developmental disabilities councils, early intervention programs, Parent-to-Parent programs, parks and recreation programs, Ronald McDonald Houses, school districts, schools for the deaf, and University Centers on Disabilities. We have found that Sibshops are well within the reach and abilities of most communities. They are not expensive to run and logistically are no more difficult to coordinate than other community-based programs for children such as Scouts or Camp Fire USA.

WHO RUNS SIBSHOPS?

We believe that Sibshops are best facilitated by a team that includes service providers (e.g., social workers; special education teachers; physical, occupational, and speech therapists; nurses; child life specialists) and adult siblings of people with special needs. At the very least, the team of facilitators will need to be knowledgeable about the disability or illness represented, possess a sense of humor and play, enjoy the company of children, and respect the young participants' expertise on the topic of life with a brother or sister with special needs. Qualifications for Sibshop facilitators are further discussed in Chapter 5.

WHAT IS THE OPTIMAL NUMBER OF PARTICIPANTS FOR A SIBSHOP?

Sibshops have been held for as few as 5 children and as many as 45. About a dozen children, with at least two facilitators, is a comfortable number.

WHEN ARE SIBSHOPS OFFERED?

Sibshops are often held on Saturdays from 10:00 A.M. until 1:00 or 2:00 P.M. This allows ample time for games, discussion, and information activities and for making and eating lunch. Of course, Saturdays from 10:00 A.M. to 2:00 P.M. will not be ideal for all families or communities. Each community will need to determine the best day and length for its Sibshop, as further discussed in Chapter 5.

HOW OFTEN ARE SIBSHOPS HELD?

Depending on the needs and resources of the community, Sibshops may be offered as frequently as weekly (as with a 1½-hour after-school program) or as infrequently as yearly (as with an all-day Sibshop that is a part of an annual conference for families from around a state or the nation). Generally, however, Sibshops are presented monthly or bimonthly.

Sibshops may be offered like a "class"—that is, five Sibshops meeting once a month with one registration. Offering Sibshops this way can provide a stable group that can form an identity during the months the participants are together. It can be difficult, however, for some participants and families to commit to a series of dates because of conflicts with other activities. More often, Sibshops are offered in a "club" format with monthly or bimonthly meetings. This format offers families and participants greater flexibility, but participants may vary somewhat from Sibshop to Sibshop. These and other considerations are discussed further in Chapter 5.

WHAT ARE THE GOALS OF THE SIBSHOP MODEL?

Goal 1: Sibshops will provide brothers and sisters of children with special needs an opportunity to meet other siblings in a relaxed, recreational setting.

The chance to meet other brothers and sisters in a casual atmosphere and join them in recreational activities has several benefits for participants. First, it can help reduce a sibling's sense of isolation. Participants quickly learn that there are others who experience the special joys and challenges they do. Second, the casual atmosphere and recreational activities promote informal sharing and friendships among participants. Friendships begun during Sibshops and continued outside the program through e-mails, visits, or perhaps instant messages offer siblings ongoing sources of support. Third, the recreational aspect of the Sibshops makes them enjoyable to attend. If children perceive Sibshops as yet another thing they have to do because of their sibling, they may find it hard to be receptive to the information and discussion presented in the workshop. Furthermore, when a workshop does not offer anything that is personally satisfying for a participant, he or she is unlikely to attend in the future.

Recreational activities and the importance of play during Sibshops are discussed further in Chapter 9.

Goal 2: Sibshops will provide brothers and sisters with opportunities to discuss common joys and concerns with other siblings of children with special needs.

At Sibshops, participants share stories, experiences, and knowing laughs with peers who truly understand the ups and downs of life with a sibling who has special needs. This opportunity allows participants to learn that they are not alone in their experiences and their often-ambivalent feelings.

Goal 3: Sibshops will provide brothers and sisters with an opportunity to learn how others handle situations commonly experienced by siblings of children with special needs.

Brothers and sisters of children with special health and developmental needs routinely face situations that are not experienced by other children. Defending a brother or sister from name-calling, responding to questions from friends or strangers, and resenting the time and attention required by the sibling with special needs are only a few of the problems siblings may experience. At Sibshops, participants learn how others handle difficult situations. This experience can offer a sibling a broad array of solutions from which to choose.

Activities that promote discussion among sibling participants are presented in Chapter 8.

Goal 4: Sibshops will provide siblings with an opportunity to learn more about the implications of their brother's and sister's special needs.

As noted above, brothers and sisters have a need for information to answer their own questions about their siblings' special needs as well as the questions posed by friends, classmates, and strangers. Sibshops offer participants opportunities to learn about the effect that a sibling's illness or disability will have on the special child's life, schooling, and future.

Informational Sibshop activities are discussed in Chapter 10.

Goal 5: Sibshops will provide parents and other professionals with opportunities to learn more about the concerns and opportunities frequently experienced by brothers and sisters of people with special needs.

Because they may be unaware of the wide range of sibling concerns, some Sibshop activities attempt to help parents and service providers better understand "life as a sib." One activity allows parents and professionals to meet with a panel of young adult and adult siblings to learn about the special joys and challenges of growing up with a special brother or sister. Parents learn about what the panelists appreciated in their parents' treatment of the children in their family, and also what they wish their parents had done differently. This and other programs for parents are discussed further in Chapter 11.

HOW DO WE BECOME A REGISTERED SIBSHOP?

To assure that when parents send their children to a Sibshop, they are sending them to a program that is true to the spirit and goals of the Sibshop model, sibling programs wishing to call themselves "Sibshops" and to use the Sibshop logo must register their program. This straightforward registration process is described in the Sibshop Standards of Practice (Appendix A).

To advocate effectively for increased services for brothers and sisters of people with special needs, it is critical to learn more about issues affecting their lives. The chapters that follow provide an overview of the unusual concerns and opportunities experienced by brothers and sisters of people with special health and developmental needs.

Chapter **2**

Unusual Concerns

• • • We are not heroes any more than we are victims or sufferers. I am just a person, with a brother whose condition makes an added complication in my life. And that, like everything else in life, has both its pluses and minuses. (Pat, in Remsberg, 1989, p. 3) • • •

Is there a relationship more ambivalent than the relationship between brothers and sisters? In families with only typically developing siblings, brothers and sisters fight and argue and laugh and hug, often within the same hour. A 3-year-old's name for her 8-year-old sister may be "dummyhead" one minute and "sweetieface" the next.

Siblings, because of their shared experiences, know one another in ways no one else ever will. Being a sibling, someone once told us, is like living in the nude, psychologically. Sisters and brothers know the chinks in the armor all too well. Like younger siblings, older siblings can be both brutal and loving. As another sister told us, "I can always count on my sister to give me an unvarnished view of how I am leading my life. Yet she will be the first to defend me if she feels I am being attacked by someone else."

• • • I was green with envy at first. My sister was just lying in bed and receiving all this merchandise: nightgowns, sheets, stuffed animals, and books. Will it ever end? Then I thought: What am I jealous of? Here I am being healthy and standing upright; my sister was lying in bed with her life being threatened. These presents were not going to help her sickness any. Then I started to feel sorry for her! I was so confused! (Amy, 14; in Murray & Jampolsky, 1982, p. 45) • • •

• • • My sister's autism pulled us apart and brought us together many times in the past, and will probably continue to do so in the future. (Seltzer & Krauss, 2002) • • •

• • • Siblings of children with chronic health problems are simultaneously vulnerable for psychological problems and precocious development. In fact, both outcomes may be true for an individual over time. What can be interpreted as inconclusive literature may be an accurate reflection of sibling status. (Leonard, 1992, p. 501) • • •

Given that most brothers and sisters harbor a wide range of feelings toward their siblings, it is not at all unusual to learn that siblings of people with special needs also experience ambivalent feelings about their brothers and sisters. After all, a relationship in which one sibling has a disability or illness is still a sibling relationship. Adding a special need to the equation appears to enhance the inherent ambivalence.

Though they may be similar, there can be some important differences when one of the siblings has been diagnosed with a special health or developmental need. In this chapter we review the unusual concerns that siblings of people with special needs may experience. This overview is based on the clinical and research literature and what we have learned working with siblings and parents for almost 25 years. Whenever possible, we let siblings speak for themselves. One unusual concern not covered in this chapter is siblings' lifelong and ever-changing need for information. An extensive discussion of siblings' informational needs may be found in Chapter 3. Chapter 4 reviews the equally important but less reported unusual opportunities recounted by brothers and sisters of people with special needs.

It is difficult to make generalizations about siblings who have brothers and sisters with special needs. After all, having a sibling with a disability or illness is only one aspect of their lives. Factors that have nothing to do with disabilities will influence their personalities. And many disability-related variables will make each sibling's experience unique; for example, age, gender, type and severity of the disability, responses of family members, services and supports available, financial resources, and personal and cultural beliefs (Seltzer, Greenberg, Krauss, Gordon, & Judge, 1997; Williams, 1997). As disabilities and illnesses affect people from all walks of life, siblings will experience these conditions in innumerable ways. If we listen to brothers and sisters long enough, however, we hear recurring themes. Here, then, is a discussion of these themes. To be sure, no one brother or sister will experience all of the concerns discussed below but all will share some of them.

OVERIDENTIFICATION

• • • Yes, I worry a lot. I worry that my leg will get cut off also. I think about it and then I wake up and I go into the kitchen. All the time I worry about it. (10-year-old brother of a sibling with osteogenic sarcoma in Sourkes, 1990, p. 6) • • •

• • • Our pediatrician announced to our entire family that Nick would be a vegetable and that my parents should put him in a state institution. Even though my parents never placed Nick in an institution, I often wondered when they would put me in Apple Creek—and what I would have to do to make them do that to me. (Barbara S., personal communication, 2004) • • •

• A 4-year-old boy worries that he might catch his sister's cerebral palsy and lose his ability to walk.

• Because her older brother and sister have seizures, a 10-year-old girl wonders when hers will begin.

- Unable to see the blackboard clearly, an 8-year-old boy wonders whether he will lose his vision the way his brother did.

- After doing poorly on a spelling test, a 9-year-old girl thinks that perhaps her brother isn't the only one in the family with a learning disability.

- When her social life is not going the way she would like, a 14-year-old girl is concerned that her twin brother is not the only family member who has Asperger's.

- On the eve of his 16th birthday, a boy worries that he, too, will start showing signs of schizophrenia, just as his sister did soon after her 16th birthday.

Overidentification occurs when a sibling wonders whether he or she shares—or will share—a sibling's problem or fate. Frequently (but not always) irrational, these fears can be very real, especially to young children, who often indulge in "magical thinking" and who have an immature concept of contagion. "Well, we all got strep throat," a sibling may wonder. "Why shouldn't we all catch cancer?" Although younger children are more open about fears of catching a disease or acquiring a disability, Sourkes (1990) doubted that there are many siblings who haven't worried about acquiring their sibling's special needs.

Severity appears to influence overidentification. Grossman's 1972 study of college-age siblings of people with disabilities suggested that overidentification is more likely to occur when the disability is mild, and especially if it is "invisible." The logic is apparent: Jennifer's sister has been diagnosed as having epilepsy, an invisible disability. Michelle's sister was diagnosed as having a genetic disorder that causes her to look and act differently from other family members. Because Jennifer's sister is like her in so many ways, Jennifer may be more likely to worry that she, too, has epilepsy.

Age also appears to influence overidentification. Miller (1974) suggested that overidentification is less likely to occur if the child with the special needs is younger than the typically developing child. A 10-year-old child whose older siblings all have learning disabilities may be more likely to fear that he or she also has a learning disability than a 10-year-old child whose younger brother just began experiencing seizures.

The risk of overidentification is one of the many reasons that brothers and sisters need accurate information about their siblings' disabilities and illnesses. Information that may be obvious to adults may be not be obvious to children. For instance, younger children need to know that they cannot "catch" their sibling's disability. One third of the siblings interviewed by Koocher and O'Malley (1981) said that they worried about getting cancer themselves. Compounding this is the difficulty families often have communicating effectively about a child's disability or illness and the effects it can have on the family (Faux, 1993; Williams, 1997).

Siblings who are at higher risk for acquiring a disability or illness need to know what their chances are. Usually their risk is much lower than they might imagine. For instance, siblings who have seen their previously healthy siblings develop serious mental illnesses frequently worry that they also will succumb to the illness, although their chances are only 1 in 10 (compared with 1 in 100 in the general population) and negligible after age 30 (Dickens, 1991). Most siblings appreciate straight talk about their siblings' special needs and, as we'll learn later, benefit from parents' and professionals' efforts to provide information proactively.

EMBARRASSMENT

• • • My friends and I were watching movies one night and all of a sudden my brother came bolting downstairs with nothing on! I was so embarrassed. My friends are like, "Does he do that often?" (Kathryn C., 14, in Meyer, 2005) • • •

• • • Embarrassed me? I don't know where to begin. My brother told my friend about a surprise party we were throwing her. He has said VERY inappropriate things to my friends — more times than I can count. He has fully combusted and acted out in front of my friends a million times. He is like a big ball of embarrassment on legs. (Miri L., 16, in Meyer, 2005) • • •

A sibling with a disability or illness can be a source of embarrassment for typically developing brothers and sisters. They may get embarrassed by the unwanted attention the child, and consequently the family, receives when the child with special needs has behavior problems:

• • • At church, the pastor began to pray. In the middle of the prayer David started to play his favorite tune — "Happy Birthday" — on the kazoo! (He must have sneaked it in with him!) Everybody laughed! I felt so embarrassed. I was glad when it was time for Sunday school and David went off for a walk with one of his helpers. (Angela, 10, in Burslem, 1991, p. 13) • • •

Differences in appearances can also make siblings feel overly conspicuous:

• • • As Red got older, people would stare at him and speak under their breath, as if my brother was some kind of side show. To this day, people still do that. (A. Jones, personal communication, 1991) • • •

In some instances, siblings may be acutely sensitive about the appearance and behavior of their siblings, lest others—peers especially—conclude that they share their brothers' and sisters' special needs.

• • • I was certain that everyone was looking at my brother with his obvious handicap and wondering what was wrong with the rest of us. (Marge, in Helsel, Helsel, Helsel, & Helsel, 1978, p. 110) • • •

In these instances, embarrassment will be more common when the problems are mild or invisible. Visible disabilities, siblings tell us, at least provide a reason for unusual behavior. A brother with a mild learning disability who is given to asking strangers rude questions can be more embarrassing than a sister who uses a wheelchair and makes occasional noises.

• • • Even though I am 49 years old, my brother Marty still occasionally embarrasses me. His disability is less obvious than my other two disabled brothers, and I think this has something to do with it. Marty talks very loud, is unkempt, and appears just plain odd to most people. I know I shouldn't feel embarrassed but I can't seem to help myself. (Nora H., personal communication, 2005) • • •

Siblings may experience embarrassment and unwanted attention when they are asked questions about their brothers' and sisters' special needs. These questions can come from friends, classmates, and even strangers:

• • • When I finally found out what happened, it was so hard to talk about it, especially when someone says, "Hey, what's wrong with your sister? Why is she in a wheelchair?" People can be such jerks sometimes! They just don't understand!! (Joanne, 16, in Murray & Jampolsky, 1982, p. 36) • • •

Developing strategies to spare a typically developing child embarrassment first requires analyzing the cause of the embarrassment. Is it something that can be changed, such as an age-inappropriate bib on a sibling who drools, or a behavior, such as singing during the sermon at church, that could be changed through a carefully considered behavior program? If changeable, then the family can work toward decreasing the sibling's embarrassment and improving the life of the person with special needs at the same time.

It is just as likely, however, that the source of embarrassment is something about which little can be done. In these instances, there are two strategies parents may wish to consider. First, they should remember that most children go through stages when they are easily embarrassed, and these experiences may be unavoidable. Early adolescents have a particularly strong need to conform. It can make a teenager miserable to be seen with her parents, much less a sister who looks and acts differently.

• • • Being in a public place, as a teenager, with my sister who was saying, doing, and/ or wearing something inappropriate would have had to have been the worst! (Seltzer & Krauss, 2002) • • •

• • • Being an older sister to David was difficult. When I became a teenager, I tried to pretend he didn't exist. Adolescence is an emotional roller coaster, and I spent most of those years on unsteady ground. It was too uncool to admit to having a retarded brother. And there were times when I wanted to drop through the earth rather than acknowledge our relationship. (Herndon, 1992, p. 2) • • •

During this time of raging conformity, the best strategy may be to give the typically developing child "space"—psychological and otherwise—and model the resilience and sense of humor parents hope their children will someday have. Given permission to walk on the other side of the shopping mall or attend a different church service, most siblings will eventually reintegrate their brother or sister according to their own agendas:

• • • As time moved on, I pretended I wasn't embarrassed by Jennifer. But I really was when friends were around. By the time I was 14 or 15 though I realized my good friends loved her too. I hadn't realized that before. I hadn't given her a chance. (Cassie, 19, in Binkard, Goldberg & Goldberg, 1987, p. 16) • • •

• • • When I was 10 and 11 I hated going to the mall because she'd scream and try to sit down and just make everyone stare at us. She's completely different now and I hate how I used be so embarrassed by her doing that. It doesn't even bother me now if she gets a little upset when out shopping. If people are that bored with themselves that they have to stare, let them. (Sarah S., 17, in Meyer, 2005) • • •

A second strategy is to acknowledge the embarrassment. Featherstone (1980) wrote that parents can help their children by allowing them some control over situations. One mother told us, "When my son comes up to me and says, 'Mom, I get so embarrassed when she does that!' I tell him, 'Yeah, I really get embarrassed when she does that too!'"

Denying siblings "permission" to be embarrassed by their sibling (as in "He's your brother; you shouldn't be embarrassed by him!") is more likely to invoke feelings of guilt and resentment than to reduce embarrassment. It also will send a message that children cannot bring their concerns to their parents. Acknowledging that a sibling with special needs is sometimes difficult to live with not only reflects reality (after all, what sibling—special needs or not—is always easy to live with?), but it also sends a message that brothers and sisters can feel free to talk about their feelings with their parents. Good communication among siblings and parents is, along with information, the primary means of minimizing siblings' concerns.

• • • My parents always wanted us to express our feelings. They'd say, "If you're uncomfortable when Jennifer is around your friends, don't feel guilty. Those feelings are very normal." (Andrea, 19, in Binkard et al., 1987, p. 18) • • •

Luckily, for most siblings, embarrassment is transitory. As described in the section on unusual opportunities, most brothers and sisters have a remarkable ability to reframe difficult situations in a more positive light:

● ● ● I don't feel embarrassed about him. With his kind of handicap, well, he does strange stuff. But it's like the stuff everybody's little brother does. It's sort of what you'd expect from little brothers. (Mary, 17, in Binkard et al., 1987, p. 11) ● ● ●

● ● ● I'll never forget my brother shouting out in the middle of a crowded movie theater that he had just passed gas. My mom and I both shrunk down in our chairs, embarrassed, but laughing all the way! What else could we have done! (Kameron P., personal communication, 2004) ● ● ●

GUILT

● ● ● I often feel trapped by him, as though my life will have to revolve around him. I don't want to be stuck caring for him after my parents are gone, and yet I feel guilty for saying it. I don't like having to take so much care of him, I don't like having to wonder what he would have been otherwise, I don't like that he may keep me from other opportunities. And I don't like that I can't accept it. (Allison S., 17, in Meyer, 2005) ● ● ●

Relationships between brothers and sisters and their siblings who have special health or developmental needs resemble those of typically developing siblings in most ways. Siblings of individuals with special needs, however, are far more likely to experience guilt than siblings of individuals without special needs. And guilt, although it represents the darker end of the emotional palette, nevertheless comes in many hues. Brothers and sisters may feel that they caused their siblings' disability; they may experience survivor's guilt; they may feel guilty about their own abilities or they may harbor less-than-charitable feelings about their siblings.

Feeling Responsible for the Disability or Illness

● ● ● When I was little, I worried that the reason that my sister wasn't learning to talk was because I would often speak for her and tell people what she wanted. (Stephanie G., personal communication, 2004) ● ● ●

Siblings who feel somehow responsible for their brother's or sister's disability or illness may experience irrational, but nonetheless real, guilt. They may feel that they are somehow being punished for something they said, did, or thought near the time of the diagnosis. Koch-Hattem (1986) reported on interviews with 33 siblings of pediatric cancer patients. Of the 33 siblings, 9 reported that when the individual patients were diagnosed, they considered the possibility that the illnesses would not have occurred if they had treated their brothers or sisters differently.

● ● ● I blamed myself [for my sister's illness]. I constantly felt guilty around her. I wanted to punish myself somehow. . . . I knew inside it wasn't my fault but I was so hurt, lost, and mixed up that I blamed myself. (Joanne, 16, in Murray & Jampolsky, 1982, p. 37) ● ● ●

One teenage member of SibKids, a listserv for young siblings, wrote that she was responsible for her little brother's autism. When they were younger, she wrote, she had chicken pox. Her brother, then a baby, caught her chicken pox. Shortly after his chicken pox resolved, he began showing behavioral signs later diagnosed as autism. Consequently, she believed (erroneously, of course, as there is no known link between chicken pox and autism) that she caused her brother's autism. The implication of this type of guilt is obvious: brothers and sisters, especially younger siblings, will need to be reassured that the disabilities or illnesses did not result from anything they did.

Survivor's Guilt

Brothers and sisters may experience a form of survivor's guilt. A sister's secret prayer might be:

"Dear God, why did this have to happen to Katie? She's so little and so sweet and now she's in the hospital with all these tubes coming out of her. She has all these seizures and seems in such pain. She doesn't deserve this. Why couldn't it happen to me?"

Three of the siblings interviewed by Koch-Hattem (1986) expressed a desire to trade places with their siblings. One 15-year-old sister of a 9-year-old boy with acute lymphoblastic leukemia said:

● ● ● Sometimes when I'm in there with him taking shots, I'll just say, "Why couldn't it be me instead of him?" He's so little and so young that I probably could take shots better than he could. (p. 114) ● ● ●

Guilt over Abilities or Health

● ● ● Since we were twins, my brother and I were always together. And so from the earliest time I can remember, I had the responsibility of watching after him. A lot of times I felt guilty because I was invited to go to parties, and I went to school. They enrolled him in first grade, but he was only there a very short time. I of course was allowed to go and I felt very guilty about that. (Fish, 1993) ● ● ●

Brothers and sisters of people with special needs often learn to value and appreciate their health, independence, family, and other aspects of their lives that their peers may take for granted. While they appreciate the ability to do things that others—such as their siblings—cannot do and the advantages they have, they sometimes feel guilty for their good fortune.

● ● ● I guess it was in junior high that I started to be aware of some of Tom's disorders and be sad for him. He was falling behind me. When I got to junior high and was having such a good time myself, I realized that the whole experience wasn't going to be the same for Tom as it was for me. I was sad but I didn't know what I could do. (Mark, 24, in Binkard et al., 1987, p. 27) ● ● ●

● ● ● I feel bad when John sees me going off with my friends and wonders why he doesn't have many. He'll be at home when I'm out having fun, and it makes my mom feel bad. I feel guilty and don't know how to handle it. (Sue, 17, in Binkard et al., 1987, p. 13) ● ● ●

• • • One of the hardest things is leaving for a long period of time. Or going somewhere with my family when I know my sib wouldn't be able to go because of his disability. Whenever I leave, my sib always says "Sissy? Sissy?" and it just melts my heart every time. (Cassandra W., 15, in Meyer, 2005) • • •

• • • I've lived away from home for almost 10 years now, but every time I go back for a vacation or holidays, I can almost guarantee that my mother is going to give me the "Why-don't-you-just-do-more-for/with-your-brother?" speech. (Kameron P., personal communication, 2005) • • •

Guilt over Typical Sibling Conflicts

• • • The toughest thing about being a sib is admitting that you don't always like your sib and that sometimes you yell at them and treat them unfairly. It's weird, but you can't fight with them like you could do with a typically developing kid and so you are forced to share your anger with someone else and then you feel like an idiot. (Caitlin M., 14, in Meyer, 2005) • • •

• • • I remember hitting my brother once when we were 8 or 9 for being stubborn. Immediately, I was overcome with guilt. The expression of betrayal and hurt on his face was one I'll never forget. The memory of that episode still hurts my heart. (Kameron P., personal communication, 2005) • • •

One 9-year-old girl described often being angry at her 4-year-old sick brother who "... was a pest, interfering with my homework and possessions." She related how in a moment of acute fury she chased her little brother around the apartment. Her mother picked up the child and shouted: "Don't you hit my child!" The sibling described feeling during this episode, as well as during many others in her life: "My parents act as if I wasn't also their child." (Bendor, 1990, p. 23)

Although difficult for parents to watch, teasing, name calling, arguing, and other forms of conflict are common among most brothers and sisters. While parents may be appalled at siblings' harshness toward one another, much of this conflict can be a beneficial part of normal social development. Bank and Kahn (1982, p. 199) noted that a "constructive function of sibling aggression is that it forces the participants into a social 'laboratory' where they learn how to manage and resolve conflicts." They further noted that

> The ability to deflect aggression, to use it wisely and at the right moment, to use humor, to surrender without debasing oneself and to defeat someone without humiliating that person are all skills that children and adolescents can eventually use in relationships with peers, spouses, and ultimately with their own children. (p. 199)

Bank and Kahn also reported that children they have interviewed have told them that a moderate amount of aggressive interaction (i.e., not interfered with by parents) is a necessary and positive part of the sibling relationship.

Presumably, lessons taught and relationships built through sibling conflict will also apply to the sibling who has a disability or illness. A brother who has Down syndrome might be better equipped to face life in the community if he has learned to defend himself within the essentially loving confines of a family. A sibling who has shared a rich if sometimes rocky relationship with a sister who has a disability may be more likely to continue that relationship as an adult.

•　•　•　It wasn't until I lived with a host family while studying abroad during college that I truly learned that typical siblings really do fight and pick on each other just as much as my sister and I did—that in some ways, my real family was more normal than I thought. (Stephanie G., personal communication, 2004)　•　•　•

Regardless of how adaptive or developmentally appropriate it might be, however, typical sibling conflict is more likely to result in feelings of guilt when one sibling has a special health or developmental need. When conflict arises, the message sent to many brothers and sisters is, "Leave your sibling alone. You are bigger, you are stronger, you should know better. It is your job to compromise." Because of their "advantages," brothers and sisters may feel they are not permitted to get angry or tease or argue with their siblings.

•　•　•　You know, I would complain about something my brother did and everyone would say, "Now you know he doesn't really know what he is doing. You're the one who is okay and you need to understand." And I used to get so frustrated and really copped a lot of resentments about that it was not okay for me to get angry with him, but it was okay for him to do whatever he wanted. (Fish, 1993)　•　•　•

Although no parent should ever tolerate physical abuse among siblings, brothers and sisters—even those with special needs—should be allowed to work out their conflicts as best they can. Because sibling squabbles can be painful for parents to watch, it is often helpful to remove oneself from the situation. It has been our experience that sibling squabbles resolve in 30 minutes when parents intervene and 30 minutes when they do not. Parents who deny their children the right to have conflicts run the risk that "the children may express their anger in secret and forbidden ways" (Bank & Kahn, 1982, p. 203).

Guilt Over Caregiving

• • • I would give my brother anything. I would love to have him with me, but he needs constant supervision and structure that can be better provided at a residential care setting. I also want to give my children (in the future) all that I have, and if he was with us, I know that would be difficult if not impossible. (Seltzer & Krauss, 2002) • • •

• • • My sister has much more of the caregiving burden for our three disabled brothers. I feel a huge amount of guilt over that since they are no more her brothers than mine. What's worse is that it has always been that way. Even as a child, Margaret — the oldest — had the lion's share of helping my Mom with the brothers. My living situation and marriage make a larger role almost impossible, but it doesn't lessen the guilt I feel. (Nora H., personal communication, 2005) • • •

• • • I am Douglas' sibling. I wanted to be a sister and very much wanted a baby brother. But I never planned on being his everything. For years I was just that. (Zatlow, 1992, p. 15) • • •

Some family theorists such as Duvall (1962) have observed that families, like individuals, proceed through a life cycle consisting of overlapping stages. Just as an individual grows, develops, matures, and ages, families also are "born," grow, change, and age. Events such as divorce, desertion, or death will profoundly affect the family life cycle. As noted elsewhere (Meyer, 1986), few changes will have a greater effect on the life cycle than the presence of a child with special health or developmental needs.

One poignant example is Duvall's (1962) seventh stage, "families as launching centers," which begins when a family's first child leaves home and ends when the last child leaves. For a family with a child with special needs, this "launching" stage may take place much earlier (for families who institutionalize their child) or may extend for the life of the child if the child lives with the parents as an adult. Regardless, entering adulthood will be an especially troubling milestone for families of people who have disabilities. For the families Wikler (1981) studied, the 21st birthday for a young adult with a disability was the second most stressful crisis for parents, following the initial diagnosis. The 21st birthday can be a double crisis: Although it normally symbolizes independence, parents may be reminded of their child's many needs before he or she can achieve independence. Furthermore, the 21st birthday will signal a transitional crisis: Schools cease to provide services after this age, and adult services are often inadequate.

Crises such as these will affect other family members as well. Brothers and sisters, who would otherwise be planning to "launch" from their families, may feel guilty about moving away from home and leaving their parents to care for their siblings' special needs (Grossman, 1972). One sister commented that going away to college was initially a relief: She did not have to care for her brother who has Down syndrome; she could sleep in. By mid-college, she felt guilty about not helping and felt the need to provide her parents with respite (Nester, 1989, p. 1). Other siblings have expressed similar feelings:

• • • As Paul finishes his college years, he's thinking more and more about leaving their family home, but finds it difficult to imagine his mother coping with their home and sister by herself. His father died a couple of years ago, and the loss of a good and kind man . . . is still keenly felt. (Binkard et al., 1987, p. 24) • • •

•　•　•　When I moved out of my mother's house, I was distraught and overwhelmed by responsibilities. Even the process of moving had to be negotiated on a compromise; I agreed to be near enough to my mother and brother so that I could get to them quickly in the event of problems. This proved to be prophetic, for there were countless days and nights when I was called upon by my mother to help her in a crisis and handle my brother on difficult days. (Zatlow, 1992, p. 13) • • •

•　•　•　I knew I could never move too far away. I always insisted my husband limit his career search to areas within a reasonable driving distance to my Mom's home. Then I would feel guilty that my family limited his career choices. (Nora H., personal communication, 2004) • • •

According to Harland and Cuskelly's study (2000), siblings who were unable to assume an active role in the lives of their adult siblings with disabilities reported feeling guilty. Even when siblings do stay to offer assistance to their siblings, however, conflicting loyalties and needs can produce guilty feelings:

•　•　•　It was grueling; I had no relief, no support, no options. My life was revolving around Kevin and his care. If I wanted to go away for a few days, I couldn't. The guilt was overwhelming. What do you tell your friends? No, I can't go out; I have to feed my brother? (Pat, in Remsberg, 1989, p. 10) • • •

Torn between loyalties to their sibling and a natural desire for distance and independence, adult siblings frequently experience stress and conflict about caring for their brother or sister with disabilities. Difficulty finding enough time and managing their brother's or sister's behavior compound this issue (Harland & Cuskelly, 2000). Siblings report that parents' failure to plan often resulted in parents seeking deathbed vows or making assumptions about the caregiving roles their typically developing children would play (Gorelick, J., 1996, p. 7).

•　•　•　I had to go to my parents and make them talk about it. It was always this given that I was going to take the responsibility over and what ended up happening is that I got really miserable. I love my brother dearly, but I don't want to be a parent. I had to set a very strict boundary: No, he cannot live with me, and I still stand by that. They felt I had really let the family down. They said: ''You're going to let him live on the street!'' No, that's not what I'm saying. What I am saying is that we have to look into other options. Living with me is not one of them. (Fish, 1993) • • •

Shame

Shame, where guilt intersects with embarrassment, is a powerful and painful experience for some brothers and sisters. Because of the stigma of a disability or illness, siblings can feel that their family is now "marked" and wish that their family would just fade into the woodwork (Sourkes, 1980).

•　•　•　Julie went through a long stage of being embarrassed about her sister. This continued into her teenage years. ''There's a constant conflict in you,'' she remembers. ''You don't want to say anything because you don't want your parents to feel that you are ashamed." (Remsberg, 1989, p. 15) • • •

Shame can have long-lasting consequences. One prominent professional in the field of developmental disabilities told us that much of her success is "shame-driven." She grew up with a brother who had Down syndrome, although she did not learn the name of her brother's disability until after his death when they were both in their early teens. Life with a brother who was different was a constant source of embarrassment for this individual. When her mother would pick her up from school, she would dive into the back seat of the car, afraid that classmates might see her with her brother. After his death, guilty feelings about her embarrassment gave way to shame. Now in counseling, she tells us that her pursuit of academic degrees and work in human services is a means of compensating for her perceived transgressions against her brother. Her shame, she feels, keeps her from enjoying her successes.

Although little has been written about this topic, siblings we know who have shared similar stories seem to share characteristics. First, most were born before the 1960s, an era when John F. Kennedy, Hubert Humphrey, and others sought to reduce the stigma of disabilities and illnesses by discussing them publicly. Today, with legislation assuring access to public education and increased visibility of people with special needs in popular media, the stigma of having a brother or sister with health or developmental needs is not what it once was. One can easily imagine, however, the stigma felt by a sibling whose brother or sister is HIV positive or has a resistant strain of tuberculosis.

Second, they came from families where the disability was rarely, if ever, discussed, and the disability was clearly traumatic for the parents.

• • • The guilt from my brother's institutionalization was internally twisting. It became a fact that he had been "placed" so [that] we could grow up having a "normal" life. The absence of real information — not to mention a brother — was eerily accepted as being for my benefit. So rarely were we told what was going on that I felt untrusted — and finally untrustworthy. (M.K.R., personal communication, 2005) • • •

• • • In our family, there exists a way of being, a denial of the truth. . . . There was a strong message that you don't go outside of the family for anything. You stay inside, you keep family secrets, and you don't seek outside help from anyone. I'm the first one in this family to seek therapy and I've had to go through a lot of shame and guilt about doing that. (David, 29, in Leder, 1991, p. 26) • • •

Finally, these instances often occur in families where there are only two children: one who is affected and one who is not. Additional children in the family, as Dyson (1989) and Kazak and Clarke (1986) have found, appear to dilute the consequences of growing up with a sibling who has a disability or an illness. Other siblings can provide a typically developing child other children with whom he or she can identify and a built-in informal means of support.

For the simple reason that they are healthy and their sibling is not, sisters and brothers of people with special needs are at risk for a variety of guilty feelings. Although open communication is desirable for any parent–child relationship, it is especially important when that child has a sibling with special needs.

ISOLATION, LONELINESS, AND LOSS

In *A Difference in the Family*, Helen Featherstone (1980) wrote: "In dealing with the wider world of friends, classmates and teacher, able-bodied children at times feel painfully different" (p. 144). A sibling's disability or illness can cause brothers and sisters to experience various feelings of loss and isolation.

Especially if there are only two children in the family, typically developing siblings may miss having a brother or sister with whom they can seek advice or share their thoughts, hopes, and dreams. They may also long for the rough-but-loving relationship many siblings share:

••• It was hard. They were telling me stuff that I really didn't understand. At that time he and I were really close. He was getting sick and we couldn't do much. I was wondering why he couldn't do things anymore. And if I got into an argument and hit him I was always afraid my hit would cause him to die. I felt lonely not having a brother to play with or beat up. (Don, 18, in Murray & Jampolsky, 1982, p. 40) •••

••• At times, I really missed having a "normal" sister or brother. Sometimes I wished I had someone to talk to, play with, to tease, argue with, confide in, and have fun with. I could tell my sister and know for sure she wouldn't tell anyone—because she didn't talk! But she never fought with me, never argued. It's not a big thing, but I think I missed out on opportunities to deal with criticism or rejection. I never had anyone yelling at me or telling me I was ugly as most siblings do and therefore didn't really learn how to cope with even the slightest bit of conflict until I entered the workforce after college. (Amy S., personal communication 2005) •••

••• It's hard seeing other siblings interact. I watch them talk, exchange advice, confide in each other, and even fight, and I realize: I won't ever have that kind of sibling relationship. (Althea R., 13, in Meyer, 2005) •••

Isolation from Parents' Attention

When parents are consumed with a child's disability or illness, typically developing brothers and sisters can feel neglected and isolated from their parents. These feelings are especially keen during times of stress for the family such as diagnoses or hospitalizations. Of course, this comes at times when siblings need more, not less, emotional support.

••• When I was 9, my brother had a stroke the same week that my grandpa passed away. It was really scary because my parents had to be out of state with my sib and we were being kind of "passed around" the family so we would have a place to stay and have someone to talk to. (Cassandra W., 15, in Meyer, 2005) •••

••• Even if you feel bad for your sick brother or sister, you still want your parents too. (12-year-old girl, in Bendor, 1990, p. 24) •••

••• I spent a lot of time with baby-sitters and television, and less with my parents and the relatives who visited only to see Lisa. It seemed as though she were the only one anybody cared about. In this, I was the typical sibling of a victim of childhood cancer. (Ellis, 1992, p. 2) •••

Cairns, Clark, Smith, and Lansky (1979), in a study of school-age children with cancer and their healthy siblings, found that siblings showed greater distress than did patients in the areas of perceived social isolation, perception of their parents as overindulgent and overprotective of the sick child, fear of expressing negative feelings, and (for older siblings only) concern with school failure. Siblings of children with cancer have the most difficulty adjusting when their brother or sister has to spend more nights in the hospital, disrupting family life (Sloper & White, 1996). Parents, overwhelmed by a child's many needs, may be too exhausted or simply unable to recognize a brother's or sister's calls for attention (Schorr-Ribera, 1992).

• • • Sometimes I feel as though my parents don't care about what I do or don't do. They are so preoccupied with my brother and all his friends that I don't really seem to matter. Almost all my time is spent in my room watching my TV, listening to music, doing homework, or talking on the phone. You would think somebody would notice that I spend all my time in my room, away from everyone else and all the problems that surround their lives. (Alisa A., 18, in Meyer, 2005) • • •

Several brothers and sisters of children who have epilepsy reflected on how their sibling's disability caused them to feel isolated from their parents:

• • • • I probably will never forget the loneliness during that period of time. The feeling that I had was that I wasn't worth as much as Jessica.

- The only way I could get them to pay attention to me was to get mad. That would get their attention.

- I wouldn't talk to my parents about being lonely because I wasn't sure that they'd understand me — the way I felt.

- I didn't do my schoolwork. I guess I wanted to see how my parents would react.

- I wanted to see if they would pay attention or yell at me or ground me or something. (K. Collins, in Collins & Emmerling, 1991) • • •

Other siblings, seeing the pain caused by a sibling's special needs, may elect not to come to their parents with their troubles. Featherstone (1980) wrote:

These siblings may, then, endure many of [their] feelings alone and without support, even when parents are tactful and eager to help. Conscientious, sensitive parents often have conscientious sensitive children; seeing how pushed and saddened their parents already are, such children hesitate to burden them further. (p. 61)

• • • When I was growing up, it never crossed my mind to turn to my parents for support. It seemed like they already had too much to deal with, so I didn't want to burden them with my problems as well, since they wouldn't have been easy to fix. (Stephanie G., personal communication, 2005) • • •

One adult sibling we met told us that it took her 5 years to tell her parents that she had been raped. She thought they had "enough to worry about" with her brother, who has autism. Another sister wrote:

• • • I felt I had to hold my feelings in when I was around my parents. I let my feelings out only when I was with my close friends. (Honey, 16, in Murray & Jampolsky, 1982, p. 54) • • •

Of course, when a child is facing a health or developmental crisis, it may be impossible for parents to meet all of their children's needs for emotional support. During trying times, many families enlist the support of a favorite relative or adult friend who provides the healthy child with time, attention, and an "open ear."

Isolation from Information, the Process

• • • My parents, my two older sisters, and my grandparents would all leave to go to the hospital while I sat at home with a baby-sitter. All I wanted to know was what was happening and why everybody always left me. No one took the time to explain to me that my sister was basically dying. (Doherty, 1992, p. 4) • • •

• • • Several [sibling group] members described the pain of having to give up a beloved bird or dog after the sick child began treatment. Pets carry germs and pose a serious threat to the infection-prone child whose immunity is suppressed when he receives chemotherapy. Two parents did not give an explanation to the healthy siblings for putting a pet to sleep or giving him away. The siblings felt devastated and angry. (Bendor, 1990, p. 24) • • •

Adult brothers and sisters occasionally report growing up in families where their siblings' disability or illness was rarely discussed. They report the irony of this situation: In many ways, they knew their siblings better than anyone, yet they knew little about the illness or disability or its implications.

• • • My brother was institutionalized in the 1960s when he was 5 and I was 8. We didn't talk about it much, as our parents followed the prevailing advice to "place and forget" their son. Visits were entirely forbidden—for my "protection" apparently. Growing up, I had so many fears, and so many questions. And nobody to talk to. There was a "correct" silence, enforced, in part, because of my parents' obvious pain about my brother. (M.K.R., personal communication, 2005) • • •

There are several reasons for this situation. Some siblings tell us that their parents wished to protect them from the stress and sadness they experienced and therefore "spared" them information about their siblings' special needs. Other siblings grew up with a sibling whose disability (e.g., epilepsy) or illness (e.g., schizophrenia) was so stigmatizing that their parents sought to keep the problem a family secret. Topics that were taboo outside the home were also frequently taboo inside the home, leaving siblings to feel alone with their questions and concerns.

Other siblings report feeling left in the dark for legal reasons. Foster brothers and sisters of children who have complex psychosocial needs have told us of their frustrations: They must live with a foster sibling's often-difficult behavior, yet they are not permitted (interpreted to mean *trusted*) to know details of the foster sibling's background.

Regardless of the reason, when there is insufficient communication about the brother's or sister's problems, a typically developing sibling can experience a unique loneliness. One brother shared what it was like to be spared information about his sister's cancer. He felt his parents sheltered him, assuring him "not to worry." He now feels that remaining uninvolved and uninformed has a cost:

•　•　•　I didn't understand the full extent of my sister's disease—I just thought that the doctors would take care of everything and I didn't think about how tough it was for my sister in other ways. (Peter, in Ellis, 1992, p. 5)　•　•　•

Not understanding the implications of his sister's illness and being reassured that he need not worry caused Peter to feel isolated and confused, especially when his parents left and went to the hospital:

•　•　•　I became a latchkey child in a lot of ways—always left by myself—so I feel that essentially I became a peripheral member of my family during that time. I wasn't included at all. (Peter, in Ellis, 1992, p. 5)　•　•　•

Whereas parents may accurately estimate their child's need for and understanding of information about a sibling's disability, they may overestimate how well their child understands the implications of the disability (Glasberg, 2000). This underscores the need for ongoing family communication and developmentally appropriate information that matches the sibling's level of understanding.

Isolation from Peers

•　•　•　Because of SibKids, I have met—or rather heard from—tons of siblings from around the world that I would never have otherwise met. It's really great to know that I am not alone. (Laura P., 15, in Meyer, 2005, p. 90)　•　•　•

•　•　•　Until this group, I had never met another sibling [of a person with a disability]. It wasn't until the tender age of 39 that I met another person like myself. (Marilyn, in Fink, 1984, p. 6)　•　•　•

•　•　•　Right now, I think it would be helpful if I could understand more about what he goes through and why my folks have such different expectations for him. If there were groups for siblings, I'd like to talk to them about parents and their different expectations. (Mary, 17, in Binkard et al., 1987, p. 11)　•　•　•

Since the 1980s, we have learned one simple yet far-reaching lesson from the hundreds of parents and siblings we have met, and it is this: Siblings' experiences parallel parents' experiences. Brothers and sisters will encounter joys, concerns, and issues regarding the person with special needs that closely correspond to those of their parents. And, although brothers and sisters have the longest-lasting relationship in the family, siblings (as we see again and again) have, compared to their parents, far fewer opportunities to gain access to programs, services, and professional support.

Nowhere is this more evident than in the area of peer support. Many parents count on sharing the good times, the not-so-good times, and helpful information with a peer who is also the parent of a child with special needs. Some parents connect with other parents through common-sense efforts in programs such as Parent-to-Parent, or fathers' programs, or mothers' groups (Meyer, Vadasy, Fewell, & Schell, 1985). Many parents maintain informal contact with other parents of children who have similar special needs. For most parents, the thought of "going it alone," without the benefit of knowing another parent in a similar situation, is unthinkable. Yet this happens routinely to brothers and sisters. The siblings Bendor (1990) interviewed made periodic but vain attempts to share feelings of frustration and loneliness with friends. The siblings reported that friends were either uninterested or unable to respond helpfully (p. 25).

••• I am part of SibKids, so I know lots of sibs from all over the world, but only through the computer. It's nice having people who understand where you're coming from. Most of my friends don't want to hear about it and don't know how to respond when I have concerns or worries about my siblings, health, or home life. (Rebekah C., 17, in Meyer, 2005, p. 91) •••

••• I'd like to join a group for siblings if there were one. I guess I'd even be willing to try to start one if I knew other brothers and sisters who would like to join. Sometimes you feel like you're the only one who's gone through this. I haven't ever been able to share most of my feelings. (Beth, 16, in Binkard et al., 1987, p. 6) •••

Despite the tremendous success of peer-support programs for parents, there remains a dearth of such programs for brothers and sisters of children with special needs. The need for such opportunities is clear: McKeever's (1983) study of children with cancer revealed that siblings were more in need of support than were other family members. Numerous authors (Cramer et al., 1997; Lobato, 1990; Murphy, 1981; Powell & Gallagher, 1993; Seligman, 1991) have suggested that support groups can provide young siblings with opportunities for "catharsis, support, and insight concerning relationships with family members and others and techniques for managing various situations" (Murphy, 1979, p. 359). Like their parents, brothers and sisters appear to benefit from groups in which they can voice their fears, hopes, and doubts. Groups specifically for brothers and sisters demonstrate that somebody cares about the issues facing them and values the important role they play in the family.

••• I cannot express what a powerful thing it was to realize I was not the only person in Seattle who had a sib with a disability! There is power in numbers and it certainly helped me through some rough patches. (Oh, and we made some wonderful lunches together!) (Sister, 32, who attended Sibshops as a preteen, in Johnson & Sandall, in preparation) •••

As discussed in subsequent chapters, brothers and sisters, although they have unique concerns, do not routinely have negative experiences, as once described in the research literature. Like their parents, the vast majority of brothers and sisters of people with special needs do well despite challenges brought about by the siblings' disability or illness (Cuskelly, Chant, & Hayes, 1998; Dyson, 1996; Eisenberg, Baker, & Blacher, 1998; Faux, 1993; Hannah & Midlarsky, 1999; Orsmond & Seltzer, 2000). Consequently, programs for brothers and sisters should reflect siblings' and families' strengths while acknowledging their concerns. (To be sure, there will be some family members— parents or siblings—who will have needs that go beyond what a peer-support group can provide. In Chapter 8, we discuss how to recognize siblings in need of therapeutic programs and where to refer them.)

RESENTMENT

•　•　•　"How is Andrea, your sister, doing today? Is she home from the hospital yet? Will she get better soon? Send her my love." When your brother or sister is sick, this is what you might hear. This is all I heard for about a year after Andrea was sick. I was so sick of hearing about all this stuff about Andrea I could scream. Why doesn't anyone ever ask me how I am doing!! (Amy, 14, in Murray & Jampolsky, 1982, p. 51)　•　•　•

•　•　•　Living with my sister [with autism] made my childhood unbearable. Between her physically violent outbursts, to her imposing rules and obsessions, life with her was a constant challenge. As a child (and teenager), I was very resistant to the controls she imposed on the household. I was often filled with resentment toward her, and my parents for trying to appease her demands. (Seltzer & Krauss, 2002)　•　•　•

•　•　•　Someday, if I do marry and have children, I really hope that no one person will have needs that have to be so much more important than everyone else's. (Paul, 21, in Binkard et al., 1987, p. 23)　•　•　•

Resentment, a strong sentiment frequently expressed by brothers and sisters of people with special needs, is unlikely to go unnoticed by parents. A group of parents of children with muscular dystrophy with whom we met said that among the most pressing concerns their typically developing children experienced was resentment. Their observations serve as an overview of the types of resentment mentioned by siblings of children with diverse special needs. The parents volunteered that their children resented the attention the siblings with muscular dystrophy received, the amount of care and time the siblings required, the perceived unequal treatment for children in the family, being expected to do more around the house and help their siblings with toileting and other needs that the siblings cannot do for themselves, and the limitations on their and the families' lifestyle imposed by the disability.

Loss of Parental Attention

•　•　•　I remember the toys, gifts, and candy that were given in surplus to Lisa in a futile attempt to ease her pain. I felt jealous, neglected, and isolated because of Lisa's illness and the subsequent attention that was given her and taken from me. (Ellis, 1992, p. 2)　•　•　•

••• The toughest thing is always coming second to your sib. Often feelings and wants are put on the back burner so that things work out for your sib. (Amanda M., 19, in Meyer, 2005) •••

One form of resentment occurs when siblings perceive that the child with special needs is receiving more than his or her share of the family's emotional or even financial resources. From the sibling's perspective, the child with special needs becomes the sun in the family's solar system. The siblings of children with cancer interviewed by Koch-Hattem (1986) said that their siblings were receiving more attention, caring, and material possessions since having been diagnosed with cancer. Although many were realistic about the need for the changes, all displayed some degree of envy.

Young siblings may lack the cognitive and affective capabilities to appreciate that their parents' behavior is a response to the genuine needs of the child with a disability, rather than a lack of love or appreciation for their typically developing children. Bendor (1990) noted that some of the children interviewed were frightened by their feelings of anger, and, developmentally, the options available to them for expressing or mastering their negative feelings were limited.

Even when they do comprehend their siblings' needs and their parents' stress, however, brothers and sisters may be faced with another dilemma. One sibling to whom Bendor (1990) spoke summed it up this way: "The worst thing about all the anger you feel inside is that there is no one to blame" (p. 24). Without the target that blame provides, siblings may turn inward, feeling guilty about their anger.

Unequal Treatment and Excessive Demands

••• "You should be ashamed of yourself," her mother told her. "You should be able to control your temper. She can't help it. You can." (Julie, in Remsberg, 1989, p. 15) •••

• • • I guess I have more resentment now about the attention my brother gets than when we were younger. When we were younger, he seemed like a little kid and it was OK for him to get a lot of help. Now it seems like my mom will sit for hours with him while I'm just expected to do my own homework for myself. . . . Nonhandicapped kids can get pushed aside when their brothers or sisters have handicaps. Andrew seems to get help naturally — it's like attention to his needs is "built in to the system." (Mary, 17, in Binkard et al., 1987, p. 10) • • •

• • • I get mad when I get into trouble for things that Vickie gets away with. I try not get mad because I know that she doesn't know any better about some things, but sometimes I just lose it! (Michelle O., 17, in Meyer, 2005) • • •

• • • I mostly missed my mom a lot. She was always away at the hospital with my sister. My brother and I had to stay with Mom's friends or our neighbors all day. When my sister came home and she was mean or bad, she got away with it. If I hit her I got spanked. Why was she so special? (Forrest, age 10, in Murray & Jampolsky, 1982, p. 48) • • •

Brothers and sisters report resentment when children with disabilities or illness are indulged or overprotected or permitted to engage in behaviors unacceptable by other family members. Miller's (1974) study revealed that parents were much less tolerant of siblings' negative behaviors toward their siblings with mental retardation than they were of similar sibling behaviors toward other, typically developing siblings. Further, Miller found that siblings without disabilities were more likely to be punished if they did not engage in a prescribed activity with a sibling with a disability than if they avoided a similar responsibility for a typically developing sibling. Podeanu-Czehotsky's (1975) study of the families of children with cerebral palsy found that in some families life was normal, whereas in other families the child with the disability was indulged and became "a tyrant causing hidden or open conflicts among siblings" (p. 309).

• • • My brother liked to lie on the floor in public places — especially at the mall. As Mom tried to convince Thad to get up, I'd think: "Why doesn't she just yank him up off the floor so these people will stop staring? I would never be able to get away with this behavior." (Kameron P., personal communication, 2004) • • •

Growing up, siblings may find themselves facing a difficult dilemma: They may appreciate that their siblings have bona fide needs, yet, because of their still-egocentric view of the world, they resent them for having these needs. One 16-year-old responded this way when asked what was the most difficult aspect of having a sick sibling: "Having to care so much and being burdened by the responsibility of caring" (Bendor, 1990, p. 28). The girl then described staying home night after night to help her mother when her sick sister had high fevers and was vomiting. She wondered if she was selfish for resenting this role.

When we listen to brothers and sisters at Sibshops or during sibling panels, they sometimes complain that their siblings "get away with murder." Family rules about behavior, chores, bedtime routines, and so forth often do not apply to the child with special needs. Brothers and sisters frequently insist that their sibling could comply with many of the family's rules and requirements "if only my parents would make him [or her] do it."

Siblings' views deserve to be heard, even if as children they lack a parent's understanding of the "bigger picture." Their alternative perspective—which almost always focuses on what they believe their sibling *can* do—can provide parents and service providers with fresh insights regarding a child's actual abilities. "My brother never has to unload the dishwasher because he has Down syndrome," one brother told us. "But he can do it. I know he can, because when my parents aren't home, I make him unload the dishwasher."

Parfit (1975) has recommended that parents avoid overprotecting children with disabilities by discussing with their typically developing children the behaviors that are unavoidable due to the siblings' disabilities and the discipline that can help modify the problem behaviors. Brothers and sisters, then, can advise parents of behaviors for which their siblings should be held responsible: "Children are often more sensible and sensitive about such matters than adults" (Parfit, 1975, p. 20).

Resentment Regarding Failure to Plan for the Future

•　•　• Julie feels that her mother overprotects Kathy and babies her more than necessary. But, "It's too sensitive an area between us to talk about. If I ask 'What's she going to do if you're gone?' the subject is changed." (Remsberg, 1989, p. 16)　•　•　•

•　•　• I worry a lot about what will happen when my parents die, and somewhat resent that I will be the primary caregiver—which I'm ashamed about. (Seltzer & Krauss, 2002)　•　•　•

In families where there is a child with developmental disabilities, frequently there is an assumption—often unspoken—that brothers and sisters will someday become guardians of their sibling as adults. From parents and siblings we have met, we know that some siblings are conceived in order to fill a role: someone who will look after the family member with the disability when the parents no longer can.

Not surprisingly, their siblings' future and the role they will play in that future is an especially poignant concern for many adult brothers and sisters. Psychiatrist E. Fuller Torrey (1992), a brother of a woman who has schizophrenia, has noted: "Demographically, we will outlive our parents; demographically, we will get involved with our siblings."

When parents fail to involve siblings in planning for the future of the person with the disability, resentment is likely to occur. "My parents won't consider letting Bobby try a group home," one sister told us. "That's all well and good now, but what happens when they die? Will he have to come live with me?"

•　•　• In the planning for my three disabled brothers' future, my mother did not include any of the typical sibs. And the plan she had was outdated and inadequate and forced us into crisis mode when she passed away. This has had a huge impact on our lives and marriages. I was always quite sympathetic about the burden my mom had but this lack of planning made me mad at her at the same time that I was grieving her death. (Nora H., personal communication, 2005)　•　•　•

••• My brother lived with my parents until they died. He was about 39 and he was very depressed, not because they died but because he had no life. I am his guardian and I took care of him for a while but came to realize that I could not do a very good job. He needed more stimulation than I could give him. He now lives in a group home with five other people, three guys and two gals. He has gotten so much better since he moved there. But I have to admit that I cried for 6 months trying to figure out what would be best for both of us for the long term. Making the decision was the hardest thing I have ever done. I don't think I will ever get over the anger with my parents for leaving me with the decision. (Victoria L., personal communication, 2002) •••

We will never forget the testimony of a young woman who participated in a sibling panel we hosted. This woman, a mother with two young children, clearly loved her parents and her sister, who has cerebral palsy and emotional problems. Her resentment toward her parents, however, was unmistakable. With tears welling in her eyes, she told how her parents, who had grown too frail to take care of her sister's many special needs, "dropped the sister on her doorstep." Her sister's presence and many demands, she said, had been extremely difficult for all members of her young family.

Failure to plan adequately can cause resentment among surviving siblings as well. Adult siblings—generally sisters—have told us how they have somehow inherited all of the responsibilities associated with caring for the sibling who is disabled. "[My siblings] are all patting me on the back, telling me what a good job I'm doing and all that, but they don't help at all" (Fish, 1993).

Even when parents plan for the future, their expectations can cause guilt and resentment. "My parents never wanted my brother to live outside the family home," one sister told us, "and when we talked about what we would do when they were gone, it was apparent that they wanted Jim to come live with me. I love my brother. I will always be involved with my brother. But I don't want him to live with me." Other adult siblings have told of promises extracted by dying parents that they will take in their sibling with disabilities.

Advanced medical technologies allow people with disabilities to live longer than in previous generations. Social policy and diminishing economic resources dictate that people with disabilities will live in the community and closer to their families than in previous generations, when the state assumed an in loco parentis role for adults with disabilities. Therefore, it is reasonable to expect that adult siblings of the baby-boom and post-baby-boom generation will be more involved in the lives of their brothers and sisters with disabilities than any previous generation. At the same time, these adult siblings face increasing uncertainty about their own retirement and health care access. Unless parents and service providers involve siblings in planning for their children's future, many adults with disabilities will soon have sibling guardians who are both ill-prepared for the job and potentially resentful of the responsibilities placed on them.

INCREASED RESPONSIBILITIES

••• When my parents went out for the evening, they would hire a baby sitter, but baby sitters didn't know how to handle a little girl who screamed all night and bit herself and did things like that, so they would get me up to take care of her. So from the time I was 5 years old, I was being responsible and helping and doing things. My two brothers have had a much harder time with it, especially the brother who is less than a year older than my sister. He won't even talk about her, and this has been 30 some years and he will not talk about her. (Fish, 1993) • • •

• • •   From age 6, I had to help with both my typical and disabled sibs. After coming home from first grade, I fed my baby sister. Starting at age 8, I changed diapers and did laundry. On weekends, I got up early to supervise my three disabled brothers. Starting at age 12, I babysat all seven of my younger siblings by myself. (Margaret H., personal communication, 2005) • • •

• • •   The toughest thing about being a sib are the sacrifices you have to make. It means being flexible 24/7 and always being aware that there are often changes that need to be made. (Alli J., 15, in Meyer, 2005, p. 141) • • •

• • •   As soon as I could see over the counter in the kitchen, I was making my own school lunch right beside my mother—who was making the exact same lunch for my brother. (Kameron P., personal communication, 2003) • • •

• • •   The responsibility definitely stinks. I get few privileges for all the work I do for my family and my little brother. (Daniel C., 17, in Meyer, 2005, p. 141) • • •

About caregiving responsibilities, Milton Seligman (1979) wrote:

• • •   The extent to which a sibling may be held responsible for a handicapped brother or sister bears a strong relationship to the perception and feelings children, adolescents, and adults have about their handicapped sibling and their parents. Available research supports the notion that a child's (especially a female child's) excessive responsibility for a handicapped sib is related to the development of anger, resentment and guilt, and quite possibly subsequent psychological disturbance. (p. 530) • • •

Early research on siblings of children with developmental disabilities frequently focused on the caregiving demands assumed by siblings—especially sisters. Authors such as Farber (1960) and Fowle (1973) observed that sisters, especially oldest sisters, were more adversely affected than brothers by the presence of a child with a disability. Other researchers from this era, including Cleveland and Miller (1977) and Gath (1974), felt that oldest daughters were often pushed into a surrogate parent role with the child with special needs, especially in large and low-income families. This heavy caregiving responsibility, they felt, often isolated them from their age mates. If they have too many responsibilities, older sisters may be at risk for educational failure and increased disturbances (Gath, 1974) and stress (Farber, 1960).

Cleveland and Miller's (1977) research suggested that the oldest female siblings may experience a sibling's disability as a double-edged sword. Their research revealed that oldest sisters were most likely to enter helping professions and to remain involved with the sibling with a disability as an adult; it also showed that this group was most likely to seek professional help for personal problems.

How much of this research—some of it 30 years old—remains valid? What effect, if any, have programs (e.g., respite care, special sitters, "Special Saturday," child care for children with disabilities) and movement toward community-based schooling and life had on the caregiving demands placed on brothers and sisters?

In a 1987 study of preschool siblings of children with disabilities conducted by Lobato, Barbour, Hall, and Miller, sisters were found to have the greatest degree of responsibility for child care and household tasks, although the difference was not statistically significant when compared with brothers of children with disabilities and with siblings of typically developing children. The sisters of children with disabilities, however, received significantly fewer privileges and experienced more restrictions on social routines compared with matched controls. Brothers of children with disabilities experienced the opposite—more privileges and fewer restrictions on social activities. According to Lobato and her colleagues, the sex of the typically developing siblings appeared to shape the daily living routines among families with children who have disabilities but not among control families.

Stoneman and colleagues have conducted extensive research on caregiving responsibilities of siblings of children with developmental disabilities (Stoneman, Brody, Davis, Crapps, & Malone, 1991). In one study of younger siblings of children with and without disabilities, they found that younger siblings of children with disabilities babysat, monitored, and helped care for their older siblings while the comparison group performed significantly less total child care and never baby-sat their older siblings.

During observational studies conducted by Stoneman, Brody, Davis, and Crapps (1987, 1988, 1989), children with disabilities (ages 4–8 years) were videotaped with their older siblings (ages 6–12 years). According to the authors, siblings of children with disabilities—especially older sisters—more readily assumed the role of manager or caregiver for their brothers or sisters.

Adult sisters seemed to continue to be more involved in caregiving and planning for their sibling with a disability (Gorelick, 1996). In Orsmond and Seltzer's 2000 survey of adults who had a sibling with mental retardation, sisters reported more involvement with their sibling than brothers. Sisters were more knowledgeable about their sibling's skills and needs, had more discussions with their parents about their sibling, and had more contact with their sibling. These findings—similar to those found by Pruchno, Patrick, and Burant (1996)—are echoed in the membership of SibNet, the leading listserv for adult siblings. Over 95% of the 600 members of SibNet are sisters.

That older sisters assume greater caregiving responsibilities in families where there is a child with a disability is hardly surprising. After all, many oldest daughters find themselves assuming the role of surrogate mother, regardless of the presence of a child with a disability in the family. When Stoneman et al. (1988) compared older sisters in families where there is a disability with a comparison group, however, they found that the older sisters of children with disabilities baby-sat and had more child care responsibilities than any other group of children. Also, the more family responsibilities these sisters assumed, the less they participated in their own activities outside of the homes, and the more conflict was found with the children who had the disability.

In their 1988 study of older siblings, Stoneman et al. found that for brothers and sisters of children with disabilities, an increase in observed sibling conflict and a decrease in positive sibling interaction was associated with child care responsibilities, which was not found with the comparison group. This finding apparently does not apply to other domestic chores. In fact, the authors noted, increased older sibling responsibility for other household chores corresponded to less, rather than more, observed sibling conflict.

As expected, Stoneman and colleagues (1988, 1991) found that responsibilities assumed by the siblings of children with disabilities (e.g., helping with dressing, feeding) tended to be greater when the child with the disability had fewer adaptive skills. Less adaptively competent children, suggested Stoneman and Brody (1993), seemed to place greater demands for caregiving on siblings, regardless of the birth order.

It would be far too easy and unrealistic to recommend that brothers, and especially sisters, of children with special health and developmental needs be spared domestic duties. After all, "special needs" invariably translate into increased caregiving needs and household chores. Besides, the responsible attitudes that so many siblings seem to have are in part a result of successfully handling duties performed in service to their siblings and families.

• • • I didn't resent [her] dependency, though. It's been my whole life. I always had to bring Sandy to the bathroom and help her get ready before I could go to school. (Rachel, 21, in Binkard et al., 1987, p. 20) • • •

• • • As a child, I know I was a very important part of Martha's life. I was the only one she would go potty for. I was the only one who could braid her hair, take her into a store, and stop her tantrums. (Westra, 1992, p. 4) • • •

The research of Stoneman et al. (1988) suggests some general guidelines for assigning domestic chores to siblings of children with special needs. First, the type of chores assigned should be considered. Are child care demands causing the conflict described by Stoneman et al. (1988)? If so, parents may wish to consider offering siblings a choice in the household responsibilities they assume. Parents can offer siblings an opportunity to contribute to the family in other ways—shopping, meal preparation, or cleaning.

Second, the number of demands placed on the typically developing child should also be considered. Parents should be advised to compare their children's level of child care and household duties with those of their peers to determine if their chores are excessive or preventing them from participating in at least some activities outside of the home. Responsibility is good, but so is soccer, being in the school play, or learning to play the saxophone.

Third, who is assuming the caregiving demands should be considered. In their research on siblings of adults with mental retardation, Orsmond and Seltzer (2000) found that brothers have the most negative feelings when their sibling with a disability is a sister. The researchers stressed the importance of increasing the involvement and building a strong relationship between these brothers and sisters. It is not surprising that it is sisters who bear the brunt of the caregiving responsibilities. Brothers, according to Grossman (1972), are often exempted from demanding caregiving duties. Parents should be encouraged to ensure that the chores and opportunities for interactions are spread equitably among brothers and sisters.

PRESSURE TO ACHIEVE

• • • Ever since I was a child, I have been put into that role—rescuer, perfect child, the one who would make everything right. And all the time while this craziness was going on in my family, I was trying to maintain my grade point average to go on to college and become a doctor. (David, in Leder, 1991, p. 22) • • •

• • • I couldn't express anger. There was lots of denial and I had to remain well-behaved all the time. (Selma, family therapist, in Fink, 1984, p. 6) • • •

Over the years we have had the good fortune to talk to many parents about their children. Some of these parents have told us of a situation they believe to be unusual: One child attends a special education program, while another child is enrolled in a program for gifted children. The perceived pressure on siblings of people with special needs to excel in academics, sports, music, or even behavior has long been noticed by clinicians. Earlier writings suggested that parents placed the pressure on their typically developing children, as if to compensate for the "failure" resulting from the other child's disability. Whether consciously or unconsciously, parents can pressure their children to compensate for the limitations of the child with a disability, creating resentment and anxiety for typically developing siblings (Murphy, 1979; Schild, 1976).

Grossman (1972) found that this pressure to achieve was especially true when the child with the disability was a son. Older only daughters are particularly prone to dual stresses, suggested Cleveland and Miller (1977). These daughters feel pressured to make up for the parents' unfulfilled hopes for the sibling with the disability; they also experience the increased parent-surrogate responsibilities that are most often delegated to daughters rather than sons.

• • •   I definitely put pressure on myself to achieve. It's just my brother and me, so I'm the only one who can make good grades, get my driver's license, go to the prom, graduate from high school, college, graduate school, get married, have a career and children — all by myself — of course that's pressure. (Kameron P., personal communication, 2004) • • •

Although parents may be the source of some of the pressure siblings experience (as one brother told us: "My parents expect me to take up all the slack!"), it may be that siblings place much of the pressure on themselves. Coleman (1990) studied 12- to 14-year-old siblings of children with developmental disabilities and compared them with siblings of children who had (only) physical disabilities and siblings of typically developing children. Specifically, Coleman investigated the siblings' self-concept, their need to compensate for the child's deficit, their actual achievement, and parental demands. Coleman found no significant differences among the groups with regard to the subjects' self-concept. There were significant group differences with regard to the need for achievement, however, with siblings of children with developmental disabilities scoring higher than siblings of children with physical disabilities only or with no disabilities.

For the siblings of children who have developmental disabilities, Coleman (1990) found that as their academic achievement increased, their self-concept decreased. Coleman speculated that this could be the result of internal conflict and could stem from survivor guilt or setting unattainable achievement goals. No such relationship was found between self-concept and achievement for the other two groups. Finally, Coleman found no significant differences among the three groups regarding siblings' perceptions of parental demands.

• • •   I put pressure on myself; whether my parents encouraged that stance I don't know. (Cynthia, in Leder, 1991, p. 210) • • •

Suggesting that parents attempt to compensate for the loss associated with having a child who has special needs by placing pressure on their typically developing children may be too simplistic and unidirectional. Siblings may place pressure on themselves for a variety of reasons. This hypothesis would certainly apply to the sister mentioned earlier in this chapter who felt that her success in human services was "shame-driven" and could not enjoy her many accomplishments.

But there can be other reasons as well. The motivation may be attention: As one sister told us, "Growing up I did well in school because that was my way of getting attention from my parents." Another brother said he did well in school to counteract the profound loss that his parents experienced about his sister's disability. Another sister volunteered that success in academics was her way of demonstrating to the world that it was her sister, not she, who had a disability.

• • •   I never exactly sat down and decided to do this, but I put a lot of pressure on myself to always "be good" and to excel in school. I think this was, in part, to show the world that I'm different from my sister. It took me a long time to be able to be okay with not being perfect, to allow myself to be human. And trying to keep up the facade of being perfect is an incredibly isolating and tiring experience! (Stephanie G., personal communication, 2005) • • •

High achievement in academics, sports, or behavior may seem like a dubious "unusual concern." After all, Grossman's (1972) study revealed that not only were there no significant differences between college-age siblings of people with and without mental retardation in academic achievement, overall academic functioning (including social adaptation), intelligence, and anxiety levels, but also that the siblings of people with mental retardation scored higher on measures of overall college functioning.

Indeed, the conscientious attitude some siblings have for their schoolwork would suggest that their need to achieve is, in fact, an "unusual opportunity." And it may well be. Parents and service providers, however, should be alert for siblings whose efforts are compulsive or neurotic (e.g., the sibling who cannot be satisfied with a B + average), or for siblings who are unhappy, despite many successes.

Chapter **3**

Information Needs of Siblings

   • • • The hardest thing is the uncertainty—not knowing what's coming next—and the feeling of vulnerability if something does happen and that you're open to being really hurt. Also, not knowing if my little brother will wake up in the morning or when a kiss I give him will be the last. (Rebekah C., 17, in Meyer, 2005) • • •

   • • • It's kind of frustrating not always knowing what they are saying about him. I am a member of the family, too, and I deserve to know what's going on with him just as much as they do. I mean: What if they aren't always there to take care of him? How am I supposed to be able to take care of him if I really don't know anything about him or the problems he has had in the past? Or what meds he is allergic to? That kind of stuff. I need to know, too, and I don't think that they realize that. (Alisa A., 18, in Meyer, 2005) • • •

Throughout their lives, brothers and sisters will have a need for information about their siblings' condition. Their need will closely parallel the informational needs of their parents, yet parents have distinct advantages. As adults, parents' understanding of the world and the way it works is more mature and benefits from a lifetime of experiences. Also, parents have far greater access to information—written and otherwise—about their child's condition and its implications than their children do.

    Siblings of children with disabilities have a compelling need for information about the condition of their brother or sister with a disability and its implications. They need information for reassurance, to answer their own questions and questions posed by others, and to plan for their future. And, unless their brother or sister has a terminal condition, the need will be lifelong and the topics ever-changing. Throughout their lives, the types of information siblings need—as well as how it is optimally presented—will vary according to the siblings' age.

INFORMATION NEEDS ACCORDING TO AGE

Preschool brothers and sisters will have a need for information about their siblings' special needs—and so will siblings who are senior citizens. What they will want and need to know will evolve throughout their lives and their family's lifespan.

Preschoolers

Debra Lobato (1990) has written that children's understanding of their siblings' special needs "will represent a unique blend of what they have been told, overheard, observed, and conjured up on their very own" (p. 21). When siblings lack adequate, age-appropriate information, and a mature understanding of the world, misunderstandings will be neither unusual nor surprising.

• • • I remember walking into my sister's room one morning [and] seeing large clumps of blond hair on her pillow. "Mommy, why is Lisa's hair falling out?" I asked. "She's sick," was the only reply possible from my mother; she had no time for lengthy explanations to a 3-year-old. So I was left to solve the mystery by myself. (Ellis, 1992, p. 1) • • •

Typically, young children interpret their world in terms of their own immediate observations. Because they have a limited range of experiences from which to draw, they frequently engage in magical thinking.

• • • "My kitty is sick!" said a 6-year-old girl who came to me, crying. Her cat had been coughing up hairballs, and this little girl was afraid that it caught cancer from her brother, who had been throwing up from his chemotherapy treatments. She looked at me, sighed deeply, and said, "This chemo has been hard on all of us." (Schorr-Ribera, 1992, p. 2) • • •

To prevent such misconceptions, preschoolers need to know that they cannot catch their siblings' disability and they did not cause the condition. These concepts—while obvious to adults—may not be clear to a young child who has caught her sister's cold and has a preschooler's sense of causality.

Children ages 2–6 are concrete thinkers. Explanations of disabilities or illnesses to children at this age should be as clear as possible. Debra Lobato (1990) noted that children as young as 3 can recognize some of their brothers' and sisters' problems, especially when they have had contact with other children and their siblings are older.

• • • John plays cars with me and he loves to break dance. Sometimes he pulls off a shoe and I have to put it back on, but he's just slower than us, that's all. (4-year-old brother, in Fink, 1984, p. 6) • • •

Lobato counsels that 3 years is not too early to share comments about a child's disability or illness. One means of explaining a disability is to describe it in terms of differences in behavior or routine. Thus, a 4-year-old who accompanies his 2-year-old sister to an early intervention program may understand his sister's disability this way: "Down syndrome means that you have to go to school to learn how to talk." To another preschooler, cerebral palsy might mean "you have a hard time walking, and a lady comes to your house to help you learn how to eat." Although clearly incomplete, these definitions can be the foundation for more involved explanations at later ages.

School-Age Children

During their grade-school years, typically developing siblings need information to answer their own questions about the disability or illness as well as questions posed by classmates, friends, or even strangers. Older children may harbor private theories to explain their siblings' problems—even when accurate information has been provided. Sourkes (1990) recounted the observation of a 10-year-old boy whose teenage sister had a leg amputated due to osteogenic sarcoma:

● ● ● My sister hurt her leg on the chain of her bike. She didn't even notice it until I pointed it out to her. I don't ride my bike anymore. I'm afraid to. One night I went out and I broke the chain on my bike so that I couldn't ride it. I told my mother that the bike broke by itself, but I really broke the chain. (p. 3) ● ● ● ●

Other siblings may hold beliefs about the cause of the condition that place the blame on the child with special needs. "She probably got it because she never drank water or something" said one 13-year-old sister of a 7-year-old Wilms' tumor patient. Blaming the patient "may be a reflection of the sibling's own anger, a part of the belief system of the sibling or family, or a projection of guilt onto the patient." (Koch-Hattem, 1986, p. 113)

● ● ● My sister's diagnosis is very strongly connected in my mind to nail polish. She was getting into that kind of stuff and I wasn't and so I thought it was kind of gross. I thought she got a rash because of the nail polish, which then caused the cancer. (Naomi, 22, in Sourkes, 1990, p. 12) ● ● ●

● ● ● I always knew that Nick had spastic quadriplegia. But it took years for me to know what that meant. (Barbara, personal communication, 2005) ● ● ●

School-age children may have more specific questions than preschoolers. They may ask, "Why does she have to go to the hospital?" "Why can some people with cerebral palsy walk and some can't?" "What does amniocentesis mean?" "What's physical therapy? Does it hurt?" "Why is Stephanie getting so fat?" "What does retarded mean?" Yet obtaining this information can be a problem for siblings of this age.

Even teenagers may have misconceptions about their siblings' problems. Some may assign a psychological or metaphysical reason for the diagnosis. One teen commented:

● ● ● Well, I think maybe it was God's way of telling our family to pull together. There had been a lot of arguing and a lot of dissension in my family and maybe this was his [sic] way to bring us together. (Sourkes, 1990, p. 4) ● ● ●

Teenagers

Like preschoolers and grade-school children, teenagers often have specific questions about the special needs of their brothers or sisters.

• • • Why was his hair falling out? Why was he going to the hospital all the time? Why was he getting bone marrows all the time? It never occurred to me that he might die. What was happening? I didn't get to go to the hospital to see him. What was leukemia? Why was he getting so many presents? (Chet, 14, in Murray & Jampolsky, 1982, p. 35) • • •

AVOIDING MISCONCEPTIONS ABOUT THE CONDITION

• • • My mother didn't tell me what was going on because she wanted to protect my feelings. I was so angry because Jeana and I were so close. I was so terribly afraid. I didn't know what was happening; I was afraid of the unknown. If you know what the problem is, you can face up to it and work it out; but if you don't understand, you can't handle it. (Joanne, 16, in Murray & Jampolsky, 1982, p. 36) • • •

How a family handles the dissemination of information about the disability or illness will greatly influence a typically developing sibling's adjustment to the condition. Some parents, seeking to protect their children from the sadness they are experiencing, choose to tell their children as little as possible. This, siblings tell us, is to be avoided. When left in the dark about what is happening to a brother or sister, siblings may make up their own stories that will be worse than the truth. They may even blame themselves for their siblings' conditions. Obtaining information, then, can be reassuring, even comforting for a brother or sister. They tell us that they still worry, but their concerns will be easier to manage because they are based on facts rather than fantasies.

• • • My advice is that doctors and parents ought to give information to the *brothers and sisters straight*! Sometimes, instead of telling them the truth, parents and doctors tell siblings a lot of baloney. It is easier to handle when at least you have all the facts. (Maria, 15, in Murray & Jampolsky, 1982, p. 43) • • •

Or, as Callahan (1990) noted, "Information, even concerning a painful subject, is preferable to ignorance distorted by imagination" (p. 157). Traditional sources of information available to parents usually are not available to brothers and sisters. With rare exceptions such as the resources noted in Appendix B, most books, web sites, and materials about disabilities and illnesses have been created for adults.

Siblings are also frequently excluded from another traditional source of information: the teachers, physicians, therapists, nurses, and other providers serving children with special health and developmental needs. Brothers and sisters seldom accompany their parents to clinic visits, or individualized family service plan (IFSP), individualized education program (IEP), or transition planning meetings, and if they do, their opinions, thoughts, and questions are unlikely to be sought. Left out of the loop or relegated to waiting rooms, siblings report feeling ignored or isolated.

• • • I went with Lisa and my mother several times a week to the hospital where Lisa would get finger pokes and sometimes bone marrows (which I thought of as "bone arrows" because the procedure entailed being punctured in the back by a large needle). She lost all her hair. . . . Sometimes she threw up and sometimes she stayed overnight at the hospital. I remember not understanding at all what was happening to my sister, and not receiving any explanations. (Ellis, 1992, pp. 1–2) ● ● ●

● ● ● Once when I was little, Monica had a seizure in the middle of the night. My parents had to rush her to the hospital because she was not breathing and left me at home with a baby sitter. My mother and sister stayed in the hospital for a week while I sat at home wondering what had happened. My parents hadn't informed me so I wasn't sure what was going on. (Martha P., 13, in Meyer, 2005) ● ● ●

● ● ● My sister came here for therapy. She got to go on these scooters, but I had to sit in the waiting room with my mom the whole time. Why isn't there something for brothers and sisters to play with while they're there? When you are a kid you don't understand. All your parents are telling you is that she's special and has to go to these special programs. Well, I wanted to be special too! (Fish, 1993) ● ● ●

● ● ● My parents sometimes include me in conversations, but most of the time I have to listen in on discussions with doctors or discussions between my parents. For example, I had to find out about one of Sarah's surgeries from when the doctor called to remind my parents of the surgery and I answered the phone. I do wish that my parents would include me more because I'm going to find out what's going on eventually. (Stephie N., 15, in Meyer, 2005) ● ● ●

The isolation, loneliness, and loss some siblings experience will be complicated by a lack of information about their siblings' special needs (Seligman, 1983). In some families, siblings receive a clear (if unspoken) signal that the condition is not to be discussed, leaving siblings to feel alone with their concerns and questions. A. Tashiro wrote about growing up in an extended family in Hawaii:

● ● ● Joyce was born soon after me. Joyce, Sharon, and I sunbathed together and explored the property between the houses, with cousin Miles as our fearless leader. Then Joyce got very sick and didn't ''grow up'' like the rest of us. . . . Joyce was no longer at home. We would ask, ''Where is Joyce?'' ''How is she?'' ''What's Joyce doing?'' Simple questions from children. We received no answers, except, ''Don't ask those questions anymore.'' ''Never ask Aunty Florence about Joyce.'' How were we to know any better? Our friend, our neighbor, our cousin, was no longer in the front house. We were only 8 and 10 at the time. (A. Tashiro, personal communication, 1992) ● ● ●

Even when parents are happy to answer questions, some siblings will keep their questions and concerns to themselves. These brothers and sisters are reluctant to ask questions, having witnessed their parents' sadness caused by the disability or illness. "Why would I ask my parents about something which makes them cry?" one sister told us.

　　Some parents are unaware that their children harbor questions they feel will cause discomfort for either the child with a disability or the parents. Often parents will be willing to answer any question their child asks, but when the child does not ask the questions, parents may assume that the child has no interest in the topic. Sisters and brothers tell us that parents must be proactive in offering information:

• • • I would like people to understand that children need information, that both handicapped and normal children have feelings and fears. I would like to let people know that they need to be open with their children, all their children, that just because the sisters and brothers don't ask, it doesn't mean that they don't want to know. (Pat, in Remsberg, 1989, p. 4) • • •

PROVIDING BROTHERS AND SISTERS NEEDED INFORMATION

What, then, are the best ways to provide a sibling with information? Siblings, young and not-so-young, recommend a variety of approaches. Few, however, are as important as the family's attitude toward the topic.

Keep the Sibling's Special Needs an Open Topic

• • • Parents have to sit down and talk to the brothers and sisters who aren't handicapped about what the handicap really means. Kids don't automatically understand it by themselves. Maybe the other kids need some help, too, understanding that the handicap won't go away, that it will be there and is a fact of life. . . . I love my brother, but I'd like to understand more about his handicap. (Beth, 16, in Binkard et al., 1987, p. 5) • • •

Although Beth encourages parents to "sit down and talk" to their typically developing children, many siblings report that this is an uncomfortable situation for all parties and have likened it to being told about the birds and the bees. A far better way, they tell us, is to keep the topic of the special needs open and to offer information frequently, preferably in small doses. If brothers and sisters observe their parents openly discussing the disability or illness, they will learn to do so as well.

Answer Siblings' Questions About the Condition

If parents answer children's questions about siblings' special needs in a forthright manner, and if they make their children feel glad that they asked, their children will not only gain an understanding of their siblings' special needs but will also become confident enough to approach their parents whenever they have questions. Of course, not all siblings will ask questions. Parents need to adopt some strategies that can help all siblings—school-age and older—acquire the needed information.

Provide Siblings with Written Materials

• • • My lack of information about my brother's disability led me to read everything and anything about cerebral palsy, including the novel *Karen* and textbooks on cerebral palsy and speech. When I was in college studying to become a speech-language pathologist, I laughed when I learned I was going to read the revised versions of the two textbooks I had read as a sixth grader. (Barbara, personal communication, 2005) • • •

Another way to help siblings learn more about their brothers' and sisters' special needs is to utilize print and web-based materials on the disability or illness. Appendix B lists various books—both fiction and nonfiction—that can help young readers learn more about various disabilities. Also, parents, family members, and service providers can contact agencies or associations representing the child's disability or illness and request information prepared for young readers. If the agency does not have such materials or web content (and many do not), they should be challenged to create them or provide links to them.

Include Siblings in Visits with Service Providers

•　•　•　Let him be as involved in the medical side as he wishes to be. Ask him if he would like to visit his brother or sister in the hospital. Let him ask questions and discuss treatments with you and the medical staff. (Schorr-Ribera, 1992, p. 1)　•　•　•

•　•　•　I wish the doctor had told me his hair would fall out. It surprised me when I saw him bald. It would scare me when he was throwing up because I thought he was dying. Later on, I found out that his baldness and his throwing up were side effects of medicine. . . . My advice to others is to try and get as much information as you can. I was one of the last ones in my neighborhood to find out he had cancer. (Kurt, 13, in Murray & Jampolsky, 1982, pp. 38–39)　•　•　•

There has been a growing recognition that a child's disability or illness will affect more than the child and his or her mother. The professional literature today more often refers to the family unit, whereas in the past, the focus was primarily on the mother, or the parents, and the child with the disability or illness. Even when an agency claims to offer family-centered service, brothers and sisters rarely are invited to clinic visits, or involved in the IEP, IFSP, or transition-planning process. Service providers who fail to address siblings' concerns squander significant opportunities and resources.

　　　Inviting—but not requiring—siblings to attend meetings with service providers can benefit all parties. When included, siblings can obtain helpful, reassuring information about a sibling's condition (e.g., behavior, schooling, future plans). Brothers and sisters can contribute to the team by providing information and a unique, informed perspective. Their views on issues such as barriers to inclusion with same-age neighborhood peers or a sibling's ability to accomplish household responsibilities are likely to be insightful—if frequently unsentimental. Parents gain a fresh perspective on the siblings' concerns, which can result in improved communication about the child's disability.

Furthermore, when invited to meet with service providers, siblings are brought into the loop. A message is sent to family members and service providers alike that brothers and sisters are valued members of the child's team. Including them acknowledges the important roles they currently assume in their siblings' lives and, for many, roles they will have as adults.

Finally, information can promote understanding. Iles (1979) found that when healthy siblings had sufficient knowledge of their siblings' illness and treatment, they had increased empathy for their parents and greater compassion for their ill brothers and sisters. To be sure, it will not always be appropriate to invite a brother or sister to a meeting: A sibling may be too young or a meeting may be about delicate issues best discussed first with parents. Whenever possible, however, parents and professionals should invite the child's brothers and sisters. At the very least, this will prevent siblings from experiencing the emotional exclusion of sitting alone in a waiting room.

Determine the Sibling's Knowledge of the Condition

Although the above strategies—keeping the topic open, answering siblings' questions, providing written materials, and inviting siblings to meetings—will go a long way toward meeting siblings' informational needs, the only way to be certain siblings understand the disability or illness will be to have them explain it to someone else. One time-tested strategy is for parents to check in with their typically developing children approximately once per year during the school years.

To do this as unobtrusively as possible, parents should choose a time when they are alone with their children, perhaps on the way to soccer practice or play rehearsal. As the child with special needs naturally enters the topic of conversation, parents pose a hypothetical situation to the typically developing sibling: "If someone asked you, 'What's the matter with David?' what would you say?" Asking the question like this will provide the parent with a fairly accurate window on the child's understanding of his or her sibling's disability. Because the question, as asked, is typical of questions asked of most siblings at one time or another, siblings are likely to be interested in discussing what a satisfactory response might be. Parents then listen carefully to their child's response. If the child seems to have a good grasp for his or her age, parents should compliment the child for his or her knowledge and consider adding a few facts to the knowledge base. If the answer needs some corrections, this will be an ideal chance to improve the understanding of the sibling's condition. If the typically developing child does not have a satisfactory answer, parents can provide some elementary information. Even a "canned" response will help the child respond when asked this question.

WHEN SIBLINGS THINK ABOUT THE FUTURE

• • •   As she grew toward womanhood, fears about the future began piling onto Pat's slim shoulders. "I thought about someday having children of my own," she says. "It seemed like a terrible worry." Late one night, sitting in the kitchen with her mother, Pat started to brood, and then to cry. "I wanted to ask her about it," Pat says, "but I didn't know how." Finally, she just blurted out her question. "If I have children, will they be like Kevin?" (Pat, in Remsberg, 1989, p. 7) • • •

• • •   I am terrified to have a child with a disability such as my brother's. I don't think I could handle it. Genetics counseling before planning pregnancy is definitely a necessity. (Seltzer & Krauss, 2002) • • •

• • •   Mother kept repeating that sooner or later I'd have to face my responsibility; that I would have to take care of Connie when she was "gone." At that time I did not equate "gone" with the word "dead." I soon realized what it meant after several suicide attempts by Mother during my teen years. And I finally understood years later that Connie was ultimately my responsibility after Mother was really "gone." (Royal, 1991, p. 4) • • •

• • •   We all have to worry. Who else is going to be there? I will have to worry and it will be my responsibility; I think about it all the time. I think about the person I am going to marry. When I meet someone, they are not going to just marry me, but they are going to have to love my brother and know he is going to be around all my life. (Fish, 1993) • • •

One very difficult topic for brothers and sisters to discuss with their parents is their concern about the future. A typically developing child may wonder, "Will my own children have disabilities?" and "What responsibility will I have to my sibling when my parents die?"

Childbearing Concerns

Siblings' concerns about their childbearing potential may be rooted in their often unexpressed but nevertheless real fears about the hereditary nature of the disability (Parfit, 1975). Often these fears are unfounded, but siblings need information and reassurance to that effect. In the event that the condition does have a hereditary basis, older siblings, prior to their childbearing years, need an opportunity to learn about genetic implications of the disability (Murphy, 1979).

• • •   I really don't know what we'd have done if the tests had shown I could pass on osteogenesis imperfecta. I've always loved kids and assumed I'd have some someday. I hadn't really thought about what my mother's and sister's osteogenesis imperfecta could mean for myself. But my husband did bring it up when we were engaged and thought it was something to explore. Luckily, we found out there was no way I could pass it on. (Rachel, 21, in Binkard et al., 1987, p. 20) • • •

Concerns About Future Responsibilities

•　•　•　The future is so unpredictable. Most likely, my parents will care for Nathaniel and Sophia as long as they are capable. I'll probably go off to college, start a career and a family, and visit whenever it's possible. When my parents can't care for them anymore, I'll probably help choose a place for them to live because I don't think I'd be able to provide the care they need as much as I would like to. It's painful to think about, but I will still make them a priority in my life. (Althea R., 13, in Meyer, 2005)　•　•　•

•　•　•　My sister and I have this picture of the future, this plan. We are going to buy a house together. Neither of us will get married. When we get jobs, one of us will work days, the other will work nights. That way we can take care of our brother. (17-year-old sister, at a sibling panel)　•　•　•

•　•　•　I have a lot of fear inside for Allen. I think I have a good future ahead—I work very hard in school and do well—but what will happen to him? I'm sure he'll stay at home with my mom and dad a lot longer than I will, but will he ever be able to get married and have kids? (Beth, 16, in Binkard et al., 1987, p. 7)　•　•　•

•　•　•　I worry about my brother many times during the day and I confess that in the darkness of night I pray that I may outlive him so I can advocate for him during his lifetime. . . . No matter how good a facility or staff may be, I contend that nothing can take the place of the love and caring of family members. (Liska, V., 1996, p. 10)　•　•　•

It is not at all unusual for school-age children to express a desire to care for their sibling when they become adults. They may reveal this sentiment in statements such as, "When we all grow up, I want Alicia to come live with me." Like other children when they reach their teens, however, it is also common for them to dream of a life beyond their immediate family. Unlike other teens, siblings of people with disabilities or illnesses may feel that their future options are limited by their siblings' many needs. They may feel that whom they marry and where they may move will be restricted because of their sibling with special needs.

•　•　•　I just keep thinking that even if I do move away, if I go away to school or if I have a job away, I am going to have to come back to Columbus. Gilbert is only comfortable in certain surroundings. If you take him away from those surroundings, he won't function. So this is going to be my home someday.
Interviewer:　*Do you think about this a lot? How much?*
Well—now planning my major—very much. There are only so many jobs in Columbus. (Fish, 1993)　•　•　•

•　•　•　Right now it's as if I don't have plans for the future. Partly it might be because Jean doesn't either. I guess at some point we all had dreams. I used to have very distinct dreams and goals about an acting career. But right now I'm not strong enough to make a decision and go after something. I'm still too tied in with what's going on at home to break the cycle and reclaim my life. I guess Jean and I are in the same boat. (David, 29, in Leder, 1991, p. 24)　•　•　•

● ● ● I don't know the options. I would watch him, but I can't do it alone. I would need help. (Seltzer & Krauss, 2002) ● ● ●

Siblings' concerns about their future options are compounded when they are unaware of their parents' plans for their siblings' adult years. Fish and Fitzgerald's (1980) work with adolescent siblings revealed that 9 of 10 siblings lacked an understanding and awareness of future plans for their brothers or sisters. They reported that they experienced varying degrees of anxiety regarding how the child with the disability would be cared for in the future, and their role in that care, a finding reported by other researchers (Eisenberg, Baker, & Blacher, 1998; Harland & Cuskelly, 2000).

● ● ● Even though my mother asked my husband and me to care for my brothers, I was not allowed any input into the planning. She even wanted us to move into her home and take over her business so my brothers wouldn't have to move. As it turns out, her financial planning was not done correctly. This almost forced us to assume caregiving as soon as she died. The only other alternative was emergency placement, which we feared would not give my brothers good care or would place them far from family. (Margaret, personal communication, 2005) ● ● ●

Siblings tell us that in many families the future is often not discussed. Parents, perhaps unaware of their children's concerns, or reluctant to confront their own mortality, often fail to make adequate plans for the child's future or to share whatever plans they have made with their typically developing children. Many brothers and sisters assume that they will someday shoulder many more responsibilities than their parents actually intend.

● ● ● Johnny lives at home, and he has been up on the list for a group home at least 6 times, and he has been ready. I keep telling my parents to at least try it. Johnny is very demanding and they have not had a life of their own. "Now, Mary," they say, "Don't worry about it. He's fine here." If something happened to my parents, I always ask them, what then? Are you just going to throw him into the situation? You know, that's going to kill him. I think it will break his heart. (Fish, 1993) ● ● ●

Many families plan for the future, involving siblings in this process. In these families, there is a spoken and accepted agreement about the responsibilities that siblings will one day assume. Unfortunately, in other families, there is an unspoken assumption that brothers and sisters will take over the roles previously assumed by the child's parents.

● ● ● I don't really know what's going to happen. I don't know if Jean can hold a job to support herself. She's not incapacitated by the illness. . . . But she's very backward socially and doesn't know how to get along with people. She's very demanding and will throw a tantrum if things don't go her way. I hope that she will be able to do something to support herself. . . . My parents are ignoring the issue, denying a potential problem. I have no idea what they plan to do in terms of finances. I know they don't have a lot of money. So when they go, I don't know if there will be a trust or something. I worry about what is going to happen. (David, 29, in Leder, 1991, pp. 22–23) ● ● ●

Older adult siblings who care for their brothers and sisters with disabilities have an additional concern: What will become of our siblings if we die before they do?

• • •   I think of what if I die first? I am the person he goes to the movies with. Is he going to be all by himself? Sometimes I think it would be better if he was a little more retarded, because he could fit into a group home where he would have friends and planned social activities. But he doesn't fit in. If I am not there, who is going to invite him over for the holidays? (Fish, 1993) • • •

• • •   I worry that at my age, I'm not going to be here forever and who is going to take care of her when I'm gone. I can see if she were worked with a bit more she could go into a smaller group home or semi-independent living. I hate the thought of her living with 23 other adults, on a third floor dorm for the rest of her life. (Fish, 1993) • • •

Unless parents make specific arrangements, responsibility for support of the family member with special needs may ultimately rest with the typically developing siblings. When this happens, siblings can become resentful and may not take adequate measures to meet their sibling's ongoing needs.

• • •   It is like no one else wants to do it. I'm just thrown into the role which, you know, I don't actually like a lot. I have three brothers and three sisters. They could help out a little, but they don't, actually. (Fish, 1993) • • •

McCullough (1981), in a study of 23 middle-to-upper-class families of children with developmental disabilities, learned that 60% of the parents said they had not made plans for someone to care for the child with special needs if they could not. Sixty percent of the siblings from these families, however, assumed that their parents had made plans. Similarly, 68% of the parents had not made financial arrangements for the child's future, and an equal percentage of siblings had assumed that their parents had made those plans. The picture that emerges from McCullough's study is one of parents who have not prepared for their children's future, and, if they have made plans, have not shared this information with their typically developing children. Various authors (Murphy, 1979; Parfit, 1975; Powell & Gallagher, 1993) have strongly urged parents to "openly and firmly" face the question of the future, perhaps with the assistance of a specialist, before the need is at hand. When they interviewed young adult siblings who had a brother or sister with a disability, Harland and Cuskelly (2000) found that the siblings had many concerns about the future. They realized that their parents could not indefinitely care for their brother or sister, and they felt unprepared to take over. Yet the siblings expected to help manage the finances and advocate for the welfare of their brother or sister. Siblings reported that their biggest contribution would be the emotional support they provided to their brother or sister. Several studies confirm that siblings continue to provide emotional support to their adult brother or sister with a disability (Harland & Cuskelly, 2000; Krauss, Seltzer, Gordon, & Friedman, 1996; Seltzer, Begun, Seltzer, & Krauss, 1991). Because they can envision a life beyond their parents, teenagers and young adults will require additional information about their siblings' future and what role they will play in that future. If parents have not made plans, it is critical that they begin to and that they encourage the brothers and sisters to be a part of the planning. During their teen years, siblings' perception of their future roles must be discussed with their parents.

When parents plan for their family's future—by writing wills that address the family members' future needs, naming a guardian, setting up trusts—they can reassure their children. They can allay worries by telling them at an early age, for example, "If you want Alicia to live with you when you grow up, that's fine, but if you don't, that's okay, too, because Mommy and I are planning for when Alicia grows up."

In other words, brothers and sisters need to know that when they are adults, there will be a continuum of ways for them to remain lovingly involved with a sibling with special needs. Parents need to be reassured that many, if not most, siblings will choose to remain actively involved in the lives of their brothers and sisters with special needs.

• • • They've always told us that Jennifer's problems are theirs to worry about and that Jennifer's future is for them to deal with. I know that they've made plans so that her future can be happy and secure and left us free to get on with our lives. (Andrea, 19, in Binkard et al., 1987, p. 18) • • •

• • • I will be there whenever I can. I don't want him to forget me at all or think I don't love him. (Kathryn C., 14, in Meyer, 2005) • • •

INFORMATION AT SIBSHOPS

The ongoing need of brothers and sisters for information creates the rationale for the fourth Sibshop goal (see Chapter 1): to provide siblings with opportunities to learn more about the implications of the special needs of their brothers and sisters.

Ultimately, attempts to provide siblings with information at Sibshops are limited: Many Sibshops serve siblings of children with various disabilities or illnesses, precluding an in-depth look at any single condition. Although this type of information is usually best provided by parents and primary service providers, Sibshops can provide participants with overviews of services, therapies, and conditions (as further discussed in Chapter 10). Sibshops can also be a safe place to seek information.

• • • I never really understood what my sister's sickness was. My mom and dad didn't ever talk to me about it but I knew something was real unhappy. [At the group] I got to ask things I never asked before. (Forrest, 10, in Murray & Jampolsky, 1982, p. 16) • • •

ADULT SIBLINGS

••• Mike has only one sibling, a brother Chris. Chris, who has Down syndrome, lives at home with his mom in another state. Mom is in her late seventies; Dad died last year. Mike and his parents have never really discussed what will become of Chris after his parents are no longer around to care for him. Mike figures that because Chris has Down syndrome, his parents always assumed they would outlive Chris. Mike, who has a young family, worries deeply about Chris's future. Should he bring Chris to live with his family or in his community? What would be the impact on his own family? What services are available for a person with a disability, especially one who is new to the state? (Meyer & Erickson, 1993, p. 1) •••

Of all the age groups, adult brothers and sisters frequently have the most compelling need for information. Many will find themselves increasingly responsible for meeting the ongoing needs of their siblings. Consequently, adult siblings express a desire to learn more about services for their brothers and sisters (Eisenberg et al., 1998; Harland & Cuskelly, 2000). They say that they need this information to help their siblings make informed choices and to plan for a future that considers the needs of all family members. The few programs specifically for adults whose siblings have special needs all attempt to address the participants' need for information. According to organizers of one such program in New Jersey, many members are "apprehensive about what will happen when their parents die" (Meyer & Erickson, 1992, p. 3) and wish to learn about options available for their siblings. One Seattle-area program for adult brothers and sisters surveyed 60 adult siblings to determine their informational needs. They identified the following topics, listed in decreasing order of interest:

- Recreation and leisure opportunities
- Community living and residential options
- Sexuality, socialization, and friendship
- Family communications
- Employment and day-program options
- Eligibility for services
- Legal issues
- Advocacy
- Respite care options (Meyer & Erickson, 1992)

The New York City-based Association for the Help of Retarded Children (AHRC) periodically hosts meetings for local adult siblings on specific topics, including family teamwork and future planning, guardianship, the caregiver experience, entitlements and benefits, and family and professional partnerships. Despite their need for information, few agencies serving adults with disabilities reach out to adult siblings. Ironically, many personnel from these agencies have been heard to complain that they have difficulty attracting parents of adults with disabilities to meetings, workshops, and other events. Instead of targeting parents (who may feel they have already attended enough meetings to last several lifetimes), these agencies should be encouraged to market their informational efforts to the family member who will have increasing involvement in the life of the person with the disability.

Chapter 4

Unusual Opportunities

When asked to reflect on how their children's needs have changed their lives, most parents will acknowledge that, in addition to the many challenges, there have also been unique, significant, and often unexpected rewards. These parents have told us that, as a result of having a child with special health or developmental needs, they have met the person who is now their best friend or spouse, helped create services for people with special needs, edited a newsletter, written a book chapter, testified at a state legislative hearing, or embarked upon a new career. Having a child with special needs was, perhaps ironically, an opportunity for personal growth.

Earlier research about siblings of people with disabilities, and the families in which they grow up, focused almost exclusively on their concerns, taking a *pathogenic* perspective. The child with special needs was seen as a burden to the family, and the family itself was assumed to be dysfunctional, experiencing chronic sorrow and pervasive guilt. Positive traits, such as optimism, were frequently interpreted as a sign of denial, not as a sign of strength. Families, of course, knew better.

• • • My experience with my sister has been one of the most important in my life. It has definitely shaped my life and channeled my interests in ways I would not have otherwise pursued. (Itzkowitz, 1990, p. 4) • • •

• • • My overriding impression of siblings is of amazing resilience. They go through the experience with the same intensity as the patient and the parents, but often on the sidelines. They come out whole, with a maturity, with a different view of things. (Sourkes, 1990, p. 11) • • •

• • • I continue to be a meaningful part of Martha's life and she is a significant part of mine. I am proud of her and her accomplishments. There are many people with more intelligence than her who cannot hold down a job, practice good grooming habits, and help run a large household. Sometimes I mourn the loss of an ideal sister, but I remind myself that other sisters fight, argue, and even hate each other. I have a much better relationship than that. (Westra, 1992, p. 4) • • •

••• We are a very close family, and are all heavily involved with Special Olympics, which is a direct impact from my brother. Having him in my life reminds me not to take my health, sanity, or freedom for granted. (Seltzer & Krauss, 2002) •••

Parents, especially the growing number of parents who work in social services, medicine, education, and academia, began to challenge this paradigm (see Gerdel, 1986). On a daily basis in their homes, they witnessed dynamics that apparently had eluded many researchers. They knew that their families and the vast majority of the families of children with special needs they knew were—all things considered—doing quite well.

Researchers and parents such as Ann and Rud Turnbull and their many colleagues began to seek a fresh, balanced view of families of people who have disabilities and health impairments. They sought a view that acknowledges the challenges faced by these families but that also appreciates families' many strengths. This view, described as a *salutogenic* perspective (Antonovsky, 1993; Ylvén, Björck-Åkesson, & Granlund, 2006), has been proposed as an alternative to the pathogenic view of families that has dominated the research and clinical literature.

> The salutogenic perspective calls for theorists, researchers, families and service providers to identify factors that contribute to families' successful functioning. This perspective assumes that families inevitably will be faced with stressors but have the potential for active adjustment. Accordingly, the role of service providers is to enhance family strengths rather than to focus solely on deficits. For families, the salutogenic perspective implies discovering and learning how best to use one's resources to meet the challenges of life. (Turnbull & Turnbull, 1993, p. 11)

Like their parents, brothers and sisters are not the at-risk population described in the early clinical and research literature. Empirical investigations and clinical observations are beginning to substantiate what most family members have believed all along: Siblings of people with disabilities display many strengths and report many opportunities. As Drotar and Crawford (1985) noted, increasing evidence for psychological strengths among well siblings suggests that future research could effectively focus on the study of competencies among this population. (p. 360)

What follows are some of the unusual opportunities reported by brothers and sisters. Since viewing families from a salutogenic perspective is still largely a new research paradigm, this section is briefer than the previous section, and we will rely more upon siblings speaking for themselves. We look forward to more research on brothers and sisters that proceeds from a salutogenic perspective.

Despite its relative brevity, however, this section's topic is no less important than the previous section's topic. If we are to help those families who are truly burdened by the challenges imposed by an individual's disability or illness, it is critical that we understand how so many families adapt and, in fact, thrive. We must learn what strategies, philosophies, and resources have sustained these families during difficult times. Appreciating the family members' many strengths and opportunities for growth should not be viewed as interpreting their lives from a "Pollyanna" perspective. Many of the insights and opportunities, although invaluable, are hard-earned.

MATURITY

••• When my sister got sick, I kind of became a big brother. I was younger, but I felt like I had to take some initiative and take care of her myself. (Chad, 16, in Sourkes, 1990, p. 13) •••

● ● ● Because I had a lot of responsibility as a child, I have become a responsible, loyal, even-tempered adult. However, I also worry a lot! (Seltzer & Krauss, 2002) ● ● ●

Brothers and sisters, noted Simeonsson and McHale (1981), are often well-adjusted and characterized by greater maturity and responsibility than their typical age peers. There are several possible explanations for siblings' frequently observed maturity.

Their Experiences Are Different from Those of Their Peers

● ● ● When I was in high school, I remember thinking that I was far more mature than the people around me but also less mature at the same time. I was very responsible and thought that my peers focused on such petty and insignificant things. But I also had never dated and didn't know how to fit in. I felt like such an odd mix of old and young. (Stephanie, personal communication, 2005) ● ● ●

Because of the impact of their siblings' needs, some siblings may feel that their peers' current concerns appear trivial by comparison.

● ● ● I have a different outlook on life than many other people my age. I understand that you can't take anything for granted. And you have to be able to look at the positives. . . . With Jennifer, there are negatives, but there's so much more that is good. (Andrea, 19, in Binkard et al., 1987, p. 19) ● ● ●

● ● ● I guess I've always felt I've been 10 years older than my peers when it comes to responsibilities. (Seltzer & Krauss, 2002) ● ● ●

● ● ● I think after something large like this happens in your family, you feel a lot more mature. When I went back to school after the summer, it seemed like everybody else was so immature. How could they be moaning because they lost a girlfriend or something like that? I felt I had real adult problems now. (Chad, 16, in Sourkes, 1990, p. 15) ● ● ●

A Loss of Innocence

Like Chad, above, a sibling's maturity may also be coupled with a loss of innocence. This loss is frequently mentioned by parents who have a child with a serious illness such as cancer or who has experienced a traumatic injury. For these siblings, maturity will be hard-won: They learn early that life can be unfair, things might not get better in the long run, bad things do not always happen to other people, and they, like their brothers and sisters, are not indestructible.

● ● ● I definitely felt I had more responsibilities compared to friends. I grew up faster because of it. (Seltzer & Krauss, 2002) ● ● ●

● ● ● I have a greater sense of compassion and sensitivity toward people who are different from the norm, but I am acutely aware of ignorance and prejudice through inflictions on my family. I may have acquired maturity at an early age, but in the process lost a degree of my innocence and childhood. (Cobb, 1991, p. 3) ● ● ●

Increased Responsibilities

A child's special needs are usually synonymous with increased caregiving demands and, as we saw earlier, siblings—especially sisters—frequently are expected to assume an active role in that care. Successfully handling the tasks assigned them can increase siblings' sense of maturity and pride.

● ● ● Being a sib has made me grow up twice as fast. Because I've had to grow up and mature faster, my personality expects other people to be as mature as I am. (Elizabeth T., 19, Meyer, 2005, p. 50) ● ● ●

● ● ● I learned to be responsible, and I know what it's like to have people rely on you. (Seltzer & Krauss, 2002) ● ● ●

Gaining Perspective

Siblings of people with special needs inevitably gain a unique perspective into the human condition. This expanded understanding frequently adds to their mature view of the world.

● ● ● Deaf-blindness causes you to look at yourself. You see how much he has affected your life; being around you all the time and helping you grow up. By dealing with his deaf-blindness, it causes you to become more mature. It causes you to deal with life in an "adult" manner. You also find out just how much you love your brother and how much a part of life he is. (Harkleroad, 1992, p. 5) ● ● ●

● ● ● I can't really separate what's just me and what's been a part of my experience as a sib. I am mature for my age and have learned a lot about the world. I like to think that knowing Caroline has made me less of an "oblivious teenager." (Caitlin M., 14, in Meyer, 2005, p. 50) ● ● ●

● ● ● He has helped me appreciate the freedom I have—whenever I do something or go somewhere new and exciting. I get sad knowing he'll never be able to do such things, but at the same time, I am reminded to appreciate it doubly for both of us. (Seltzer & Krauss, 2002) ● ● ●

As Dudish (1991) has noted, siblings of children with a disability or illness have multidimensional lives. They see that life has many, varied facets. From and with their families they learn determination, patience, and other qualities that can help them grow into mature, sensitive adults.

Although maturity is certainly an attribute desired by parents (and many siblings we have met have been delightfully mature for their years), we realize that maturity is an attribute on a continuum: Early maturity can also be a source of concern. On occasion we have met young siblings—usually sisters—who have little in common with their age peers and seem to be very young adults. Most of these siblings are involved in many aspects of their siblings' lives, especially their care. A reasonable amount of responsibility, it seems, can help develop a sibling's sense of maturity; excessive demands can cost a sibling his or her childhood. These children (and their parents) will need to be encouraged to attend to equally important aspects of their development that have little to do with the sibling who has the special needs.

• • • There have been times when I have had to tell my parents, "I am not the parent, you are!" Because when I was ten years old, I was probably giving them advice on how to help her out and how to raise her. (Fish, 1993) • • •

• • • For as long as I can remember, people have always told me that I "seem so mature for my age." I took pride in that when I was younger. I wanted to be more mature. But as I get older, this isn't such a compliment anymore. Some days I don't want to be "more mature" than usual. (Kameron, personal communication, 2005) • • •

SELF-CONCEPT AND SOCIAL COMPETENCE

• • • Growing up, I enjoyed linking my identity to my brother. I always asked my parents to bring him to school assemblies, after-school activities, birthday parties, etc. I liked the praise, support, and attention that I got from teachers and friends after they met him. And, of course, my parents were usually beaming with pride at my request. To this day, my self-concept is largely intertwined with his presence in my life. (Kameron, personal communication, 2005) • • •

Self-Concept

Existing studies on the self-concept of brothers and sisters of children with special needs are inconclusive; however, most studies suggest that siblings' self-concepts compare favorably with those of their peers in the community. For instance, Harvey and Greenway (1984) found that brothers and sisters of children with physical disabilities had lower self-concepts than did controls. Coleman (1990), however, found no significant differences in the self-concept of siblings of children with physical disabilities when compared with siblings of children with mental retardation and siblings of children with no disabilities.

Kazak and Clarke (1986) compared 8- and 9-year-old siblings of children with spina bifida with a control group. Subjects completed the Piers Harris Self-Concept Scale (Piers, 1984), which measures their self-concept as well as their perspectives on their own happiness, popularity, level of anxiety, physical appearance, school performance, and behavioral functioning. The authors' results indicated that there were no differences in self-concept between the two groups.

Coleman's (1990) finding that siblings of children with mental retardation were not significantly different from a control group concurs with studies by Dyson (1996), who found that siblings of children with disabilities displayed the same levels of self-concept, behavior problems, and social competence as matched siblings of children with typical development. Other studies (Dyson & Fewell, 1989; Hannah & Midlarsky,

1999; Lobato, Barbour, Hall, & Miller, 1987) also have reported that siblings of children with disabilities do not display lower self-concepts.

Studies of the self-concepts of siblings of children with chronic illnesses are similarly inconclusive. Spinetta (1981) found that 4- to 6-year-old siblings of children with cancer had lower self-concepts than did the patients. Tritt and Esses (1988) found that preteen siblings of children seen at three specialty clinics (diabetes, juvenile rheumatoid arthritis, and gastrointestinal) had significantly more behavior problems than did controls; however, their levels of self-concept did not differ.

Social Competence

In virtually all studies of the subject, siblings' social competence compares favorably with peers who do not have siblings with a disability or illness. One study (Abramovitch, Stanhope, Pepler, & Carter, 1987) revealed that both younger and older siblings of children with Down syndrome were significantly more prosocial than children in the normative sample. Ferrari (1984) compared siblings of boys who had diabetes or pervasive disabilities or were healthy. Comparing the three groups, Ferrari found no overall group differences in self-concept or teachers' ratings of self-esteem. He found that the siblings of children with diabetes were reported by teachers as displaying the most prosocial behaviors toward other children in the school, and the siblings of children with pervasive disabilities were given the highest ratings of social competence. He concluded that his study fails to support the view that siblings of children with a health impairment or disability are uniformly at greater risk of psychosocial impairment than siblings of children who are healthy.

Gruszka (1988) as reported in Lobato (1990) compared 45 siblings (ages 3–17) of children with mental retardation with a control group of equal size. Mothers of these children were asked to rate the children's behavior problems and social competence, and the children completed a standard assessment of their own self-concepts. Gruszka found that the two groups did not differ in their mothers' ratings of their social competence, or in the number and type of behavior problems. The children held similar positive views of their cognitive and physical abilities and their relationships with their mothers and peers. The way they thought about themselves and the way they thought that others felt about them, concluded the author, was not influenced by the presence of a sibling with mental retardation.

Dyson (1989) also found that children with siblings who had disabilities were better behaved and less aggressive and hyperactive and tended to have fewer acting-out behaviors than did controls. And in a later study, Dyson (1996) reported the positive self-concept of siblings with a brother or sister who had a learning disability. In a study that compared equal numbers of siblings of children with either autism, mental retardation, or no disabilities, McHale, Sloan, and Simeonsson (1986) found that, as a group, siblings of children with autism or mental retardation were significantly less hostile, less embarrassed, more accepting, and more supportive than siblings of children with no disabilities. The authors did note, however, that there was a much wider variation in the attitudes of the siblings of the children with disabilities than in the control group—that is, some attitudes were extremely positive and others much more negative.

● ● ● I have learned to be less self-conscious and less concerned with what others think about me. It made me defend the disabled more than I probably would have otherwise. It made me feel better about myself and any problems I might have. (Seltzer & Krauss, 2002) ● ● ●

INSIGHT

● ● ● When my husband asked me to marry him 6 years ago, I answered with an excited yes, and then stepped back and said I wanted him to really think it over because I was a package deal. My sister will always be a priority to me. If he marries me, he must understand that at some point if my parents are gone that my sister will need our support and I will be there no matter what. That is the thing: I think you learn early on to spot out quality people. Somehow, and without many words, my sister taught me what was important in relationships and life. She taught me to accept people for who they are, to accept and appreciate myself, how to be quiet and enjoy someone's company, to slow down and to look at what's around you. She did all this without trying. (Summers, 2004) ● ● ●

● ● ● Even though Ellen is no longer here on earth, she is ever so alive within me. It is amazing that a person who has never spoken a word or even looked me straight in the eye could have such an influence on my life—but she does. I find my greatest source of strength comes from God and my memory of Ellen. It is a strength [that helps me] raise my own family with a sense of optimism. For these reasons, I take back the statement that Ellen may not have had anything to do with a ''great life'' growing up. She had and still has everything to do with it. (Dudish, 1991, p. 3) ● ● ●

Perhaps the greatest of opportunities experienced by any family member of a person with a disability or illness is the insight one gathers on the human condition. Brothers and sisters frequently mention how their siblings have influenced their perceptions and philosophies, giving them reason to reflect on aspects of life that their peers may take for granted. For instance, young brothers and sisters frequently discuss the meaning of friendship during a Sibshop. A friend, they often say, is not someone who makes fun of a person with special needs. Brothers and sisters, first as grade schoolers, then as teenagers, and later as adults, may use the treatment of a sibling with special needs as a "litmus test" when screening potential friends, dates, or even spouses.

● ● ● I tend to pick friends who are likely to get along with Nathaniel and Sophia because it's easier that way. And besides, my take on it is that if they're not going to try to get along with Nathaniel and Sophia, they're really not my friends. (Althea, 13, in Meyer, 2005) ● ● ●

● ● ● I think Gene's having albinism has made me more accepting of people and to look differently at them. If you are exposed to something you do change. I tend to look harder and deeper at my friends, at the kind of people they are in handling themselves and treating other people. (Bill, 16, in Binkard et al., 1987, p. 9) ● ● ●

● ● ● When I was in my early 20s, I met a girl and fell in love. After a few months I brought her home to meet my family. When my mother went to the kitchen to prepare dinner, I asked the girl, ''Would you like to see Oliver?'' for I had told her about my brother. ''No,'' she answered.

Soon after, I met Roe, a lovely girl. She asked me the names of my brothers and sisters. She loved children. I thought she was wonderful. I brought her home after a few months to meet my family. Soon it was time for me to feed Oliver. I remember sheepishly asking Roe if she'd like to see him. "Sure," she said.

I sat at Oliver's bedside as Roe watched over my shoulder. I gave him his first spoonful, his second. "Can I do that?" Roe asked with ease, with freedom, with compassion, so I gave her the bowl and she fed Oliver one spoonful at a time.

The power of the powerless. Which girl would you marry? Today Roe and I have three children. (de Vinck, 2002, p. 33)　•　•　•

Appreciating the distinction between mere ignorance and actual rudeness at a young age, many brothers and sisters can be philosophical (and sometimes forgiving) even of those who do not appreciate their siblings' qualities.

•　•　•　First you have to really know someone like my sister to really understand and appreciate her achievements. (Cassie, 18, in Binkard et al., 1987, p. 18)　•　•　•

•　•　•　I tell them that my brother has Down syndrome, which affects him physically and mentally. Sometimes they ask questions and I am always pleased to answer. Questions only mean that they are interested and want to learn more. I take it as a positive sign. (Lindsay, 17, in Meyer, 2005, p. 60)　•　•　•

•　•　•　The people who know him don't tease him. The kids who are my age and my sister's age are more curious than wanting to ridicule. (Bill, 16, in Binkard et al., 1987, p. 8)　•　•　•

•　•　•　There are a lot of people who don't understand. The people who are just being "ignorant" I usually don't waste my time with. But people who try to understand, I usually explain the situation. Then they get the full picture and see that he is a person, just slower than others. This taught me to respect people, because I can understand how it feels not to be wanted, held, and cared for. (A. Jones, personal communication, 1991)　•　•　•

Many siblings, realizing how their families differ from others in the community, often express appreciation for things that may go unnoticed or unappreciated by their peers.

● ● ● Among people we know, we were unique in having an autistic sibling. We're proud of him, proud of my mother for all her support of him, proud that he's part of a close-knit family. (Seltzer & Krauss, 2002) ● ● ●

Appreciation for Their Siblings' Abilities

Perhaps because they perceive that there is a societal emphasis on their siblings' disabilities, brothers and sisters frequently describe their siblings in terms of their strengths, not their deficiencies.

● ● ● The label autism does not cover the breadth of my brother's personality. It does not explain why he prefers contemporary jazz to other types of music, why he will spontaneously initiate verbal games with my fiancé, or why he chooses to bond with certain peers over others. If the word "autism" were the sum total of my brother's personality, would he have learned to be affectionate and communicative? (Shanley, 1991, p. 2) ● ● ●

● ● ● I'd like people to know that although my brother may express his skills differently, he is very talented. And although he may not be able to carry on a philosophical conversation, he ain't stupid. (Carly, 17, in Meyer, 2005, p. 41) ● ● ●

● ● ● Sometimes nothing makes Ray happy and it is frustrating. Then there are days when he is so happy. He can be listening to music or, you think, to your conversations. You really marvel at how your brother copes with deaf-blindness. You appreciate the fact that he "loves" to work as often as he can. (How many people feel this way?) These are some of the things that make me feel he is a very special person. (Harkleroad, 1992, p. 5) ● ● ●

● ● ● Peter was the golden thread that held our family together. (sister speaking at a sibling panel) ● ● ●

● ● ● Even now, 5 years after his death, Oliver remains the weakest, most helpless human being I ever met, and yet he was one of the most powerful human beings I ever met. He could do absolutely nothing except breathe, sleep, eat, and yet he was responsible for action, love, courage, insight. (de Vinck, 1985, p. 28) ● ● ●

Life with a sibling who has special needs, many say, has profoundly influenced their values. These brothers and sisters claim that their siblings have taught them at an early age that there are human qualities to appreciate in a person besides intelligence, popularity, and good looks. Their siblings have taught them about compassion, humor, loyalty, and unconditional love.

● ● ● She taught me how to love without reservation, without expectation of returned love. She taught me that everyone has strengths and weaknesses. Martha is no exception. She taught me that human value is not measured with I.Q. tests. (Westra, 1992, p. 4) ● ● ●

● ● ● Here's what I have learned as a sib: The odds may be against you, but if you strive for success, it will come to you. I have watched Stephen beat the odds many times, and I remember that when the odds are against me. (Kevin, 14, in Meyer, 2005) ● ● ●

•　•　•　Douglas has a boundless capacity for love which to this day is evident in his smile and affection. His devotion to me has never wavered. For this reason, and many others, my love for him was always stronger than my rage over his actions. (Zatlow, 1992, p. 13)　•　•　•

•　•　•　Kevin possesses virtues that I lack. He is not judgmental and he is quick to forgive. He does not expect too much out of people or bear grudges. . . . Although I am the ''oldest'' in my family, it is his example I follow. He has the virtue of simplicity. It's too bad that simple is often considered a synonym for stupid. They are worlds apart. (Cobb, 1991, p. 3)　•　•　•

Appreciation for Family

•　•　•　I don't have my own children yet, but when I do, I will aspire to be at least half the parent that my mother and father were to my brother and me. My brother is living at home once again after being in a group home for 7 years. My parents' love, support, and dedication to him is unwavering and continues to amaze me. They absolutely personify the definition of ''good parents.'' (Kameron, personal communication, 2005)　•　•　•

Koocher and O'Malley (1981) reported that while one fourth of the siblings of patients who had been treated for cancer reported feelings of jealousy, others reported feelings of enhanced closeness toward other family members, and most appeared to resolve their anger toward the patient once the treatment ended. Adaptation to the special needs of a sibling with chronic health needs or a disability is a process, and family roles and activities change and evolve (Glasberg, 2000; Williams, 1997). Brothers and sisters, because they and their families experience challenges unlike those faced by others in the community, often express gratitude for their parents' efforts during difficult times.

•　•　•　My parents treated us equally — but to be equal, Jennifer had to have more direct attention from our parents. We never felt shut out because of her needs though. Our whole family always got attention. (Cassie, 18, in Binkard et al., 1987, p. 17)　•　•　•

•　•　•　My parents went out of their way to give me significant attention. I understood that sometimes my mom needed to take care of my sister's problems. My parents would take turns taking me out to eat or to the park. I would get time alone with them away from my sister. I also went to Sibshops. (Ty, 17, in Meyer, 2005, p. 56)　•　•　•

•　•　•　People tend to think in simplistic terms, not in reality. My mother, for example, is not a saint. In some ways she has still not come to terms with my sister's disability. Yet I see her as a tower of strength. I don't know if I would have that much strength. (Julie, in Remsberg, 1989, p. 3)　•　•　•

•　•　•　I really admire our family for how well we accept Kim like anyone else. . . . My parents give Kim everything she needs: love, acceptance, understanding, patience, discipline, proper hygiene, entertainment. Everything any other child needs. That's not to say she isn't spoiled, but who does not spoil their children? (Hanson, 1985, p. 6)　•　•　•

Appreciation for Health and Capabilities

Many children grow up feeling indestructible. Brothers and sisters who have witnessed their sibling's struggle to learn or simply stay alive are often less likely to take the blessings of good health and abilities for granted.

● ● ● Most of my friends have lived very sheltered lives — and I admit I have as well. But because they have never suffered a loss, they don't appreciate the little things. (Catherine, 13, in Meyer, 2005) ● ● ●

● ● ● Jennifer wasn't going to have all the positive things the rest of us would. I was never jealous. I couldn't be. I have so much, can do so many things, and have all the friends that I do. (Cassie, 18, in Binkard et al., 1987, p. 17) ● ● ●

● ● ● I have a greater appreciation for my opportunities and capabilities. Yet, I am painfully aware of what I, and others as fortunate waste. . . . My "special" brother has taught me through his life that my dreams are only as inaccessible as I let them remain. (Cobb, 1991, p. 3) ● ● ●

● ● ● Living with Melissa's handicaps makes me so much more cognizant of my own blessings. She provides a constant reminder of what life could have been like for me if I had been my parents oldest daughter. This encourages me to take advantage of my mental capacities and to take care of my healthy body. (Watson, 1991, p. 108) ● ● ●

TOLERANCE

● ● ● Lucy is constantly teaching me stuff. . . . She has taught me to be more patient in accepting people where they are and not putting my expectations on them. (Skrtic, Summers, Brotherson, & Turnbull, 1983, p. 18) ● ● ●

● ● ● I tend to see things that are different or strange as just "normal" and I know there is no real definition of "normal" — it's just what you think. My friends notice people's differences and think of them as weird, rather than unique. (Alli, 15, in Meyer, 2005, p. 48) ● ● ●

● ● ● My brother [with autism] has such a different perspective on life, and he makes life much more interesting. It gave me more of a focus for helping people in my career. (Seltzer & Krauss, 2002) ● ● ●

The college-age siblings that Grossman (1972) studied reported that the benefits of growing up with a sibling who has a disability include greater tolerance, understanding of people, compassion, and a dedication toward altruistic goals. Parents, as well as brothers and sisters themselves, have reported that siblings of people with special needs are more tolerant and accepting of differences than their peers are. The siblings of children with chronic illnesses that Tritt and Esses (1988) studied remarked that they had developed more patience, understanding, sensitivity, and awareness about how to deal with someone who is sick.

• • • In spite of his I.Q., Kevin has taught me many valuable lessons. Growing up with a handicapped brother has fostered perseverance and patience. I am accepting of not only the shortcomings of others, but those in myself as well. (Cobb, 1991, p. 3) • • •

They are more tolerant, siblings frequently note, because life with their brothers and sisters has made them keenly aware of the consequences of prejudice. Intolerant of intolerance, brothers and sisters bristle when others make assumptions about their siblings based on their physical appearances.

• • • Sometimes kids at school look at Elizabeth and say, "Is that your sister?" "Who is she?" They think because she looks different that she's different inside. But she's just like us inside. And she doesn't want to be stared at and laughed at or ignored. ("Jennifer," 1990, p. 2) • • •

• • • Disabilities make life rich and experiences different; they're not all bad. It's the reactions to them that cause problems. (Rebekah, 17, in Meyer, 2005, p. 125) • • •

• • • My brother does look kind of different, but that doesn't really affect him. If that's a problem for other people, well, that's their handicap. (Bill, 16, in Binkard et al., 1987, p. 8) • • •

PRIDE

With a tendency to focus on their siblings' abilities, brothers and sisters frequently testify to the adaptations their siblings have made to their disabilities or illnesses:

• • • When my brother had his leg amputated, I wondered if he would ever be able to skateboard or ride a bike again. Then the first day out of the hospital he rode a skateboard. Now he can ride a bike, a horse, and do anything. My brother Tony's ability to deal with the problem helped me to have the strength to deal with it too. (Eric, 16, in Murray & Jampolsky, 1982, p. 41) • • •

• • • What makes me proud of my brother? He has dreams and goes after them. Some people sit around just thinking about what they want to do with their life, and Alex makes an effort to make his dreams become reality. Alex is also an incredible bowler, and a great friend. (Stephanie, 16, in Meyer, 2005, p. 53) • • •

• • • Jennifer has probably achieved more than I have. She's been through so much. She couldn't even talk when she started school; now she can, and she can understand others. She's really fulfilling her potential. I'm not sure the rest of us are. (Cassie, 18, in Binkard et al., 1987, p. 17) • • •

• • • My sister [with autism] is outstanding! She loves working and she does her best in spite of her disability. I admire her loving personality. (Seltzer & Krauss, 2002) • • •

• • • Living away from home, I am able to escape from my label of being "Melissa's sister." I don't have to compete with Melissa for my friends' attention, and I can avoid unwanted attention from little children staring and pointing at her. My freshman year in college I welcomed this opportunity and purposely neglected to tell my roommate about Melissa. I immediately felt guilty and knew that I was not being fair to myself or Melissa. I am proud of Melissa, and I am proud to be her sister. I soon realized that I wanted everyone to know that I am Melissa's sister. (Watson, 1991, p. 108) • • •

VOCATIONAL OPPORTUNITIES

• • •   I have found my upbringing to have been very positive, in spite of the emotional hardship that [my sister's] cystic fibrosis placed on the family. At the age of 9 I perceived myself as being a vitally important participating member of the family. My parents encouraged me to assist in the care of my newborn sister, and I learned to crush pills and mix them in applesauce, do postural drainage, and clean and fill the mist tent. Through this experience, self-esteem was enhanced, responsibility was learned, and maturity was developed. Although I occasionally feel that I grew up too fast, for the most part the experience gave me a personal insight and compassion that I carry with me in my practice as a pediatric specialist. (Thibodeau, 1988, p. 22) • • •

• • •   As I plan for my future, I realize how much of my life, of what makes me unique, is the result of having Alison as my sister. My desire to become a doctor, my ability to work well with children, all can be attributed to Ali's presence. (Rinehart, 1992, p. 10) • • •

Siblings, as well as Gorelick (1996), have noticed that brothers and sisters of people with special needs frequently gravitate toward the helping professions. Among siblings of people with disabilities, Cleveland and Miller (1977) found oldest daughters most likely to enter helping professions. Grossman's (1972) study of college-age siblings revealed that young adults who grew up with a brother or sister who had a disability were more certain of their own future and about personal and vocational goals than comparable young adults without a similar experience.

In a 1993 study, Konstam et al. did not find differences in the career choices of siblings with and without brothers or sisters with a disability. The authors speculated that economic and social changes since the earlier studies may influence siblings' career choices. When siblings do enter professions in social services, education, or health care, their motivations are varied. One brother of a person with mental illness noted: "It can be therapeutic to help others if you cannot help your family member" (Dickens, 1991). Another acknowledged that "Part of the reason I've chosen law as my career is to enable myself to deal with some of the problems that Tom will always face" (Mark, 24, in Binkard et al., 1987, p. 28).

Many siblings have told us that having a brother or sister with special needs has made them feel comfortable with disabilities and appreciate the diversity of the human condition. As a result of their many years of informal education on disabilities, chronic health impairments, or mental illness, these siblings feel that they have much to share. Like the growing number of parents of children with special needs who are assuming leadership roles in education and health care, the brothers and sisters who seek careers in these fields bring a welcome reality check to their professions.

• • • I am very open to ''different'' people or situations. I have patience with young children or disabled people, and I always choose to work with the ''black sheep'' of the group. (Seltzer & Krauss, 2002) • • •

ADVOCACY

• • • Melissa also gives me a sense of responsibility to inform others about the realities of Down syndrome. Although speaking in front of a class usually makes me literally stop breathing and grow dizzy, I have faced large groups without fear, arguing the right to life of babies with Down syndrome. (Watson, 1991, p. 108) • • •

• • • If I see someone with a disability walking down the street, I don't think AHHHH! or eww, I think that person is out, taking care of herself, being independent. I feel proud of them, even if I don't know them because I understand, a little, some of the things they have to overcome. (Erin, 14, in Meyer, 2005, p. 48) • • •

• • • My parents and I wondered what the purpose of special education might be when it could be suspended so arbitrarily for the crime of growing up. (Zatlow, 1992, p. 15) • • •

Because of the value they place on their siblings' abilities and contributions, and perhaps because they will likely assume increasingly active roles in the lives of their siblings, brothers and sisters often become ardent advocates for people with special needs.

• • • Today, not because of guilt, but because I genuinely want to, I am helping my mom monitor and coordinate Kim's programs. . . . I think that things go better for people like Kim when service providers know there is a family member on the scene and paying attention. (Marsha, 28, in Binkard et al., 1987, p. 31) • • •

• • • We have not fought this hard for Douglas to be thwarted by a termination of programs. Personally, I have not given so much of myself and my life to Doug only to see his existence end in despair. . . . My brother *WILL* have an option. (Zatlow, 1981, p. 2) • • •

Programs serving brothers and sisters can provide participants with information and preadvocacy skills. Sibshop discussion activities such as Moccasins and informational activities that acquaint participants with the services, therapies, career, and residential opportunities available for adults with disabilities can provide participants with a foundation of information and concepts that will be the basis for future advocacy activities.

LOYALTY

• • • Now that she is older, people treat her just fine. When we were younger, a few kids teased her and called her a retard. Once I got kicked out of Boy Scouts because this punk kid called her a retard. I punched him in the face. No one calls my sister a retard. They know I will kick their ass. (Ty, 17, in Meyer, 2005, p. 93) • • •

• • • I'm used to being kind to my brother and sister, so I'm kind to everybody else. But, if someone starts a fight, I will fight. I won't put up with anyone teasing Wade or Jolene. (Morrow, 1992, p. 4) • • •

• • • I don't have my own family yet, but when I do, they will know that there is no question as to where my brother will be when my parents are no longer able to care for him. He will absolutely be close to me, wherever I am — this is not negotiable. (Kameron, personal communication, 2005) • • •

Like most siblings, brothers and sisters of children with special needs frequently fight and argue within the family. Outside of the family, however, siblings of children with developmental disabilities or chronic health impairments may feel required to defend their brothers and sisters from cruel comments and stares. This loyalty can be a problem for some brothers and sisters.

• • • When my brother turned 4 or 5 years of age, I was a very defensive person. I felt people were treating my brother differently. I used to get into fights with other kids. (A. Jones, personal communication, 1991) • • •

• • • She caused problems for me at school too. I'd get into fights because of her, so I held her responsible for most of my problems. (Marsha, 28, in Binkard et al., 1987, p. 29) • • •

Yet, for many other brothers and sisters, these incidents can be reason to re-examine the relationship they have with their brothers and sisters and to reflect on the meaning of friendship and society's tolerance of differences.

•　•　•　I decided that I had to stop being worried about how friends might react. There were two boys whom I'd met at school and thought were my friends. The first time they met Jennifer though, they laughed. I told them to leave our house. (Cassie, 18, in Binkard et al., 1987, p. 16)　•　•　•

•　•　•　My sisters and I can turn into three really big monsters in public if someone makes fun of her when we're around. But we don't want pity for her. She deserves respect as a person. (Andrea, 19, in Binkard et al., 1987, p. 19)　•　•　•

•　•　•　We all love my brother very much. My siblings and I have and continue to support my brother to the best of our abilities. He unites us. (Seltzer & Krauss, 2002)　•　•　•

CONCLUSION

As the brothers and sisters quoted in this chapter make clear, many siblings of people with special needs experience unusual opportunities throughout their lives. We can better appreciate siblings' many strengths and coping strategies if we complement their testimony with research that proceeds from a salutogenic viewpoint. As McConachie (1982) has noted:

•　•　•　Most [scales] do not evaluate positive traits. When the researcher has given parents greater freedom to comment, they tend to demonstrate their strength, resilience, and sense of humor in coping with their own reaction . . . and also with the reactions of their family and neighbors. (p. 161)　•　•　•

In addition to research that respects the complexity of their experiences, siblings deserve more immediate considerations. These considerations should begin when siblings are young and be offered proactively throughout their lives. Parents and providers should become familiar with the wide range of issues siblings may experience growing up. All of those who work with people who have disabilities should understand the important role that siblings play and create policies that include brothers and sisters who wish to be involved in the lives of their siblings with special needs. Programs should be widely available for brothers and sisters who wish to meet and talk with their peers. When brothers and sisters receive these considerations, it is possible to minimize the "unusual concerns" they experience and maximize their "unusual opportunities."

Chapter 5

Getting Started

In this chapter we discuss the component activities required to create a Sibshop. If the information that follows appears daunting, please remember that any activity—even something as mundane as cleaning a refrigerator or washing a car—can seem surprisingly complex when broken down into component tasks. Use this chapter as a blueprint for planning your Sibshop.

COSPONSORS

As mentioned in Chapter 1, we strongly encourage cosponsorship of Sibshops and feel that the benefits of cosponsoring Sibshops are many.

The first benefit is that more siblings are served. Frequently, individual agencies will not have a sufficient number of siblings in the identified age range to create a viable Sibshop. Working with other agencies helps assure that all potentially interested families will learn about a Sibshop and, as a result, more siblings will be registered. An enthusiastic response and a healthy enrollment help create an exciting program.

Second, as discussed later in this chapter, cosponsorship allows agencies with limited resources to share costs and pool resources.

Third, Sibshops offer an extraordinary opportunity for collaboration among diverse agencies. Agencies that have worked together to cosponsor Sibshops include autism societies, chapters of The Arc and United Cerebral Palsy, children's hospitals, Developmental Disabilities Councils, early intervention programs, Parent-to-Parent programs, parks and recreation programs, Ronald McDonald Houses, school districts, schools for the deaf, and University Centers on Disabilities. We have also witnessed examples of agencies with previously competitive and even acrimonious relationships working together to cosponsor Sibshops. Sometimes, community businesses that donate to a local Sibshop are cosponsors. One Sibshop we know is cosponsored by a community hospital, three early intervention programs, a Parent-to-Parent program, and a local grocery store! A "big tent" approach seems to work well.

Of course, any agency or organization serving families of children with special needs can sponsor a Sibshop provided it can offer financial support, properly staff the program, and attract sufficient numbers of participants. Single agency sponsorship may be most appropriate if the Sibshop is to be a component of a large event, such as a statewide conference for families of children with special needs, or if it is for a specific disability, such as for children with hearing impairments, sponsored by a state school for the deaf.

Educate Potential Cosponsoring Agencies About Sibshops and Siblings' Concerns

Agency personnel may want to learn more about the need for Sibshops before they attend a planning meeting. With your letter inviting them to cosponsor a Sibshop, send them information, such as A Brief Description of the Sibshop Model (Appendix C) and What Siblings Would Like Parents and Service Providers to Know (Appendix D)—both are also available in an electronic format from the Sibling Support Project—and follow up with a phone call to answer any other questions they might have.

Ensure Family Participation in Planning for Sibshops

In many communities, Sibshops are spearheaded by what Florene Poyadue, a founder of California's Parents Helping Parents program, calls "monomaniacs with a mission": people who have a vision of what ought to be. Often, these visionaries are parents. If the representatives of your cosponsoring agencies do not include a parent or sibling of a person with special needs, by all means invite a family member to be a part of your planning committee. You will be "selling" your Sibshop to parents; consequently, it's helpful to have them involved from the start.

Ask Agencies to Send Representatives to a Planning Meeting

Once cosponsoring agencies have been determined, each agency should appoint a representative to be a part of the Sibshop Planning Committee. Ideally, the agencies will send representatives who work closely with family members of people with special needs or are family members themselves. It is recommended that all members of the planning committee read this chapter and the Sibshop Standards of Practice (Appendix A) prior to meeting as well as. The committee may find the Sibshop Planning Form (see Figure 5.1) a helpful tool as you plan your community's Sibshop.

As you and the committee begin, keep in mind that each interagency collaboration resulting in a Sibshop will be unique; the arrangements will reflect the resources each agency has to offer. Often, the arrangements made are somewhat informal, using a "potluck" style, depending on the resources available. For instance, Agency A, although committed to the program, has no funds to support the program. It does, however, have an excellent facility that the Sibshop can use. It agrees to handle the registration. Agency B has a similar lack of money but is sufficiently committed to the program to offer the services of its family specialist, who will take "comp time" for time spent on Sibshops. Agency C has neither staff nor space to support the program, but it does have $1,500 in a gift fund to help defray costs, and so on.

Sibshop Planning Form

Use this form as you plan for a Sibshop in your community. With your planning committee, discuss the following questions to determine audience, resources, and responsibilities. The format below follows the discussion in Chapter 5, Getting Started.

1. The sponsoring agencies and planning committee.

   What agencies will cosponsor the Sibshop?

   Who are the identified representatives from these agencies on the planning committee?

   Which members of the planning committee are also parents or siblings of people with special needs?

2. Identifying the brothers and sisters you wish to serve. Please define your population with regard to

   The special needs of the siblings of the children you wish to serve.

   The ages of the children who will attend your Sibshop.

   The geographic area you wish to serve.

   The maximum number of children you wish to serve.

   Will enrollment be limited to families served by the cosponsoring agencies?

(continued)

Figure 5.1. Sample planning form.

Figure 5.1. (*continued*)

| ⚬ **Sibshop Planning Form** | PAGE 2 |

---

3. Identifying resources. Please discuss what financial or other resources may be available to support your Sibshop for the following areas:

   Potential costs:

       Sibshop facilitators

       Materials and food

       Facility

       Other (postage, stationery, printing, photocopying, processing registrations, and so forth)

   Potential sources of income:

       Registration fees

       Grants, gifts, and other sources of income

4. Identifying Sibshop facilitators

   What is your desired facilitator-to-participant ratio?

   Who will be your Sibshop facilitators?

5. Where will your Sibshop be held?

6. When and how frequently will your Sibshop meet?

7. Who will publicize the program and recruit participants?

8. Who will register participants and manage the Sibshop budget?

PARTICIPANTS

Once the question of sponsorship is determined, making decisions about service populations will be easier. You and the planning committee will need to identify the brothers and sisters you wish to reach with your Sibshop.

What Are the Special Needs of Siblings of Children Your Sibshop Will Serve?

Will this Sibshop be for siblings of children who have a specific disability (e.g., Down syndrome) or illness (e.g., cancer)? Or will it be for siblings of children with various developmental disabilities, chronic health impairments, or perhaps mental health concerns? Focusing on a specific disability or illness can offer participants a wonderful opportunity to learn more about their siblings' condition. Unless you can assure sufficient numbers of participants (at least six), however, we recommend offering the Sibshop to siblings of children who have various developmental disabilities or chronic illnesses. Although there will be some differences in their experiences, there will be many more similarities. Besides, differences will afford participants a richer understanding of the diversity embodied in the term *special needs* and insight into their own families.

Will Sibshop Enrollment Be Limited to Siblings from Families Served by the Cosponsoring Agencies?

Will your Sibshop be available for all appropriate brothers and sisters, regardless of where their sibling receives services? Or, is this Sibshop just for the cosponsoring agencies' families? Will they get first priority? Although there is no right or wrong answer, this should be decided upon ahead of time.

What Geographic Area Do You Wish to Serve?

Will your Sibshop be for kids from all over the county, or just from a specific school district? This decision may affect, among other things, how you publicize your program and when you host the program.

What Are the Ages of the Children Who Will Attend Your Sibshop?

Avoid the temptation to offer a Sibshop for children of all ages. Sibshops that are hosted for children ages 4–16 will confuse the 4-year-olds and bore the 16-year-olds, and the confusion and boredom can adversely affect the flavor of the Sibshop for the children in between. Although Sibshops can be adapted for younger and older children, they were designed with children ages 8–13 in mind. Restricting the age range ensures that the siblings share the common interests and levels of emotional maturity that make Sibshops successful.

By 8 years of age, most brothers and sisters know a little about their siblings' disability and can talk about their life, their feelings, and other people. Children younger than 8 may not even be aware that their sibling has special needs and often have a difficult time grasping the topics discussed by the older children. The typical 3- to 4-hour Sibshop will be too long for children younger than 8. It is far easier to expand the target range of 8–13 to include older siblings. Many programs have successfully incorporated teen siblings as "junior facilitators." These teen volunteers now have an excuse to hang out with kids younger than they are, they will model the sharing you'll want from your young Sibshoppers, and they can even work off the service hours they'll need to graduate from high school. It's a win-win-win relationship!

If the committee determines that what they want is a program for siblings other than the target range of 8–13 years, there are alternatives. First, they may wish to stretch the target range by holding two Sibshops, one for younger siblings (i.e., 6–9 years) and another for older siblings (i.e., 10–13 years). Second, the committee may wish to sponsor a Sibshop specifically for younger children (i.e., 4–8 years) or for teenagers. Chapters 7–10 include activities that will be helpful with younger children and teens. Sibshops for younger children will need to be shorter in duration than typical Sibshops.

How Many Children Do You Wish to Serve?

Sibshops should be large enough to offer participants a vital, exciting program, yet small enough to assure that everyone gets to participate in the discussion activities. Ideally, there will be enough children in the group for a child to find another child—a future friend, perhaps—of the same sex and close in age and someone with whom he or she can share a phone number, e-mail, or IM (instant messaging) address. Somewhere between 12 and 20 kids seems to be a good number for many Sibshop facilitators.

With a recommended ratio of one facilitator per five or six participants (more with younger children; slightly less with older), the number of facilitators you have—as well as the space available in your facility—will influence how many siblings you can serve.

Open Enrollment or Closed Enrollment?

One issue you'll wish to consider is whether you want your Sibshop to have a closed enrollment (more like a class) or an open enrollment (more like a club). Each has advantages and disadvantages.

A Sibshop with a closed enrollment might meet once per week for 6 weeks. The advantage of a closed enrollment is that the "cast of characters" remains constant and a group identity can be nurtured. The disadvantage of a closed enrollment is that today's families and kids have very busy schedules. Consequently, if they can only attend four of the six meetings, they may not sign up at all. Another potential downside of closed enrollment is that families who learn about your Sibshop mid-session will need to wait until a new session is offered.

A Sibshop with an open enrollment might meet once per month throughout the school year. The advantage of open enrollment is that if a Sibshop participant cannot attend a meeting in, say, November due to a conflict with his soccer schedule, he can rejoin the group at the December meeting. Furthermore, families who hear about the program mid-year will learn that it is not too late to enroll their children. The disadvantage of open enrollment is that the participants will change slightly from Sibshop to Sibshop. Usually, however, there are enough familiar faces to make a Sibshopper feel at home after having missed a session. See Appendix E for an example of how one Sibshop successfully uses an open enrollment format.

FINANCIAL ISSUES

Most communities, organizations, and agencies have limited funds for services for families, regardless of how valuable they may be. This is true for traditional family programs (i.e., programs for parents), and especially true for less-traditional programs such as Sibshops. Consequently, most programs for brothers and sisters have budgets and funding bases that can be considered both creative and individualistic.

Sibshops rarely exist because of readily available funds. They exist because individuals and agencies share a deeply held belief that brothers and sisters deserve peer support and education opportunities despite a lack of earmarked funds. This encourages agencies to seek innovative approaches to funding: Where there's a will, there's a way. Although a typical Sibshop budget may be elusive, many local programs utilize similar strategies.

Agencies' abilities to share costs and pool resources will greatly affect a Sibshop budget. Some programs relying on volunteers and donated foods and materials have achieved a zero-based budget. Others pass on all costs to participants. Most fall somewhere in between. A discussion of costs associated with hosting Sibshops follows.

Costs

According to a survey in 2004, most facilitators lead Sibshops as part of their job or are hired to conduct the programs, often with the help of adult or teen sibling volunteers. Much rarer are Sibshops run by volunteer power alone. Volunteers can be a wonderful asset to a Sibshop. Because they donate their time, however, volunteers may be less reliable than paid staff. Hiring staff to conduct the Sibshop can help assure reliability and accountability, assuming that funds are available. Some programs have volunteers who receive a small stipend. Committing staff to conduct sibling programs is perhaps the best option. No new funds need to be identified and staff conducting Sibshops frequently take comp time during the week for their involvement in a weekend Sibshop. Many agencies profess a commitment to serving people with special needs *and their families*, when, in practice, they may simply be serving the client and his or her parents. By committing staff to facilitate sibling programs, agencies acknowledge siblings' critical role in the family.

Materials and Food

In creating the Sibshop model, an effort was made to select activities that do not rely greatly on materials. There are two reasons for this: to reduce costs and to streamline planning. Sibshops often are conducted by personnel who do not work at the facility where the Sibshop is being held. Consequently, facilitators will need to import all materials or, at the very least, seek permission to use the facility's materials. Food—even if it is just a snack—is an essential part of Sibshops. When facilitators' time and the facility are donated, Sibshop registration fees can cover materials and food.

Facility Use

Frequently, use of a facility will be a contribution of one of the cosponsoring agencies. Later in this chapter is a further discussion on preferred locations for Sibshops.

Miscellaneous Costs

Postage, stationery, printing, photocopying, and processing registrations are all miscellaneous costs that vary greatly from program to program. Generally, one program assumes responsibility for all of the above.

Income

Although some agencies offer Sibshops free of charge, it is reasonable to ask parents to pay a fee for their children to attend one. Most Sibshops cost far less than child care for the same amount of time. Fees can help offset costs associated with running a Sibshop. Perhaps most important, fees help ensure that parents bring their children to the Sibshop that facilitators have worked so hard to make rewarding.

A significant effort should be made to assure that Sibshops are available to families who cannot afford the set fee. On the registration forms of many Sibshops is a statement similar to the following: "A limited number of Sibshop scholarships are available on a first-come, first-served basis. Check here if you'd like your child considered for a Sibshop scholarship." (See Appendix E.) On the same form, other parents who do not have money woes can be given an opportunity to contribute to the Sibshops scholarship fund.

Other local Sibshops have successfully applied for grants from community mental health boards, developmental disability councils, local businesses, fraternal organizations, local private benefactors, and city block grant programs. A sample version of the "front matter" for a grant application is available as an e-mail attachment from the Sibling Support Project.

Sibshop Budgets

There is no typical Sibshop budget. See Tables 5.1–5.3 for sample budgets for three different Sibshops. For the purposes of comparison, each sample Sibshop uses four facilitators and has a 4-hour meeting once a month for 5 months. The first two Sibshops serve 20 children; the third serves 10.

FACILITATORS

We believe that Sibshops are best facilitated by at least two people. Ideally, one facilitator will be an adult sibling of a person who has a special need similar to the siblings of the participants. The involvement of an adult sibling can keep the program "honest," credible, and focused on issues important to the participants. On occasion—and as appropriate—adult sibling facilitators can share the experiences and insights that they

Table 5.1. Budget for Sibshop A

Facilitator 1	Services donated by Agency 1 (employee)
Facilitator 2	Adult sib ''paid volunteer'' services donated by Agency 1 ($240–$12/hour x 4 hours per session x 5 sessions)
Facilitator 3	Volunteer, works for Agency 2
Facilitator 4	Services donated by Agency 3 (employee)
Food	$500 ($5 x 20 participants x 5 meetings)
Materials	$300 ($3 x 20 participants x 5 meetings)
Facility	Donated by Agency 3
Other (e.g., registration, stationery, mailing, printing)	Donated by Agency 1
TOTAL	$800
INCOME	$900 registration ($10 per session x 18 paying participants x 5 sessions; two additional participants received scholarships)

Table 5.2. Budget for Sibshop B

Facilitator 1	Community volunteer
Facilitator 2	Community volunteer
Facilitator 3	Services donated by Agency 1 ($300: $60 per session x 5 sessions)
Facilitator 4	Services donated by Agency 1 ($300: $60 per session x 5 sessions)
Food	Donated by local grocery stores and individuals ($400: $4 x 20 participants x 5 meetings)
Materials	Donated by Agency 1 ($150)
Facility	Donated by Agency 2
Other (e.g., registration, stationery, mailing, printing)	Donated by Agencies 1–4
TOTAL	$0
INCOME	N/A (no registration fee)

Table 5.3. Budget for Sibshop C

Facilitator 1	$125 ($25 per session x 5 sessions)
Facilitator 2	$125 ($25 per session x 5 sessions)
Facilitator 3	$125 ($25 per session x 5 sessions)
Facilitator 4	Volunteer
Food	$200 ($4 x 10 participants x 5 sessions)
Materials	Donated by Agency 1
Facility	Donated by Agency 2
Other (e.g., registration, mailing, stationery, printing)	Donated by Agency 1
TOTAL	$575
INCOME	$600 ($15 x 8 paying participants x 5 sessions; two additional participants received scholarships)

had growing up. For young Sibshoppers, having a facilitator who has successfully adapted to life with a sibling who has special needs can be tremendously reassuring.

The other member of the team will be a service provider (e.g., a social worker, special education teacher, professor, psychologist, nurse) who will be aware of issues, resources, services, and the special needs represented in the Sibshop. This person, frequently employed by one of the cosponsoring agencies, can also serve as the liaison between the facilitators and the planning committee.

Parents, of course, can be excellent facilitators, but ideally they would not facilitate Sibshops that their own children attend. Parents are often the driving force for creating community-based Sibshops: They appreciate the value of peer support and witness on a daily basis the concerns experienced by brothers and sisters. Even if they are not facilitators, parents can make many behind-the-scenes contributions to ensure a successful Sibshop.

Based on years of conducting programs for siblings, we believe that Sibshop facilitators should share some varied core skills. Both facilitators, for instance, should be as comfortable leading discussions as they are organizing a game of Ultimate Nerf or a cooking project for 14 children.[1] It is strongly desired that Sibshop facilitators

1. Have a working knowledge of the unusual concerns and opportunities experienced by brothers and sisters of children with special needs. At the very least, future Sibshop facilitators should read Chapters 2, 3, and 4 of this book, which were written with them in mind. Facilitators and the planning committee, however, should not stop there. The sibling panel and the books, videotapes, listservs, and newsletters discussed in Chapter 11 are excellent ways to learn more about sibling issues.

2. Attend a Sibshop training offered by the Sibling Support Project. These 2-day trainings offer facilitators detailed information about siblings' lifelong issues and the implications these issues will have for facilitators, parents, and service providers. Equally important, they provide participants with detailed information on the Sibshop model and an opportunity to participate in a Demonstration Sibshop. These trainings are the best possible means for learning what Sibshops are all about, and obtaining training on the Sibshop model is required to use the Sibshop name and logo. See the Sibshop Standards of Practice (Appendix A) for details.

3. Have personal or professional experience with people who have special needs and their families. They should also possess knowledge of the special needs represented at the Sibshop. Therefore, a special education teacher, despite her experience with children with developmental disabilities, may not be the best candidate to run a Sibshop for brothers and sisters of children who have cancer. A colleague knowledgeable about the impact of childhood cancer on families (e.g., a child life specialist, clinical nurse specialist, pediatric social worker) should be there to provide assistance.

4. Be familiar with active listening principles. These skills will be valuable throughout the Sibshop and especially during discussion activities. If there is a Parent-to-Parent

---

[1] During training on the Sibshop model, we promise future facilitators three things. First, if they do it right, they will have at least as much fun as the participants; second, they will need no further exercise on the day of the Sibshop; third, they will sleep very well that night.

program in your community, you are encouraged to attend the workshops offered by the program to train "helping parents." Active listening is a key skill taught at these trainings, and these same principles can be used with Sibshop participants. (Of course, Parent-to-Parent trainings are also a great way to learn about the impact a child's disability has on families and to get the word out about your Sibshop to a key audience.) If Parent-to-Parent trainings are unavailable, consider reading Adele Faber and Elaine Mazlish's excellent book *How to Talk So Kids Will Listen and Listen So Kids Will Talk.*

5. Have experience leading groups, preferably groups of children.

6. Convey a sense of joy, wonder, and play. Having fun is an important component of a successful Sibshop. Even though we learn at them, Sibshops are not school. Even though we talk about our feelings, Sibshops are not therapy. All potential facilitators should truly enjoy the company of children. A self-deprecating sense of humor helps too!

7. Be available to meet at the times and dates identified by the planning committee.

8. Subscribe to SibGroup, the listserv for those running Sibshops, and similar sibling programs. An excellent forum for sharing activities, challenges, questions, and successes, membership in SibGroup is one of the Sibshop Standards of Practice (see Appendix A).

8. Be somewhat physically fit. Sibshops are lively, exciting events, with many high-energy activities. Facilitators will be expected to model and participate in these activities.

9. Appreciate that the Sibshop participants, not the facilitators, are the experts on living with a brother or sister with special needs. One of the rewards of facilitating the program is what we can learn from the kids we serve.

LOCATION

An ideal facility will be centrally located and kid-friendly and have a gym or large multipurpose room for games, a quiet meeting place for discussions, and a working kitchen that accommodates all participants. Ironically, although public schools may seem the best choice (as they certainly meet the above qualifications), they can also be the most problematic. Although some districts will donate the use of a school, others will charge fees to cover general rental or to pay for a custodian. In some instances, stringent contracts with food-service unions will prevent use of a school kitchen without paying an employee overtime. In this case, you may wish to inquire whether the district has a living-skills classroom with a kitchen. It may be easier and less expensive to meet in a church hall, a community center, an early intervention program site, and so forth.

TIMES AND DATES

Although many Sibshops are held on Saturdays from 10:00 A.M. until 2:00 P.M., this is not a time that will be ideal for all parties. Many programs have found that this time slot is simply the "least worst time" for most families, participants, facilitators, and agencies. Smaller communities often have greater flexibility with regard to meeting times than larger communities. If all the participants attend the same school district, Sibshops can be held on teacher in-service days. Sibshops are sometimes held on Friday evenings in communities where Friday afternoon traffic is not a nightmare.

How Often Should You Meet?

How often your Sibshops meet will be determined by the needs and resources in your community.

Annually

Some Sibshops meet only once a year. Examples of this are a 6-hour Sibshop that is part of a national conference for families who have children with a specific disability or illness, or a 4-hour Sibshop that is a part of a statewide conference for families who have children with various disabilities. Another example is the Sibshop that is a component of a camp for children or families of children who have disabilities or illnesses.

Every 6 Months or Quarterly

In rural communities, where the long distance traveled would prohibit meeting more frequently, some Sibshops are offered once every 3 to 6 months. Sometimes a simultaneous program is offered to parents.

Monthly or Every Other Month

Some Sibshops meet monthly—especially those using an open enrollment format. Often these Sibshops meet during school months only. One community does it this way: The September, November, January, March, and May Sibshops are for 6–9-year-old brothers and sisters; the October, December, February, April, and June Sibshops are for brothers and sisters ages 10–13.

Weekly

Some Sibshops, especially those with a closed enrollment, are held weekly. Usually, these are much shorter in duration (1–1½ hours) and are often held after school.

Other

Of course, there are many variations on the theme. As noted earlier, some Sibshops are held on teacher in-service days, and still others are held during the summer, perhaps every day for 3 days or even for an entire week.

Finally, when deciding how often to meet, remember this rule of thumb: It is better to meet *less* frequently and have Sibshops that are well planned, exciting, and meaningful events than to meet often and have programs that become routine.

PUBLICITY

Making parents, brothers and sisters, agencies, organizations, and the public aware of your services for brothers and sisters is not a one-time effort! How often you will need to publicize your Sibshop will depend, in part, on how frequently the program is offered. If you offer your sibling program in a series (e.g., one meeting a week for 6 weeks), expect to publicize your program prior to each series. If your program is an ongoing program (e.g., monthly meetings with open enrollment), plan on publicizing the program once per year and sending letters or emails to parents on your mailing list announcing each meeting. If you hold the program infrequently or as a one-time event, plan on publicizing your sibling program prior to each event. See Chapter 6 for a further discussion of awareness activities, sample awareness materials, and timelines.

REGISTRATION AND BUDGET MANAGEMENT

To plan for your Sibshop, you'll need more information about your young participants than you can easily gather over the phone. Consequently, we recommend that parents complete and return a registration form containing helpful information about their children (see example in Appendix E) along with registration fees (if any). Registration is usually handled by the agency that manages the Sibshop budget or donates the facility where the Sibshop will be held.

CONCLUSION

Once you have answered the questions posed on the Sibshop Planning Form (Figure 5.1) discussed in this chapter, you should have a clear idea of the following:

- Who your cosponsors are
- Who will be served by your Sibshop
- What your financial and other resources are
- Who will facilitate your Sibshop
- Where your Sibshop will be held
- How frequently it will meet
- Who will publicize the program
- Who will register the participants

If you can answer all or most of the above questions, congratulate yourself and your planning committee. If you can't, hang in there! There's a good chance that no one in your community has ever tried anything like a Sibshop before. As pioneers and history makers, you and your colleagues will be expected to be creative, resourceful, and occasionally monomaniacal. If you get stuck, seek the counsel of other Sibshops in your state and the Sibling Support Project. When the logistics are resolved, the fun begins. In the next chapter, we provide detailed information on planning your first Sibshop.

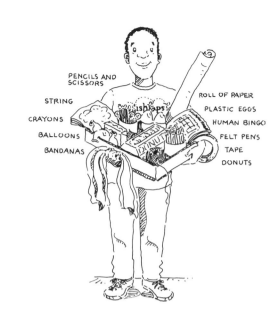

Chapter 6

Putting It All Together

As we noted earlier, Sibshops are logistically no more difficult to organize than other groups for kids (e.g., Camp Fire, Cub Scouts, Brownies). They may, in fact, be easier! In this chapter, we guide you as you plan your first Sibshop. We provide you with a timetable for publicizing your program and provide you with sample awareness materials. Furthermore, we give you and your colleagues a tested, detailed Sibshop schedule that can help you plan your very first meeting. At the end of this chapter, we suggest ways to evaluate how satisfied parents and participants are with your program. In providing the information in this chapter, we are assuming that

1. You and your planning committee have read Chapter 5.

2. Representatives from cosponsoring agencies and family member representatives have been identified and have met.

3. The population of children you wish to serve has been defined.

4. The necessary financial resources have been identified.

5. A site for your Sibshop has been identified.

6. Facilitators for your Sibshop have been identified, meet the qualifications discussed in Chapter 5, and are ready to hop into their sneakers and have some fun.

7. You have read and agreed to the Sibshop Standards of Practice.

8. Dates for your Sibshop have been set.

AWARENESS AND RECRUITMENT ACTIVITIES

Awareness activities—fliers, e-mails, and notes sent home—are good ways to get the word out about your Sibshop. But they're not enough. Especially in your Sibshop's early years, you'll need to personally invite parents to bring their children to your

Sibshop. You'll also want to encourage your colleagues to do the same. After you've developed good word-of-mouth with parents and service providers, making these personal invitations may be less necessary.

Timeline

Once resources, dates, facility, and facilitators have been identified, you'll want to develop a timeline for awareness and recruitment activities. We suggest the following:

8 weeks before—Create flier and seek opportunities to speak to groups of parents and service providers about your new Sibshop.

6 weeks before—Send fliers and letters to agencies via e-mail and "snailmail."

5 weeks before—Send fliers, letters, and e-mail to parents of children served by cosponsoring agencies.

4 weeks before—Send press releases to local media.

2–6 weeks before—Send registration forms to parents who have phoned requesting registration materials.

This chapter contains sample awareness materials you may use to publicize your upcoming Sibshops. You may, of course, adapt these in any way you see fit.

Expanding Awareness of Sibshops

An effective way to create awareness of your Sibshop program in general is to present information at local programs for parents of children with special needs and colleagues interested in the well-being of those children and their families. You may wish to request a chance to speak at staff meetings and parent support groups sponsored by chapters of The Arc, early intervention centers, schools, hospitals, disability-specific groups, or Parent-to-Parent programs. This need not be a lengthy discourse. Remembering the dictum to "be brief, be bright, and be gone," you can plug your program in 15 minutes or less. You may use the Brief Description of the Sibshop Model (Appendix C) and What Siblings Would Like Parents and Service Providers to Know (Appendix D) as a basis for your talk and as a handout.

Publicizing Your Sibshop

Letters, e-mails, fliers, and press releases can be valuable methods of getting the word out about your Sibshop. Because parents may be unsure of what you intend to do with their typically developing children, be sure to emphasize Sibshops' wellness approach and the fun and camaraderie experienced by participants.

A Sample Press Release

Sibshops and the young participants who attend them have been featured in many local newspapers. Besides calling attention to an especially deserving community, newspapers can be a great way to get the word out about your Sibshop. Sometimes,

Subject Line: New Program Dedicated to Life's Longest-Lasting Relationship   Date: 10/31/07

FOR IMMEDIATE RELEASE

Contact: Sarah Marshall, Sibshop director, DayStar Developmental Center, 368-4911; www.daystar.org/sibshops

Sibshops

A Program Just for Sibs of Kids with Special Needs

Brothers and sisters will have the longest-lasting relationship with a sibling who has a disability—*one that can easily exceed 65 years*. During their lives, they will experience most of the unique concerns and joys their parents do. But few siblings of kids with special needs ever have a chance to talk about their issues with others who "get it"—until now.

Brothers and sisters of kids with special needs from Brighton County now have a program that's just for them called Sibshops. At Sibshops, they'll have a chance to meet other kids whose brothers and sisters have special needs and talk about the good and not-so-good parts of having a sibling with a disability. Most important, they'll have fun!

Sibshops are an exciting new support, information, and recreation opportunity for siblings ages 8–13. Brighton County's Sibshops are cosponsored by Children's Hospital, the DayStar Early Developmental Center, and The Arc of Brighton County. Sibshops will be held at Olympic View Elementary School, 504 NE 95th in Lake Stevens. For more information and to register, call Sarah Marshall at the DayStar Developmental Center at 368-4911 or visit www.daystar.org/sibshops.

The first meeting will be held on Saturday, February 22, from 10 A.M. to 2 P.M. Additional meeting dates are March 21, April 25, May 16, and June 13 [year].

In addition to receiving peer support, Sibshop participants will play lively "new games," learn about their siblings' disabilities and the services they receive, participate in cooking and craft activities, and make new friends. Sibshops are a spirited celebration of the many contributions made by brothers and sisters.

Many brothers and sisters have feelings that are difficult to express, even to a friend: sadness that a sister can't learn things that others take for granted; anger when a brother's behavior prevents the family from doing things other families do; or the special pride when a sibling with a disability learns a basic but important life skill after months or years of practice. At Sibshops, they'll share these feelings with others who truly understand.

Figure 6.1.   Sample press release.

you can let newspapers and television stations know about your Sibshop by calling their "news tips hotlines" or visiting their web sites. Alternatively, you may wish to distribute a press release. According to media relations professionals we have spoken to, press releases should be sent no later than 3 weeks prior to the event or registration deadline for maximum impact (sample press release is shown in Figure 6.1).

If your agency does not already have a list of contacts and addresses for local media, consider asking well-connected colleagues in the community for their lists.

A Sample Flier

All registered Sibshops (i.e., those that have signed and submitted the Sibshop Standards of Practice [Appendix A]) may use the Sibshop name and logo in their publicity materials. Included in this chapter is a blank flier with empty boxes that you may use to publicize your program (see Figure 6.2a). The box on the left may be filled in with information about the sponsoring agencies, and the box on the right may be filled with contact phone numbers, as shown in Figure 6.2b. This flier then may be used in several ways. As long as it does not mention dates, it may be distributed to agencies for children with special needs and their families to post indefinitely. It may be photocopied on the back of the letter you send to parents, or included with your press release.

Sibshops: A program just for brothers and sisters of kids with special needs!

Sibshops are a celebration of the many contributions made by brothers and sisters.

Here's what kids say about Sibshops:

"At **Sibshops** you get to meet other brothers and sisters of kids with special needs."

"**Sibshops** have outrageous games!"

"At **Sibshops** you can talk about the good and not-so-good parts of having a brother or sister who has special needs."

"**Sibshops** are a place to learn about cool things."

"**Sibshops** have great cooking activities!"

"**Sibshops** have some of the greatest kids in the world!"

"**Sibshops** are fun!"

Sibshops are for kids who have a brother or sister with special health or developmental needs. Join us!

Sibshops: Workshops for Siblings of Children with Special Needs, Revised Edition, by Don Meyer and Patricia Vadasy.
Copyright © 2008 Paul H. Brookes Publishing Co. All rights reserved.

Figure 6.2a. Blank Sibshop flier.

Sibshops: A program just for brothers and sisters of kids with special needs!

Sibshops are a celebration of the many contributions made by brothers and sisters.

Sibshops are cosponsored by: Children's Hospital and Medical Center, The Arc of King County, and Seattle Public Schools.

Here's what kids say about Sibshops:

"At **Sibshops** you get to meet other brothers and sisters of kids with special needs."

"**Sibshops** have outrageous games!"

"At **Sibshops** you can talk about the good and not-so-good parts of having a brother or sister who has special needs."

"**Sibshops** are a place to learn about cool things."

"**Sibshops** have great cooking activities!"

"**Sibshops** have some of the greatest kids in the world!"

"**Sibshops** are fun!"

Sibshops are for kids who have a brother or sister with special health or developmental needs. Join us!

For information and registration call 368-4911.

Figure 6.2b. Filled-in Sibshop flier.

Dear Parents, ...

It gives us great pleasure to announce Sibshops, an exciting program just for brothers and sisters of kids with special needs. At a Sibshop, brothers and sisters will

- Meet other brothers and sisters of children with special needs
- Have fun
- Talk with others who "get it" about the good (and sometimes not so good!) parts of having a sib with special needs
- Learn more about disabilities and the services that people with disabilities receive
- Have some more fun!

Who are Sibshops for? Sibshops are for 8 to 13-year-old brothers and sisters of children who have special needs.

Who sponsors Sibshops? Sibshops are a collaborative effort of Children's Hospital, the DayStar Early Developmental Center, and The Arc of Brighton County.

Who runs Sibshops? Our Sibshops are run by a team of people who have a professional and, in some cases, a personal understanding of the impact a child's special needs can have on brothers and sisters. Equally important, they all have great kid skills! We also have junior facilitators who are sibs in their late teens.

When and where are Sibshops held? Sibshops will be held from 10:00 A.M. to 2:00 P.M. on the following dates: February 22, March 21, April 25, May 16, and June 13. Sibshops will be held at Olympic View Elementary School, 504 NE 95th in Lake Stevens.

What is the cost of a Sibshop? Each Sibshop is $12, which includes lunch.

A limited number of scholarships are available.

Sounds great! How do I register? For more information and to register, call Sarah Marshall at the DayStar Early Developmental Center at 368-4911 or visit www.daystar.org/sibshops. But hurry—space is limited!

....

Figure 6.3. Sample letter to parents.

A Sample Letter to Parents

The letter you send to parents provides them with details pertaining to the "who, what, when, where, and how much" of the program (see Figure 6.3). It also reassures parents about the program in which they will be enrolling their children. The letter to parents, like the flier, should present the program as a positive, fun experience for a deserving population. One common way of disseminating these letters is to ask agencies to e-mail them to the families they serve or to send them home with children who attend special education programs.

Other ways of distributing the letter include obtaining mailing lists of families from Parent-to-Parent programs, The Arc, and other parent-driven organizations, or requesting that these organizations include a copy of this letter in their routine mailings to families.

A Sample E-Mail Message to Agencies Announcing Upcoming Sibling Workshops

The letter in Figure 6.4 may be sent to other agencies serving people with special needs. It asks agencies to post a flier and offers further information on your program. An alternative to sending this letter is to send agencies a press release and a flier.

PLANNING FOR YOUR VERY FIRST SIBSHOP

The information following is designed to assist the planning committee and especially the facilitators in planning a Sibshop for 8- to 13-year-old brothers and sisters of children with special health or developmental needs. The annotated schedule describes in detail

Dear Colleague, ...

We are pleased to announce that Children's Hospital, the DayStar Early Developmental Center, and The Arc of Brighton County are cosponsoring Sibshops for 8- to 13-year-old brothers and sisters of kids with special needs. Please share this e-mail with parents and others who may be interested!

Our Sibshops are lively, action-packed, 4-hour workshops that celebrate the many contributions made by brothers and sisters of kids with special needs. Sibshops acknowledge that being the brother or sister of a person with special needs is for some a good thing, for others a not-so-good thing, and for many, somewhere in between. They reflect a belief that brothers and sisters have much to offer one another—if they are given a chance. The Sibshop model mixes information and discussion activities with new games (designed to be unique, off-beat, and appealing to a wide ability range) and special guests.

We are attaching a flier on the Seattle-area Sibshops and ask that you post it where parents and other interested professionals might see it. A letter to parents describing the program is also attached. Please feel free to photocopy it and distribute it to families.

For more information and registration materials, visit www.daystar.org/sibshops or write to me at smarshall@daystar.org

Sincerely,

Sarah Marshall
DayStar Developmental Center
333-368-4911

P.S. We'd welcome an opportunity to share information about Sibshops at your next staff or parent support meeting!

....

Figure 6.4. Sample letter to agencies.

Sibshop discussion, recreation, and food activities; component tasks; and materials that will need to be purchased or gathered. We are confident that after you have conducted a Sibshop using this schedule, you will have no problem planning subsequent Sibshops. At the end of this chapter, we discuss a planning sheet that will simplify planning for future Sibshops.

Table 6.1.　A Sibshop schedule

Time	Activity	Materials needed	Lead person
9:15	Setup	☐ Signs ☐ Tape ☐ Coffee, anyone?	
10:00	Trickle-in Activity: For parents: Enrollment For sibs: Facetags!	☐ Sibshop Registration Form ☐ Facetags sheet ☐ Pencils ☐ Stickyback nametags ☐ Felt-tip pens ☐ Scissors ☐ Boombox	
10:20	Introductory Activity: Strengths & Weaknesses	☐ Strengths & Weaknesses sheet ☐ Pencils	
10:45	Knots		
10:50	Lap Game		
11:00	Stand Up!		
11:10	Group Juggling	☐ Beanbags, stuffed animals, rolled- up socks, or — during warm weather — water balloons!	
11:30	Triangle Tag	☐ Wristbands or bandanas	
11:40	Sightless Sculpture	☐ Bandanas ☐ Rectangular table	
11:50	Lunch prep		
12:00	Lunch		
12:20	Lunch cleanup		
12:30	Dear Aunt Blabby	☐ Letters in envelopes	
12:55	Pushpin Soccer	☐ Large balloons ☐ Large, clean garbage bags ☐ 2 pushpins ☐ 2 large rectangular tables	
1:15	Scrabble Scramble	☐ 62 sheets of 8 x 11 paper ☐ 2 large felt-tip pens (different colors) ☐ 2 rectangular tables	
1:30	Sound Off	☐ Sound-Off Sheet ☐ Pencils	
1:55	Closure	☐ Day's schedule to take home	
2:05	Debriefing and planning for next Sibshop	☐ Activity Planning Form (see page 96)	

The schedule shown in Table 6.1 is intended to make your first Sibshop as smooth and successful as possible. Set a time to meet with the other cofacilitators to work through the packet and assign responsibilities as needed. *It is critical that you and your cofacilitators read the Annotated Sibshop Schedule carefully.* You and your team, of course, can feel free to substitute other activities of your choice.

AN ANNOTATED SIBSHOP SCHEDULE

What will happen during the first Sibshop is explained in some detail in this section. You are asked to photocopy some materials, gather others, and decide who will present activities.

Times on the Schedule

The times listed on the Sibshop schedule and this annotated schedule assume that your Sibshop will run from 10 A.M. until 2 P.M. If necessity dictates that your Sibshop occur during different hours, adjust the schedule. In any event, the times listed are approximate. You may not have time for all activities or you may try a game suggested by a brother, sister, or cofacilitator.

PLEASE NOTE: This schedule does not include a guest speaker or other learning activity. During the first Sibshop, we usually spend extra time getting to know one another. If you are hosting your Sibshop at a conference for a specific population (e.g., siblings of children with spina bifida), you may wish to amend the schedule to make room for an informational activity (e.g., Ask Dr. Bob!). All facilitators will need a copy of the schedule for Sibshop day.

Who will photocopy the schedule?

9:15 A.M. Setup

It is a good idea for all facilitators to arrive 45 minutes before kids are scheduled to arrive. This provides time for staff to ensure that the building and rooms are as you wish (i.e., open and clean), to arrange furniture, to post directional signs (e.g., Welcome to SIBSHOPS! Use front door), to ensure that all materials have been gathered, and to confer briefly before the festivities begin.

Materials: Signs, paper, tape, coffee

Who will gather materials?

10:00 A.M. Trickle-In Activity: Facetags (p. 104) and Registration

Invariably, some participants will be early, some will be late, and a few might even arrive on time. It is always helpful to have a few activities available while kids are trickling in. Besides keeping participants busy, trickle-in activities go a long way toward making kids feel welcome and at ease. Examples include group juggling, a pickup basketball game, a craft project, or helping the facilitators set up the food activity for the day. As mentioned in Chapter 7, Introductory and Trickle-In Activities (p. 103), a great way to add excitement and instant atmosphere is to play world-beat music on a boom box. Because this is the first day, we will ask participants and their parents for information during the trickle-in time. If the participants' parents have not completed and returned the Sibshop Registration Form online (see example in Appendix E), we will ask them to do so when they drop off their children. At least one facilitator should be available at every Sibshop to welcome kids and parents and to help participants with nametags. For the first Sibshop, however, we all will welcome families and help participants create their Facetags. Of course, each facilitator will make a Facetag too!

Materials: Sibshop registration forms, Facetags sheets, pencils, stickyback nametags, felt-tip pens, scissors, boom box, and an appropriate CD

Who will gather materials?

10:20 A.M. Introductory Activity: Strengths & Weaknesses

For our first Sibshop, we will get to know one another using a simple activity called Strengths & Weaknesses (see p. 109). In addition to introductions, this activity gives participants permission—from the start—to say flattering and, should they wish, not-so-flattering things about their brothers and sisters with special needs.

Materials: Photocopies of Strengths & Weaknesses for each participant and facilitator, pencils

Who will make photocopies and gather materials?

Who will present Strengths & Weaknesses?

10:45 A.M. Knots

The entire group ties itself into one big knot. Can it be untied? You'll find out! (see p. 111).

Materials: None

Who will present Knots?

10:50 A.M. The Lap Game (see p. 158)

This game doesn't require anyone to run laps, nor does it hail from Lapland. This *lap* refers to (as the dictionary defines it) "the front region or area of a seated person extending from the lower trunk to the knees." In short, participants and facilitators will attempt to sit on one another's lap—all at the same time. Can it be done?

Materials: None

Who will present the Lap Game?

11:00 A.M. Stand Up! (see p. 167)

Pairs of equal heights sit back to back, reach back, lock elbows, and attempt to stand up. Lots of variations on this activity!

Materials: None

Who will present Stand Up?

11:10 A.M. Group Juggling (see p. 104)

Although it can be difficult to juggle three balls by oneself, it's easier with a little help from your friends. Or is it? In a circle, we pass a ball and establish a pattern. Once established, we add another ball. And then another. Then we'll try it a different way entirely.

Materials: Three beanbags for each group of five to six.

Who will gather materials?

Who will present Group Juggling?

11:30 A.M. Triangle Tag (see p. 169)

A geometrical twist on Tag. Three players hold hands to make a triangle. One wears a wristband or a bandana around the wrist to identify her as the "target." A fourth player attempts to tag the target while the triangle moves around to protect the target.

Materials: One wristband or bandana for each group of four

Who will gather materials?

Who will present Triangle Tag?

11:40 A.M. Sightless Sculpture (see p. 166)

Can a person who is blind be an artist? Sure she can—she can even be a sculptor! This activity requires three participants: one who will be a model, one who will be a blob of clay, and one who will be a blindfolded sculptor. This can be done in groups of three. It is even better when groups of three sculpt in front of the rest of the Sibshop.

Materials: Bandanas or blindfolds, rectangular table

Who will gather materials?

Who will present Sightless Sculpture?

11:50 A.M. Lunch: Super Nachos

If you are planning on making lunch instead of bringing in pizzas or slapping together a few subs, we suggest Super Nachos for the first lunch. Most kids love nachos, and compared with other cooking activities, they require little in the way of equipment and preparation. After you use the kitchen and get to know its strengths and shortcomings, you can attempt something more adventurous. Despite their relative ease, even nachos can be difficult to prepare if an important ingredient or piece of equipment is forgotten. You will need:

Food

- Tortilla chips
- Yellow cheese (in blocks, so kids can grate)
- Mild salsa
- Black olives (optional)
- Sour cream (optional)
- Tomatoes (optional)
- Green pepper (optional)
- Mild onion (optional)
- Refried beans (optional)
- Juice, cider, or other beverage
- Fruit or dessert (optional)

Equipment

- Working oven
- Hot pads
- Metal spatula
- Bowls for salsa, grated cheese, olives, and so forth
- Cheese graters
- Can opener
- Cutting boards
- Kid-friendly knives
- Cookie sheets
- Pan for heating refried beans (or a microwave and a suitable bowl)
- Cups
- Paper or other plates
- Napkins
- Cleaning equipment and soap

Who will shop?

Who will visit the kitchen to determine equipment needs?

Who will gather the remaining equipment?

12:30 P.M. Discussion Activity: Dear Aunt Blabby (see p. 127)

A visit with Dear Aunt Blabby puts the participants in a rarely recognized role: as experts on what it is like to live with a brother or sister who has special needs. Write out five to seven letters from Appendix F and place them in individual envelopes addressed to Dear Aunt Blabby.

Materials: Dear Aunt Blabby letters in envelopes

Who will copy the letters and place them in envelopes?

· Who will present Dear Aunt Blabby?

12:55 P.M. Pushpin Soccer (see p. 163)

Soccer with a point and a caution: This game requires two players to use pushpins! Teams swat balloons toward the "popper" in their goal, who pops the balloon to score a point. For safety's sake, poppers cannot reach outside of the goal box and other players cannot reach inside. If the thought of participants plus pushpins is more than you can bear, substitute an equally lively activity such as Blob Tag (p. 148), Islands (p. 157), or something outrageous, like Body Surfing (p. 149) or The Dangling Donut Eating Contest (p. 151).

Materials: Two large balloons per participant, two pushpins, four or more large garbage bags (to store balloons after they are blown up), two large rectangular tables (to serve as goals). When shopping, aim for balloons at least 8 inches when inflated; in this game bigger is better. Dollar stores can be a good resource for balloons.

Who will gather materials?

Who will lead Pushpin Soccer?

1:15 P.M. Scrabble Scramble (see p. 164)

A fast-paced variation of the world's most popular crossword game. Watch out though: Adults are likely to be every bit as competitive playing as the kids!

Materials: 62 sheets of $8\frac{1}{2} \times 11$ paper, two large felt-tip pens (different colors), two rectangular tables

Who will lead Scrabble Scramble?

1:30 P.M. Discussion Activity: Sound-Off (see p. 124)

Sound-Off provides participants with an open-ended structure to hypothetically tell a friend, teacher, parent, or the whole world whatever they wish about being the brother or sister of a person with special needs. Responses generally cover a wide range of experiences.

Materials: Sound-Off Sheet, pencils

Who will photocopy the Sound-Off Sheet?

Who will lead Sound-Off?

1:55 P.M. Closure

Closure is a good time to check in with participants. You may wish to ask, "If your friends ask you what you did today, what would you tell them?" (Inevitable answers: "We played games!" "We ate nachos!" Continue to rephrase the question; eventually they will mention that they had a chance to talk about their brothers and sisters.) An alternative question might be, "You know, there are probably some brothers and sisters who knew about the Sibshop but weren't sure whether they wanted to attend. What would you say to them to encourage them to come to the next Sibshop?"

Finally, closure is a good time to ask participants to suggest food activities, recreational events, or guest speakers. Accommodating the group's wish to, say, make pizza or play Freeze Tag at the next Sibshop can encourage continued participation. At the very end, you may wish to have a group cheer. If this is to be your only meeting, it is also a great time to take a group picture or to hand out the Official Sibshop Certificate (see Figure 6.5). Group pictures are a wonderful way of extending the Sibshop experience. We know participants who were involved in Sibshops 10 years ago who still have their Sibshop group picture and can still identify many of the kids in the group. If you are holding a series of meetings, plan on taking a group picture during your next-to-last meeting. At your last meeting, hand out copies of the picture, along with participants' names, addresses, phone numbers, and e-mail addresses.

Who will lead closure?

Sibshops

This certifies that

has been a successful participant in Sibshops

OFFICIAL
Awesome Sibling
AWARD

Date

Facilitators

Figure 6.5. Sibshop certificate.

2:05 P.M. Debriefing and Planning for Subsequent Sibshops

This is an opportunity to discuss what went on while it is still fresh in your mind. Even though you will have had a long day, consider spending a few minutes planning for the next Sibshop. A few minutes spent at this time may mean that the group will not need to meet again before the next Sibshop.

THE ACTIVITY PLANNING FORM

The Sibshop Activity Planning Form (Figure 6.6) can greatly simplify the process of coming up with the next meeting's agenda. For each activity, the form asks you to estimate time and identify a leader, materials needed, and materials that may need to be purchased. Here is how it is done:

1. Flipping through Chapter 8, identify the peer support and discussion activity you want to try at your next Sibshop. For a 4-hour Sibshop, three will be plenty; two may be enough.

2. Decide on information activities or a guest speaker, either one proposed in Chapter 10 or as identified by the facilitators. Of all activities, planning this one should get top priority; potential guest speakers need as much lead time as possible. You may wish to identify a back-up speaker or activity. Also, the times that a guest speaker is available may influence the rest of your schedule.

3. Select an introductory activity (Chapter 7).

4. Select a food activity from Chapter 9 or, better yet, create one of your own. Think through the ingredients, materials, and equipment you will need.

5. Select three or four high-energy activities and two or three quieter recreational activities from Chapter 9.

6. If you are having special events or other activities, include the estimated time, activity leader, and materials needed on the activity planning form.

7. Using the completed form, begin to build a schedule around timed activities such as introductory activities, lunch, and perhaps your guest speaker. Discussion activities are often best held after lunch, when full tummies predispose participants toward quiet conversation and contemplation. Follow high-energy activities with a quieter activity.

Materials: Activity Planning Form

Who will photocopy the Activity Planning Form?

Who will develop the schedule for the next Sibshop (based on activities suggested on the Activity Planning Form)?

EVALUATING YOUR PROGRAM

After you have held two or three Sibshops, seek feedback from participants and their parents. Contributed anonymously, this feedback will provide you with invaluable information and allow you to adjust and improve your program. At the end of a session,

⚬ Sibshop Activity Planning Form

Planning for a Sibshop need not be difficult or time-consuming. Use the following form to record the activities you select for your next Sibshop. After deciding upon your core (discussion and information) activities, decide upon complementary recreational activities. Once completed, use this information to build a schedule.

Date: _____

Discussion/Peer Support Activity: _____

Estimated time to complete activity: _____

Activity leader: _____

Materials needed: _____

Shopping list: _____

Information Activity/Guest Speaker: _____

Estimated time to complete activity: _____

Activity leader: _____

Materials needed: _____

Shopping list: _____

Introductory/Warm-Up Activity: _____

Estimated time to complete activity: _____

Activity leader: _____

Materials needed: _____

Shopping list: _____

Food Activity:

Estimated time to complete activity: _____

Activity leader: _____

Materials needed: _____

Shopping list: _____

High-Energy Recreation Activity #1: _____

Estimated time to complete activity: _____

Activity leader: _____

Materials needed: _____

Shopping list: _____

High-Energy Recreation Activity #2: _____

Estimated time to complete activity: _____

Activity leader: _____

Materials needed: _____

Shopping list: _____

Figure 6.6. Sibshop activity planning form.

○ Sibshop Activity Planning Form PAGE 2

High-Energy Recreation Activity #3: _____

Estimated time to complete activity: _____

Activity leader: _____

Materials needed: _____

Shopping list: _____

Quieter Recreational Activity #1: _____

Estimated time to complete activity: _____

Activity leader: _____

Materials needed: _____

Shopping list: _____

Quieter Recreational Activity #2: _____

Estimated time to complete activity: _____

Activity leader: _____

Materials needed: _____

Shopping list: _____

Special Event: _____

Estimated time to complete activity: _____

Activity leader: _____

Materials needed: _____

Shopping list: _____

Other #1: _____

Estimated time to complete activity: _____

Activity leader: _____

Materials needed: _____

Shopping list: _____

Other #2: _____

Estimated time to complete activity: _____

Activity leader: _____

Materials needed: _____

Shopping list: _____

NOTES: _____

_____

_____

_____

_____

distribute pencils and a consumer evaluation sheet such as the Official Sibshop Feed-back Form (Figure 6.7). As parents pick up their children, hand them a consumer satisfaction survey, such as the Parent Feedback Form (Figure 6.8). To increase your chances of having the questionnaires returned, also provide a self-addressed, stamped envelope.

CONCLUSION

In the chapters that follow, we provide detailed descriptions of favorite Sibshop intro-ductory, discussion, recreational, food, and informational activities. As you plan your first Sibshop, be sure to read the introductions to each of these chapters. They contain information that will help you plan and present Sibshop activities for the first time.

The Official Sibshop Feedback Form
PAGE 1

Date: _____

Your age: _____

Names of the Sibshop leaders: _____

Your name (optional): _____

1. What do you like most about Sibshops? _____

_____

_____

2. What don't you like about Sibshops? _____

_____

_____

3. Please tell us what you think about the Sibshop activities.

	Good	So-so	Not-so-good	Don't remember
a. Warm-up activities ( )	1	2	3	4
b. Games ( )	1	2	3	4
c. Discussion activities ( )	1	2	3	4
d. Cooking activities ( )	1	2	3	4
e. Information activities ( )	1	2	3	4
f. Guest speakers ( )	1	2	3	4

4. Are the Sibshop leaders: Helpful? _____

Interesting? _____

Boring? _____

Other? _____

(continued)

Figure 6.7.   The official Sibshop feedback form.

Figure 6.7 (*continued*)

The Official Sibshop Feedback Form

5. Is there something you want to know that we could learn during a Sibshop? _____

_____

_____

_____

_____

6. Is there something you would like to talk about with the other kids? _____

_____

_____

_____

_____

7. How can we make these Sibshops better? _____

_____

_____

_____

_____

8. Do you think other kids whose brothers and sisters have special needs would like to go to a group

like this? Yes _____ No _____ Why? _____

_____

_____

_____

_____

9. Do Sibshops make you think of your brother or sister? How? _____

_____

_____

_____

_____

10. Is there anything else that you want to say about the Sibshops? _____

_____

_____

_____

_____

⦿ **Parent Feedback Form**

Please take some time to answer each of the following questions about your child's participation in the Sibshop series. Be as honest and open in your answers as possible. Thank you for your time and attention.

Date:

Sibshop leaders:

Meeting time and location:

Your name (optional):

Rate your satisfaction with the following aspects of the group on a scale from 1 (very dissatisfied) to 5 (very satisfied). If you have no opinion or the item is not applicable, circle N.

1. Meeting time	1	2	3	4	5	N
2. Location	1	2	3	4	5	N
3. Length of Sibshop	1	2	3	4	5	N
4. Group composition	1	2	3	4	5	N
5. Communication and contact with Sibshop leader	1	2	3	4	5	N
6. Sibshop format	1	2	3	4	5	N
7. Sibshop activities/content	1	2	3	4	5	N
8. Opportunities for parent input	1	2	3	4	5	N
9. Impact on your child's knowledge of disabilities or illness	1	2	3	4	5	N
10. Impact on your child's feelings toward his or her brother or sister	1	2	3	4	5	N
11. Impact on your child's feelings toward other family members	1	2	3	4	5	N
12. Impact on your child's self-image	1	2	3	4	5	N
13. Impact on your concerns about your child	1	2	3	4	5	N
14. Impact on your knowledge/awareness of your child's needs	1	2	3	4	5	N
15. Quality of the Sibshop series overall	1	2	3	4	5	N

16. Comments regarding above items (please note item number)

_____

17. Has your child talked about what has happened during the Sibshop? Yes _____ No _____

Comments: _____

_____

_____

18. Has your child seemed to enjoy the Sibshop? Yes _____ No _____

Comments: _____

_____

_____

(continued)

Figure 6.8. Parent feedback form.

Figure 6.8 (*continued*)

⟳ Parent Feedback Form

19. Was there a particular activity that your child seemed to have really enjoyed? Yes ____ No ____

Comments: _____

_____

_____

20. Has your child seemed upset by any meeting? Yes ____ No ____

Comments: _____

_____

_____

21. Has any activity made a strong impression on your child? Yes ____ No ____

Comments: _____

_____

_____

22. What do you think your child has learned from the Sibshop? How has he or she benefited so far?

Comments: _____

_____

_____

23. Is there any way in which you feel your child may have been harmed by the Sibshop activities?

Yes ____ No ____

Comments: _____

_____

_____

24. Overall, are you glad your child participated in the Sibshop series? Yes ____ No ____

Comments: _____

_____

_____

25. Is there anything we should consider for future Sibshops to make them more enjoyable or

informative? Yes ____ No ____

Comments: _____

_____

_____

26. Any other comments? _____

_____

_____

Please return this questionnaire to:

Chapter 7

Introductory and Trickle-In Activities

When we help start a new Sibshop, one question we often ask participants is, "Not counting your own brothers and sisters, how many of you have ever met other brothers or sisters of kids with special needs?" It still surprises us to find out that usually only 20% have ever met another sibling. The introductory activities presented in this chapter will help you and your colleagues accomplish the first Sibshop goal:

Goal 1: Sibshops will provide brothers and sisters of children with special needs an opportunity to meet other siblings in a relaxed, recreational setting.

This seemingly simple opportunity—to meet their peers—may be the most important experience that Sibshops provide. How we introduce ourselves to the participants and the participants to each other will set the tone for the day. Be prepared for the day's events so that you can attend to participants as they arrive. Remember that for many first-time participants, attending your Sibshop was their parents' idea, not theirs. Consequently, from the moment they walk through the Sibshop door, your young participants should feel that the adults who are running the program are happy to see them, interested in who they are, and ready to have fun. One simple-but-effective way to set the stage is to play a world-beat CD as kids arrive. The infectious music welcomes kids, prevents stuffy silences, and creates an atmosphere that says "Something's going to happen here!" If you're new to world-beat music, visit the Putumayo web site. Putumayo specializes in world-beat music, and they have a terrific selection of irresistible music.

The activities you offer at the very beginning of a Sibshop can help break the ice and introduce participants to the facilitators and each other. "Trickle-in" activities are good to use as participants are arriving. These activities can be as simple as inviting participants to join a pick-up basketball or volleyball game or a craft or art activity or enlisting their help in making water balloons, grating cheese, and so forth in preparation for an activity later that day. Many of these activities, such as Facetags, begin as soon as the participants walk through the door.

Once most of the participants arrive, it will be time for slightly more organized introductions. Some of the activities described in this chapter, such as Strengths and Weaknesses, will introduce participants to one another. Others, like Knots, will warm up a group by putting them in close physical proximity.

FACETAGS

Materials: Standard sticky-back nametags, a good selection of fine-point felt-tip pens, a few pairs of scissors to share, and copies of the Facetags sheet

Nametags are standard issue at most Sibshops, so why not make them fun to design and wear? As participants arrive, give each a Facetags sheet (Figure 7.1), a sticky-back nametag, and access to a wide array of colorful markers. Facilitators can model artistic license by creating and wearing an outrageously designed Facetag.

Facetags allow participants to draw a self-portrait as a part of their nametags. These self-portraits can be as realistic or as outlandish as the artist desires! As participants arrive, they select a face shape that most looks like their own face from the Facetags sheet. They then fill in and color the faces to resemble themselves. Once completed, they cut out the Facetag, leaving a bit of room at the top. Next, they write their names on the sticky-back nametag. They attach the "extra room" they left on their Facetag to the bottom of the sticky back of the nametag. There will still be lots of sticky surface left, so have them use this to attach the completed Facetag to their shirts.

GROUP JUGGLING

Materials: (In order of preference) beanbags, old stuffed animals, and/or rolled-up socks; during warm weather, water balloons

Although it can be difficult to juggle three balls by yourself, it is easier with a little help from your friends. Or is it? A group of five or six participants, standing in a circle, gently toss a ball back and forth, establishing a pattern: Madison throws to Sam, Sam throws to Jorge, Jorge throws to Gina, and Gina throws to Madison. Two helpful strategies may be suggested: Call the name of the person to whom you are throwing as you throw the ball, and keep your eyes on the person who always tosses you the ball. Once this pattern is

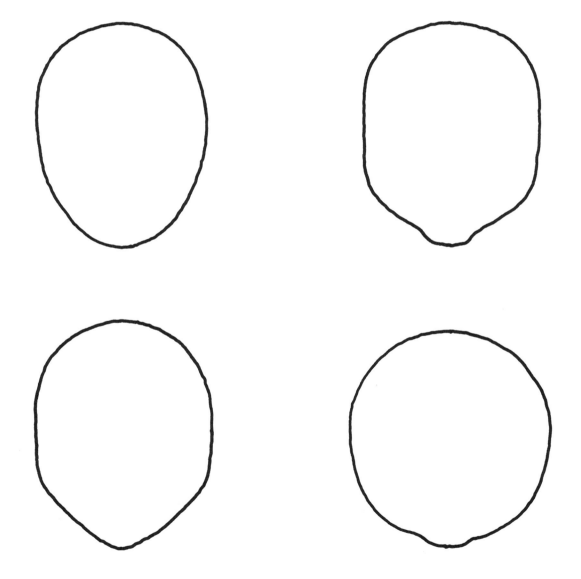

Figure 7.1. Facetags activity sheet.

perfected with one ball, another ball is added. And then another ball. And then another. (For younger children, try the Useless Machine variation of Group Juggling. To play, create a pattern just like Group Juggling, but instead of throwing the beanbags, you pass them, preferably at a rapid clip. Useless Machine has a wonderful Lucy-and-Ethel-in-the-chocolate-factory quality that appeals to both kids and adults.) A wonderful warm-weather Group Juggling variation is to use softball-size water balloons!!

Source: Adapted from More New Games (Flugelman, 1981, p. 61)

HUMAN BINGO

Materials: Human Bingo sheet, pencils. Optional: three small, silly prizes (e.g., glow-in-the-dark slugs)

This is a great introductory activity for a group of school-age siblings. It is guaranteed to warm things up in a hurry!

To begin, ask which participants know how to play Bingo. Have these participants describe how in Bingo you win by completing a horizontal, vertical, or diagonal row of boxes. Distribute Human Bingo sheets (Figure 7.2) but not pencils. Ask the participants how they think Human Bingo is played. Using hypothetical examples, let the participants know that a box is completed by filling in the name of a person in the group who meets the conditions or can perform the actions specified in the box. "If I asked Maurice if he likes blue cheese, and he answers yes, I would write his name in the blue cheese box." Explain that, like regular Bingo, the first person to complete a horizontal, vertical, or diagonal row is the winner. When that person wins, he or she yells "Bingo!" Pass out pencils, say "Ready, Set, Go!" and stand back! Kids asking questions, wiggling ears, imitating elephants, and writing simultaneously creates a funny, friendly, if chaotic, scene. You can stretch this activity out by having three winners: one who wins by the above means, another who fills in the four corners first, and a third who is able to assign names to all 16 boxes.

"I AM" POEM

Materials: Photocopies of "I Am" poem sheet, pencils

In this easy icebreaker, participants complete sentences that culminate in a poem about themselves. Below is our version of the "I Am" poem format, but feel free to tweak it any way you wish. To begin, distribute papers and share how you completed an "I am" poem about yourself. Be sure to emphasize that everyone's poem will be different and that's what makes these poems special. (And, in case they're worried, no rhyming is necessary!) Once completed, have the participants share their poems. If a participant is reluctant to read his poem, offer to read it for him (often this does the trick with shy participants). But if he remains reluctant, no worries. His poem may be too private to share.

I Am
I am (something that is special about you)
I wonder (something you are actually curious about)
Sometimes I hear (an imaginary sound)

HUMAN BINGO

Find someone (besides yourself) who . . . .

Has a bird for a pet. NAME_____	Can name the last four U.S. Presidents VAN HALEN? JACKSON? NAME_____	Has four kids in their family NAME_____	Can imitate an elephant NAME_____
Likes anchovies on their pizza NAME_____	Has been to the Statue of Liberty NAME_____	Has a dog for a pet NAME_____	Can do the splits NAME_____
Has visited their special sib's school NAME_____	Can wiggle their ears NAME_____	Can roll their tongue NAME_____	Likes blue cheese NAME_____
Was born in another state U. S. A NAME_____	Has been to Disney World or Disneyland NAME_____	Knows why their sib has a disability NAME_____	Can pat their head and rub their tummy for 10 seconds NAME_____

Sibling Support Project· Seattle, Washington

Figure 7.2. Human Bingo activity sheet.

Or I see (an imaginary sight)
I want (something you really want)
I am (the first line of the poem restated)

I pretend (something you actually pretend to do)
I feel (a feeling you have)
I touch (an imaginary touch)
Sometimes I worry (something that really bothers you)
But I laugh (something that you find funny)
I am (the first line of the poem repeated)

I understand (something you know is true)
I say (something you believe in)
I dream (something you actually dream about)
I try (something you really make an effort about)
I hope (something you actually hope for)
I am (the first line of the poem repeated)

FAVORITES I

Even though the participants will share the common denominator of having a brother or sister who has special needs, they will be different from one another in many ways. One small way of celebrating these differences is to try an activity such as Favorites I or II. Favorites II is especially good with younger participants.

Materials: A slip of paper as described below, pencils

Favorites I creates a flurry of activity and warms up a crowd quickly. At the very beginning of the Sibshop, participants are instructed to fill in a slip of paper providing the following information:

What is your favorite food?

What is your favorite hobby?

What is your favorite television show?

NOTE: DON'T WRITE YOUR NAME ON THIS PAPER!

The completed slips are collected, mixed up, and redistributed at the beginning of the activity. Participants then must find the person who wrote on their piece of paper by asking others what their favorites are (e.g., "Is your favorite hobby skateboarding?"). Because participants are simultaneously seeking the writer of the paper they are holding and being sought, the activity creates mild confusion. But don't worry—it is a pleasant, constructive commotion. Once everyone finds the person they are seeking, participants introduce their "partners" to the group and announce their favorites.

FAVORITES II

Materials: 5 × 7 index cards, felt-tip pens, safety pins

Favorites II is especially fun with younger groups (6- to 8-year olds). At the beginning of the Sibshop, instead of nametags, give each participant a 5 × 7 index card and a felt-tip pen. Have available as a model two posters illustrating index cards. One poster will describe the information you wish:

Favorite TV program

Favorite pastime

Name

Word that describes me

Favorite food

Favorite color

The second poster will have an illustration of the card as it might be completed by a participant:

The Simpsons

Jump rope

Belinda

Silly

Pizza!

Purple

Help the participants fill out a card that describes their favorites. Use a hole puncher and a safety pin or tape to attach nametags. At the beginning of the Sibshop, ask the participants and facilitators to share the information on their tags.

Source: Adapted from Child Support (Landy, 1988)

STRENGTHS & WEAKNESSES

Materials: Strengths & Weaknesses activity sheet, pencils

Strengths & Weaknesses interviews take introduction activities one step further: They help participants begin to think in terms of their sibling with special needs. Strengths & Weaknesses also serves two other purposes: First, it acknowledges that everyone has strengths and weaknesses; and second, it provides participants permission—from the start—to say flattering and not-so-flattering things about their brothers or sisters with special needs.

Introduce the activity by asking the group if they believe that everyone has strengths—things that they do well. The answer, of course, will be yes. Ask them about people who have disabilities or illnesses: Do they also have strengths? Then ask them whether most people also have weaknesses—things they do not do so well. As you introduce this activity, model the sharing you would like to see from the participants. If you are a good cook but a truly awful singer, describe, with gusto and detail, how bad and good you are at these activities.

Have the participants pair off with someone they have not met before and, using the Strengths & Weaknesses activity sheet shown in Figure 7.3, have them interview each other about their strengths and weaknesses and the strengths and weaknesses of their brothers and sisters with special needs. Distribute pencils and the activity sheet

STRENGTHS & WEAKNESSES

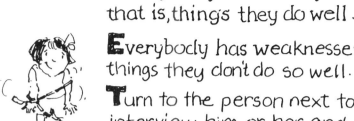

Everybody has strengths—that is, things they do well.

Everybody has weaknesses—things they don't do so well.

Turn to the person next to you, interview him or her, and find out ONE strength they have and ONE weakness.

Also, find out ONE strength and ONE weakness for their sibling with special needs.

Take good notes. You'll introduce the person you interviewed!

Name of person you interviewed:
_____

One strength: _____
_____

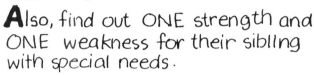

One weakness: _____
_____

Name of person's brother or sister with special needs: _____

His or her strength: _____
_____

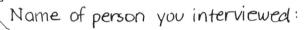

His or her weakness: _____
_____

Your Name: _____

Figure 7.3. Strengths & Weaknesses activity sheet.

and dispatch the participants to various corners of the room. Allow approximately 5 minutes for the interviews.

When the interviews are completed, regroup in a circle and have the participants introduce their partners and describe their partners' strengths and weaknesses and the strengths and weaknesses of their partners' siblings. This can be a good time to ask the person being introduced if he or she knows the name of their siblings' disability. It is also a good time to explore common experiences (e.g., "Does anyone else have a brother or sister who can't talk?" or, "Sounds like we have a few musicians here. Who else is good at music?" or, "How many other people do we have here who have a hard time keeping their room clean?" [Then in mock horror] "Oh, no, not you too!").

TWO TRUTHS AND A LIE

Materials: None

This slightly sneaky way to learn more about one another was suggested by Nanci Morris and Stacy Levin of the Sibshop at Oakstone Academy in Columbus, Ohio.

To begin, have the participants sit in a circle. Ask each player to think of two interesting facts about him- or herself that are true and to create one "fact" that is false. One at a time, the players share their facts with the group. Other players ask questions to determine which two facts are true and which one is false. For example, one player might say, "I have two sisters," "My family lives on a big farm," and "I play on a baseball team." Participants then guess which of the three facts is not true, asking questions ("What position do you play?") if they wish. Once everyone has made his or her choice, the player reveals the lie ("Living on the farm is the lie! I live in the city in an apartment!").

KNOTS

Materials: None

In Knots, a group of six to eight players tie themselves together into one big knot. To begin this activity, players stand, shoulder to shoulder, in a circle facing inward. The players extend their hands and grab two other hands, observing two rules: 1) Do not take both hands of the same person and 2) Do not take the hands of the person next to you. Once knotted, players gently try to untie the knot, stepping over and under arms and pivoting handholds without breaking their grip. Can it be untied? There is only one way to find out! This game is guaranteed to get participants close in a hurry!

INSTANT REPLAY

Materials: None

Try this decidedly silly name-learning game after a warm-up activity such as Knots, Group Juggling, or Human Bingo. In a circle, each group member says his or her name while making an extravagant motion. For instance, Mike may choose to hop around in a circle on one foot (or do a forward roll, or slap his knees), ending by shouting, "Mike!" After Mike demonstrates, everyone else does an "instant replay"; that is, they simultaneously perform the same silly act and say, "Mike!" Going around the circle, encourage the participants to introduce themselves with dramatic gestures.

Source: Adapted from More New Games (Flugelman, 1981, p. 71)

SNOWBALL FIGHT

Materials: One piece of 8½ × 11 paper (rescued from recycling is fine!) per player; pencils

Have each participant write one fact that other Sibshop participants might not know (but is not some family or personal secret!). You can decide if you wish this to be a "generic" fact (e.g., "I used to live in Alaska," "There are 12 kids in my family," "I broke my leg when I was four") or "sibling-related" (e.g., "My sister knows the movie *Shrek* so well that she can act out the entire movie," "Doctors say they have never seen a child with the same special needs that my brother has," or "Once my little sister asked this lady why she talks so much"). NOTE: Sibshoppers should NOT write their names on their piece of paper!

Tell the participants to crumple up the papers into balls. On your cue, have them toss the snowballs to the center of the room, creating a snowball-like chaos. Have each participant find a snowball, uncrumple it, and read the fact written on it. Have the participants search out the author of the fact written on their snowball. Because they will be simultaneously searching for their snowball's original owner and being asked questions, there will be some additional—albeit mild—chaos.

Once all the original authors have been found, have the participants introduce the authors to the group by reading their fact—for example, "This is Mike. He wrote that the school band he plays in will be going to New York next year."

Adapted from Heidi Springston, Horizon Middle School, Aurora, Colorado

GO STAND IN THE CORNER!

Materials: Sheets of large 8 × 14 paper and markers, or two chalkboards, chalk, and erasers

In Go Stand in the Corner!, we vote with our feet. To prepare, have two assistants stand in opposite corners of the room or gym. One assistant will have pieces of paper with the words from Column A written in large letters. The other assistant will do the same with words from Column B. Alternatively, both assistants can write the choices on chalkboards for each round. Have the participants join you in the center of the room and dispatch them to corners based on the preferences listed below.

Ask the participants: "Which describes you best?"

Column A	or	Column B
Baseball		Football
Orange juice		Tomato juice
Burger King		McDonalds
Cereal		Bacon and eggs
Donald Duck		Daffy Duck
Potato chips		Taco chips
Get up early		Sleep in
School, thumbs up		School, thumbs down
Pizza, pepperoni		Pizza, extra cheese

Once your Sibshoppers have raced to the corners to let you know whether they're Oreos or chocolate chip cookies, shoo them back to the center of the room to prepare for another round of "voting."

Have several pieces of blank paper on hand so the participants can privately suggest other choices.

Source: Adapted from More New Games (Flugelman, 1981, p. 71)

SIBTREE

Materials: Butcher paper, markers, tape, scissors, and construction paper

Marianne Barnes of the Tampa Sibshop suggested this wonderful autumn trickle-in activity. It can also be a great way to publicize your Sibshop. To prepare, draw the trunk and branches of a tree, approximately 5 feet high, on butcher paper. At the bottom of the tree, write in large letters "SibTree." On brightly colored construction paper, draw leaves—or hands—and cut them out. On these leaves (or hands), put a variety of questions such as

* What do you like about yourself and why?

* What do you like to do with your sib?

* What's one thing you would change in your life and why?

* What's one thing that's really great about my brother or sister?

* What's one thing that's a little difficult about having a sib with special needs?

Put the leaves into a box and have the kids pick one and answer the question on it. When finished, the participants tape their leaf to the SibTree. Continue to add new leaves to the tree throughout the day, perhaps during snack or lunch or even at subsequent meetings. At the end of the day, call the kids' attention to the SibTree and remind them that when they arrived, the tree was "barren" with no leaves, hands, and so forth, and they gave it "life," just the way their ideas, energy, and sharing have brought life to the Sibshop. One Sibshop moved the tree to one of the main halls in the center they use and left it up as an autumn decoration. They found that their SibTree generated much interest and was good public relations for their Sibshop!

SIBSHOP ACTION ART

Materials: White or light-colored mural butcher paper (2–3 yards), scissors, crayons or markers

Sibshop Action Art is a great warm-up activity that gives each kid a chance to "fit" his or her individuality into the group!

Prior to the Sibshop, decide on a word or phrase applicable to the group and draw it in big bubble letters on the butcher paper. Then cut the paper into puzzle-like pieces, one for each member of the group. Remember to cut through the letters, so that each piece has just a part of one or two letters.

As the participants arrive, give each one a piece of the puzzle and explain that it may be decorated however he or she wishes. Colors, shapes, and tones will vary with each child's emotions and feelings. When each participant is finished, or the time is up, explain that it is now time to fit all of the individual pieces together into a whole. Guesses are welcome as to what the finished word or phrase will be!

Tape the pieces together as they are fitted correctly and hang the puzzle on the wall for all to see as you begin your group circle or full-group activity.

THE NAME GAME

Materials: None

The Name Game, like Telephone, is a game that will be known to many readers. Although we constantly are on the lookout for innovative games, we have learned that games we might consider old warhorses are still enjoyed by young participants who have never experienced them. The Name Game helps participants and facilitators learn names; it also lets the group know that the program has begun and their attention is required. If you have many participants, you may wish to break into two or even three circles for this activity.

To play, the group sits in a circle. The first person says, "My name is Michelle." The person to her left says, "My name is Sean and that is Michelle." The person to Sean's left says, "My name is Terese, this is Sean and Michelle." Continue adding names as you go around the circle.

TRUE FACTS!

Materials: True Facts! sheet, pencils

Have the participants find someone they haven't met before and interview this person using the True Facts! sheet (Figure 7.4). Then have the participants reverse roles. Finally, have each participant introduce the person they interviewed to the group. Good with older Sibshop participants.

TELEPHONE

Materials: A bag containing sayings, such as those described below, written on slips of paper

Kids love this old chestnut. Line up the participants in a straight line. Explain that the first child will be handed a slip of paper with a message on it, such as

- Loose lips sink ships.
- A bird in the hand is worth two in the bush.
- An apple a day keeps the doctor away.
- Early to bed, early to rise, makes a man healthy, wealthy, and wise.
- What we've got here is a failure to communicate.
- People who need people are the luckiest people in the world.
- The rain in Spain stays mainly in the plain.
- Toto, I have a feeling we're not in Kansas anymore.
- Cleanliness is next to godliness.
- When the well's dry, we know the worth of water.
- Little strokes fell great oaks.
- It don't mean a thing if it ain't got that swing.
- Water, water, everywhere, but not a drop to drink.
- Live simply so that others may simply live.
- The corn is as high as an elephant's eye, An' it looks like it's climbin' right up to the sky.
- I yam what I yam and that's all that I yam!
- In like a lion, out like a lamb.

The first child turns to his or her neighbor and whispers the message. That participant whispers the message to the next person and so on. Challenge the group to be as accurate as possible. By the end of the line, you will likely have a garbled message. Have the last person announce the messages as he or she understands it or, even better, write it on a chalkboard. Have the first participant state what the original sentence was.

If desired, have the group discuss where the breakdown occurred and what this activity teaches (miscommunication can cause disagreements and even hurt feelings).

◯ True Facts!

Ladies and gentlemen, we want the dirt, the scoop, the hard, cold facts about the person you are interviewing. Please find out the following:

This person's name: _____

This person's school and grade: _____

Favorite animal: _____

_____

_____

Favorite TV show:

_____

_____

Least favorite TV show:

_____

_____

This person's response to the following question: If I could rule the world for one day, the first thing I would do is:

_____

_____

_____

_____

_____

Name and age of this person's sibling with special needs:

_____

Name of sibling's special need (if it has a name, that is!):

_____

_____

_____

What is this sibling doing today?

_____

_____

Finally, ask this person to describe an ideal weekend:

_____

_____

_____

_____

Figure 7.4. True Facts! activity sheet.

A nonverbal variation of this game is to have the first player make a face that represents an emotion and then pass along that face to other players down the line.

THE WEB

Materials: A ball of heavy yarn

Build cohesiveness in your group by spinning a web of shared thoughts and experiences. To begin, have the participants sit in a circle. Hold a ball of yarn in your hands and state, "If I were an animal, I would like to be a _____. " Hold the end of the yarn and gently toss the yarn ball to a participant. Ask this participant, "If you could be an animal, what would it be?" Once this player answers, he or she holds onto the yarn but gently tosses the ball to someone else. This continues until all have shared and a web has been created. Other possible questions include

1. What do you enjoy doing in your spare time?

2. What is your favorite color, song, place, or food?

3. Who is someone important to you and why?

4. What is one thing you always wanted to do?

WHEN YOU'RE HOT, YOU'RE HOT!

Materials: The "When You're Hot, You're Hot" activity sheet, pencils

Like Strengths and Weaknesses, this activity acknowledges that we all have different talents and limitations. With this activity, participants fill out the sheet shown in Figure 7.5 and share a sample of their findings with the group. As the participants share their results, celebrate the diversity of the responses and acknowledge similarities.

Source: Adapted from We All Come in Different Packages (Konczal & Petetski, 1983, p. 13)

M&M GAME

Materials: M&M candies, tablespoon, small disposable cups

As you will see in the next chapter, the M&M game can be a great discussion activity, but it makes an excellent introductory activity as well. To play, have the participants sit in a circle. Distribute cups and give each player a heaping tablespoon of M&Ms—but instruct them NOT to eat them—not yet, anyway! Pass a bag of M&Ms around and ask the kids to take a small handful.

Assign something to each M&M color that you'd like the participants to share (e.g., "If you have a red M&M, tell us your favorite movie"). After hearing about everyone's favorite movie, all the red M&Ms can be eaten. Here are a few other things that you could assign to an M&M color:

• Tell us your favorite hobby.

• Tell us your favorite book.

• What is your favorite food?

When You're Hot, You're Hot...

...and when you're not, you're not! Nobody does everything well. Things that are easy for some folks are difficult or even impossible for others. That is okay. Life would be pretty boring if we all did the same things well—and pretty tough if we all had problems doing the same thing! Indicate how well you can do each of these things by putting an X in one of the boxes beside it.

	For me it is...			
	Easy	Hard	Impossible	Never tried it!
Adding numbers ''in your head''				
Ballet				
Braiding hair				
Chin-ups				
Climbing a rope				
Cooking a whole meal				
Dancing				
Doing a head stand				
Doing a magic trick				
Doing cartwheels				
Doing science projects				
Drawing				
Flying a kite				
Jumping rope				
Looking up words in the dictionary				
Memorizing a part for a play				
Painting				
Playing a musical instrument				
Playing chess				

(continued)

Figure 7.5. When You're Hot, You're Hot activity sheet.

Figure 7.5   (*continued*)

When You're Hot, You're Hot...

	For me it is...			
	Easy	Hard	Impossible	Never tried it!
Riding a horse				
Rollerblading				
Saving money				
Shooting baskets				
Singing				
Skateboarding				
Skipping				
Sleeping in				
Spelling				
Swimming				
Swinging on monkey bars				
Telling a joke				
Tossing a football				
Typing				
Using a computer				
Using a yo-yo				
Whistling				
Writing a story				

- What was your proudest moment?

- What is your sibling's name?

- What is the name of your sibling's special needs (if there is a name for it!)

- What do you want to be when you get older?

- Where in the world would you most like to live?

- Who is your role model?

After the player answers the question, he or she can eat the M&M color associated with the question.

By the end of the first half-hour of your Sibshop, the young participants will have properly greeted and been introduced to one another and, with some of the more physical activities, may even be "warmed up" to a point of light sweat! Now you're ready to try other Sibshop activities, such as those described in the following chapters.

Chapter **8**

Sibshop Discussion and Peer Support Activities

Peer support and discussion among participants occur throughout a Sibshop, often in a variety of guises. Sometimes discussion is incidental to another activity, such as the introductory activities described in Chapter 7. Often the discussion and peer support opportunities are informal: One of the reasons we like cooking and craft activities is because of the sharing that takes place while Sibshoppers grate cheese for pizza or create masterpieces with pipe cleaners, Popsicle sticks, and paint. Sometimes the support offered is unspoken, with participants taking comfort in the knowledge that they are among kindred spirits.

Support and discussion are also encouraged by more formal Sibshop activities designed to encourage participants to reflect on their experiences with their siblings who have special needs. These activities offer a counterpoint to the lively recreational activities. Whether it is formal or informal, planned or incidental, the support offered at a Sibshop seeks to accomplish two Sibshop goals:

Goal 2: Sibshops will provide brothers and sisters with opportunities to discuss common joys and concerns with other siblings of children with special needs.

Goal 3: Sibshops will provide brothers and sisters with an opportunity to learn how others handle situations commonly experienced by siblings of children with special needs.

121

The majority of activities presented in this chapter are designed to allow brothers and sisters—perhaps for the first time—a chance to discuss their lives with others who share similar experiences. They also allow participants a chance to explore strategies to address situations that siblings sometimes face, such as feeling invisible or knowing what to say to classmates who make fun of their brothers or sisters. Other activities are designed to encourage discussion on a variety of topics—some personal and some disability-related. These activities may refer to the sibling with special needs, but sibling issues are not always the sole focus. Providing discussion activities on other topics acknowledges that participants are more than a-brother-or-sister-of-a-person-with-special-needs."

Although they may be therapeutic for some siblings, Sibshop peer support and discussion activities are not a form of group therapy, nor are they an adequate substitute for a child who needs intensive counseling. Children who may need to be referred for other services include

- Children showing signs of depression as demonstrated by reports of decreased appetite, sleep disturbance, chronic fatigue, apathy, loss of interest in previously enjoyed activities, changes in behavior or personality, or preoccupation with the subject of death

- Children who display outbursts of anger or emotional lability

- Children who demonstrate low self-concept or describe themselves as worthless or not appreciated by anyone

- Children who are extremely withdrawn or noncommunicative

- Children who act out in the group or are markedly defiant

- Children who report a lot of stress symptoms or physical complaints (Usdane & Melmed, 1988, p. 13)

When in doubt, facilitators should always err in the direction of safety and consult the child's parents about the child's possible need for further assistance.

The following sample Sibshop discussion activities will help get you started.

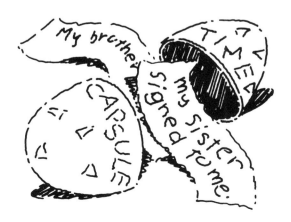

TIME CAPSULES

Materials: Slips of paper (as described below), aluminum foil, "capsules" (e.g., film canisters, paper tubes, plastic eggs), a small box

In Time Capsules, brothers and sisters get to talk about various times in their lives. To prepare, write the times, listed below, on individual pieces of paper. Then place the papers in individual "time capsules," listed above, wrapped in aluminum foil to give them a futuristic look. An alternate method is to place the slips of paper in a shoebox that is made to look like a time capsule. Participants then select a capsule or a piece of paper from the capsule for the group to discuss. Examples of times could include

- A time when I was really proud of my brother or sister
- A time when I was really proud of something I did
- A time when I really was embarrassed by my brother or sister
- A time when my brother or sister caused problems with a friend
- A time when I helped my brother or sister in a special way
- A time when my brother or sister helped me in a special way
- A time when my brother or sister really made me mad
- A time when my brother or sister made me laugh
- A time when I was confused about my brother's or sister's disability

MOCCASINS

Materials: None

Moccasins asks participants to see the world from their siblings' point of view. Share with the group the Native American proverb: "Do not judge a man until you have walked a mile in his moccasins." Discuss what this means. Each member of the group then gets to "try on the moccasins" of his or her brother and sister. Acknowledge that although no one can really speak for another person, brothers and sisters are as qualified as anyone to imagine what their brothers and sisters who have disabilities might say. Discuss questions such as

- What would your sibling say about having a disability?

- What would your sibling say about having *you* as a sibling?

- What would your sibling say about his or her life?

- What would your sibling say about school?

- What would your sibling say about his or her friends?

SOUND-OFF

Materials: Sound-Off activity sheet, pencils

Sound-Off is an open-ended activity that gives participants permission to air their feelings about life with a sibling who has special needs. To begin, hold up the Sound-Off sheet (Figure 8.1) and announce that "During Sound-Off we'll have a chance to tell others how we feel about having a sibling with special needs." Everyone will probably fill out the sheet differently. For instance, someone might write, "If I could tell the whole world just one great thing about having a brother or sister with special needs it would be: 'He's a really neat guy even though he has a hard time learning.'" Someone else might write, "If I could tell the kids on the school bus just one bad thing about having a brother or sister with special needs it would be: 'I hate it when they pick on my brother.'"

Distribute the workshop sheets and pencils and give the participants 5 minutes to complete the worksheets and illustrate them if they wish. If you have sufficient staff and kids who may balk at paper-and-pencil activities, offer to be their secretary or scribe for the day. Kids love the opportunity to have someone take dictation! At the end of 5 minutes, encourage the participants to read their Sound-Off sheet. There is frequently a wide range of responses, including some very personal comments. Respect the wishes of those who do not wish to share.

TANABATA

Materials: Strips of brightly colored paper, markers, bamboo poles or bamboo, willow, or other branches

Yasuko Arima, of Tokyo's Sibling Support Group, tells us that Japanese children love Sibshop recreational activities but can be reticent about discussing their families. She gets around the shyness by creating a Sibshop activity out of a traditional Japanese activity done during Tanabata, or the Japanese Star Festival. During Tanabata, it is traditional for people to write their wishes on colorful, small strips of paper and hang them on bamboo branches. Yasuko asks her Sibshoppers to write wishes they have for themselves, their siblings, and their families on small strips of paper and hang them on the bamboo branches, but you could use bamboo poles or a nearby tree branch. She gives them a chance to share their wishes but doesn't require them to do so.

Figure 8.1. Sound-Off activity sheet.

DREAM PILLOWS

Materials: Pillowcases, cardboard, fabric markers, pins

Dream Pillows keep participants' hands busy while they engage in a lively discussion of their dreams for themselves and their sibs; this activity is suggested by Tara Kosieniak, an adult sister of a man with a disability and a long-time Sibshop facilitator in Brookfield, Illinois. To begin, cut sheets of cardboard approximately the size of the pillowcases. Then place the cardboard inside the pillowcases; the fit should be snug. If needed, use a few pins to pin the pillowcase to the cardboard so it does not move. Using fabric markers, have the participants draw a picture of their dream for themselves on one side, and for their sib on the other side. Older participants may wish to use words instead of pictures. Encourage the participants to discuss their dreams while they create their Dream Pillows. Tell them that they can use their pillowcases on their pillows at home or, if their dreams are too private, they can tuck their new pillowcases inside the pillowcases they currently use. You may wish to send home instructions on how to wash the pillowcases. These instructions can be found on the back of the fabric marker packages.

SUPERHEROES

Materials: Paper, crayons, or markers

If your Sibshop has a plethora of young boys, you know how challenging discussion activities can be. Many prefer action and sitting down to talk is not their idea of a good time. If this is the case, let Superheroes come to the rescue! With Superheroes, kids reinvent themselves—or their sibs—as superheroes. Provide the participants with paper and markers and ask them to create themselves as a superhero. Have them annotate their drawings with comments about their super strengths (e.g., super-sense of smell allows me to locate French fries from miles away), super accessories (e.g., laser-guided atomic flying wheelchair), and any Kryptonite-like weaknesses they may have (e.g., Teletubby or Barney dolls; school-cafeteria tuna noodle casseroles). While their hands are busy, engage the participants in a discussion about how superheroes utilize their powers for the cause of justice. Ask them what their superheroes fight for. The participants may want to share a story about the hero and his or her adventures. If time permits, have them create more superheroes—this time featuring their sibs who have special needs. Other variations could include making a mural of superheroes on a long sheet of butcher paper, or using clay, playdough, or sculpey to make three-dimensional superheroes. Suzanne Salmo, who runs Sibshops at the United Services in St. Peters, Missouri, suggested this activity.

DISCUSSION GIFT

Materials: Small gift or bag of candy, wrapping paper

Discussion Gift is a decidedly rewarding activity! To prepare, select a gift that can be shared with the group, such as a bag of candy. Wrap the candy in multiple layers of wrapping paper, making a few more layers than players. On each layer, write or tape a question related to having a sibling with special needs. Especially for older sibs, you may wish to use the Slam Book questions (see page 135). Sitting in a circle, each participant takes a turn opening a layer and must answer the question that is revealed when they unwrap their layer. The last question can be: "If you get the gift, will you share it with the group? Why or why not?" If all goes well, this person will share the bounty with fellow Sibshoppers! This activity was suggested by Sibshop facilitator Michelle O'Connor-Teklinski of the Program for Exceptional Families in Lincoln Park, Michigan.

DEAR AUNT BLABBY

Materials: Letters to Aunt Blabby in individual envelopes addressed to Dear Aunt Blabby

Since it was first presented in the early 1980s, Dear Aunt Blabby has been the most durable of Sibshop discussion activities. Aunt Blabby, a bogus advice columnist, receives letters from brothers and sisters who have concerns similar to those the participants may experience. Because she is not a sibling herself, Aunt Blabby needs help from experts to answer questions posed by her correspondents. The letters are read, and the participants—experts on the subject of being a sibling of a person with special needs—provide the letter writer with advice, drawing from their own experiences. Typically, some of the advice provided by the participants is thoughtful and helpful, although some—kids being kids—is less so. Facilitators will want to accept each participant's solution to the problem and reinforce suggestions and strategies that are especially useful. Actual advice and strategies, while useful, are secondary to the experiences shared by the participants. If participants have had experiences similar to the letter writer's experience, they share them with the group. In doing so, participants learn that there are others who have faced similar situations and that there are a variety of possible solutions.

To introduce the activity, ask the group questions such as, "Who knows what an advice columnist is?" "Do advice columnists know everything?" "Can they answer any question?" "What do they do when they can't answer a question?" "What do you think all the kids in this group are experts on?" Once their expertise on being the sibling of a person with special needs is established, hold out letters (which have been placed in envelopes) and allow the participants to select a letter and read it to the group.

After the participant has read the letter, you may wish to reread it, pausing now and then to inquire whether anything like this has ever happened to any of the participants. Then ask their advice: "What should Perplexed do?" Gently challenge responses by asking the participants to consider the consequences of the advice: "What would happen if you tried that approach?" End the discussion of each letter by restating the helpful strategies offered by the group.

Similar to other discussion activities, Dear Aunt Blabby works best in groups of five to eight. A group this size encourages a variety of responses, yet allows each participant a chance to talk. Although it is a good idea to have six or seven letters in reserve, you may only respond to three or four letters in each session. To keep the interest level high, be sure to move on to a new letter before participants become bored.

See Appendix F for sample letters to Dear Aunt Blabby to use or adapt. When selecting, adapting, or creating letters, make sure that the problems presented are sufficiently common to allow discussion among participants.

M&M GAME

Materials: Small paper cups (one per participant) each filled with approximately 10 M&Ms of various colors and large sheets of paper with questions written in red, orange, yellow, brown, blue, and green

This is an effective way to get young sibs to talk! As you'll see, there are many ways you can vary this simple game.

Have the participants sit in a circle and hand each child a paper cup containing M&Ms. Tell the participants that they can't eat them—not yet, anyway. Ask the group which M&M colors they have in their cups and, with the group, establish that there are usually red, orange, yellow, brown, blue, and green candies. Ask someone to pick one of these colors. If, for instance, red is suggested, ask that all kids who have red M&Ms in their cups stand up. Tell them they may eat their red M&Ms once they've answered the "red question." Then tape the red question (which you have written with a red felt-tip pen) to the wall. Go around the circle and have each sibling answer the red question before eating their red M&Ms. Continue with the remaining colors.

The questions for each color can be about anything—sibling-related or not; the following are some ideas:

- If you were a Popsicle, which flavor would you be?

- What makes you happy about your sib?

- What makes you mad about your sib?

- What is your favorite thing to do with your sibling?

- Has your sib ever had a temper tantrum in public?

- What was the funniest thing your brother or sister with a disability has ever said?

- If you were an animal, what would you be?

- What is your favorite movie of all time?

FEELINGS-ON-A-ROPE

Materials: One rope, approximately 20 feet long

Not to be confused with Soap-on-a-Rope, Feelings-on-a-Rope transforms two participants and one rope into a human Likert scale. To begin, the participants sit on the floor facing two facilitators (or participants) who are holding a rope stretched between them. The facilitators describe the activity in a way similar to the following:

"Has anyone ever been asked to rate something on a 1-to-10 scale, such as 'What do you think about the new school lunches?' or 'What do you think about this new TV show?' When you rate things like this, '1' usually means that you don't like it at all and '10' means that you like it a lot! A '3' would mean that you don't really like it but you don't hate it. A '7' would mean that it's pretty good but you don't love it. A '5' rating would mean that it's just ok.

"We're going to do some ratings here. Julie (who is at the other end of the rope) is going to represent number 1. I'm going to represent number 10. We're going to ask for your ratings of different things. First, we'd like your feelings about The Extremely Important Pepperoni Issue. Julie, being on the low end of the scale feels that pepperoni is the worst possible thing you could put on a pizza. I, being on the high end of the scale, think that pizza is not pizza without pepperoni! It's the best stuff in the world! Now, what do you think about pepperoni on pizza? When I call on you, I want you to come up and rate how you feel about pepperoni by placing your hand on the rope. If you hate it as much as Julie does, hold the rope near her end of the scale. If you love it as much as I do, hold the rope near my end of the scale. If you are somewhere in-between in your feelings about pepperoni, hold the rope somewhere in-between. Mike, come up and show us how you feel about pepperoni!"

Have the participants come up, one by one, and place themselves on the scale. Keep going until everyone is standing, holding some part of the rope. Ask participants why they rated pepperoni the way they did. After a brief discussion, ask all to sit down. Tell the participants that you want to know what they feel about other things. Present issues for the participants to come up and "rate." These issues could include sibling-related issues such as

- Family outings with your brother or sister who has special needs (1 = I hate going out with him and 10 = I love going out with him)

- Having friends come over (1 = don't like it when my sib is around and 10 = no problem at all when he is around)

- Going to the same school as your sibling with special needs (1 = never in a million years! and 10 = It's great to have my sib there)

- Playing with your sibling (1 = I can't stand playing with my sib! and 10 = We get along great!)

- Sharing a room with your sib who has special needs (1 = I hate it! and 10 = I wouldn't have it any other way)

You can intersperse sib issues with non-sib issues such as school, local sport teams, TV shows, and so forth

NOTE: After each child has come up and chosen a place on the scale, discuss the reasons behind their ratings before going on to the next issue.

THREE WISHES

Materials: Small boxes with lids, felt-tip pens, glue, glitter, colored sand, shells, and so forth; also: tub(s) of cake frosting, pretzel rods, candy sprinkles

A fantasy art project/discussion complete with edible magic wands—does it get better than this? This activity, submitted by Sheila Swann-Guerrero of Chicago's Advocate Illinois Masonic Medical Center, works great with younger Sibshop participants. Provide participants with small cardboard boxes to decorate with colored sand, shells, felt-tip pens, glitter—almost anything will do. While the decorated boxes are drying, give each sib three strips of paper and instruct him or her to write down three wishes. The first is a wish for themselves, the second is a wish for their sibling, and the third is a wish for their family. After completing their wishes, the participants put the "wish slips" in their box for safekeeping, and each sib is given an opportunity to share his or her wishes with the group.

Sheila and colleagues do "Three Wishes" as part of a fantasy-themed Sibshop. To ice the cake, they conclude with edible magic wands. To make the wands, simply have the participants dip pretzel rods into frosting and then roll the frosted tip in sprinkles. Sheila notes: "The original recipe called for placing the pretzel wands on wax paper in the fridge to set up. We don't bother doing that. The sibs just eat them right away. They've been a big hit."

WHEEL OF FEELINGS BEANBAG TOSS

Materials: One beanbag and a sheet of poster board on which to draw a "feelings" wheel. When completed, the wheel should be at least 2 feet in diameter. Divide the wheel into pie-shaped sections and label them with feelings such as "proud," "confused," "excited," "worried," "embarrassed," "happy," "irritated," and so forth.

Have the group sit in a circle on the floor, with the feelings wheel in the center, several feet from the participants. Explain what will happen in the first round and demonstrate by taking the first turn.

During Round 1, each player takes a turn tossing the bag onto the wheel. The feelings word on which the beanbag falls determines the feeling the player will describe. The player then provides an example of when he or she felt that way. Thank each person in turn for sharing his or her feelings. Complete the first round before explaining Round 2.

During Round 2, each player again tosses the beanbag. This time each player talks about one time he or she felt that way about his or her brother or sister with a disability. If a facilitator has a sibling with a disability, he or she may wish to go first, modeling the type of response he or she wishes from the participants. This round frequently sparks discussion, as participants share similar experiences. Facilitators may wish to prompt participants with comments such as, "I wonder if anyone else ever felt that way?" At the end of each turn, be sure to return to the comment of the "tosser" and thank him or her for sharing before passing the beanbag.

Tamara Besser of the Jewish Children's Bureau of Chicago created a variation on Wheel of Feelings, which you can call Tubs of Feelings or Buckets of Feelings if you wish! She uses plastic buckets or tubs and asks the participants to choose a feeling. They then decorate their bucket with their feelings word and any objects they like such as feathers, puzzle pieces, foam pieces, stickers, and so forth. While the participants decorate their tubs, facilitators lead an informal discussion on the feelings the participants chose and how their decorations portray those feelings. When completed, the buckets are lined up against a wall. The participants take turns tossing a beanbag into the buckets and talk about the feeling written on the bucket. During the first round, the participants talk about a time when they experienced the feeling described on the bucket where their beanbag landed. During the second round, they describe when they felt that emotion toward their sib with special needs. During the third round, they describe a time when their sibling felt that emotion. And during the final round, they share any stories they may have about the feeling represented by the tub in which their beanbag landed.

SAME AND DIFFERENT

Materials: Photos of the participants and their siblings with special needs (as described below), butcher paper and markers, or chalkboard and chalk

Especially good with younger brothers and sisters, this activity reinforces what many brothers and sisters know intuitively—people with disabilities are more like their family members than they are different from them. Consider it a preadvocacy activity! Prior to the Sibshop, send a note home requesting that the participants bring two photos (e.g., school pictures) to the next Sibshop: one photo of the child with special needs and one of the child who attends the Sibshop.

To begin, select one pair of photos and post them where the participants can see them. On a piece of paper or chalkboard, make two columns, one marked *Same* and the other *Different*. Say to the participants, "Here are Melinda and Michael. How are they the same?" Have the group brainstorm as many ways as possible that Melinda and Michael are the same (e.g., same hair color, same family) before asking Melinda. Then ask Melinda to help the group out by telling other ways that she is the same as Michael (e.g., both like same television shows, both like the color blue). Record the ways that they are the same in the appropriate column. Repeat this for differences.

Finally, ask, "Is one of these kids better than the other?" Briefly discuss how *different* does not mean *better*. Ask the group, "Who would like to go next?"

MY SIB & ME

Materials: Legal-size paper (one sheet per child), crayons or colored pencils

Tina Prochaska of the Sibshop at the Tennessee School for the Deaf says that her Sibshoppers love this variation on "Same and Different" and "Favorites." To begin, have the participants fold a piece of paper in half, making a "book." Next, have them open the book and write "My Sib" on the top of one side, then "Me" on the other. On the "My Sib" side, have the participants write or draw their sibs' favorite (or least favorite!) foods, games, toys, and so forth. Then have the participants repeat on the "Me" side the child's favorite (or least favorite) things, making sure to match categories. When everyone is finished, ask the kids to compare the sides, discussing how many things are similar or different.

STRENGTHS & WEAKNESSES, JR.

Materials: Chalkboard and chalk

Try this activity with younger brothers and sisters who may not have the writing skills to accomplish easily the Strengths & Weaknesses activity found in Chapter 7. Divide a long chalkboard as shown in Figure 8.2 with the participants' names on the top and their "special needs" siblings' names on the bottom. Announce to the group: "Everybody has strengths—that is, something they do well. And everybody has weaknesses—things they do not do so well." Provide dramatic examples of abilities of which you are proud and equally dramatic examples of things at which you are truly awful. Then ask the group, "Do you think that people who have special needs have

Sibshops Kids!

Tony's strengths	Brian's strengths	Tashina's strengths	Danielle's strengths
Basketball	Soccer	Jump rope	Keeping my room clean
Video games	Math	Science	Spelling
	Pizza making	Singing	

Tony's weaknesses	Brian's weaknesses	Tashina's weaknesses	Danielle's weaknesses
Making his bed	Jump rope	Spelling	Cooking
Spelling	Saving money	Homework	Telling jokes

Our Sibs Who Have Special Needs!

Allison's strengths	Rachel's strengths	Tracey's strengths	Kelly's strengths
Funny	Soccer	Can't think of any	Very curious
Learning to walk	Likes to cook		Learning to sign

Allison's weaknesses	Rachel's weaknesses	Tracey's weaknesses	Kelly's weaknesses
Has temper tantrums	Math	Embarrasses me	Gets into Danielle's stuff
	Gets into Brian's stuff		Can't talk

Figure 8.2. Sample chart of Strengths & Weaknesses, Jr.

strengths—things they do really well? How about weaknesses—things they don't do so well?"

Tell the group that they will now have a chance to tell about their strengths and weaknesses and the strengths and weaknesses of their brothers and sisters with special needs, and that you will list these on the board. Let them know that they can add to their lists of strengths and weaknesses as you go along. Frequently, participants will be "inspired" to add another strength or weakness after hearing another participant's contribution.

TWO BUG ACTIVITIES: THAT BUGS ME! AND THE LOVE BUG

Materials: Paper plates, construction paper, scissors, stapler, writing implement (crayons, markers, pens, or colored pencils); optional material: Jiggly eyes, pipe cleaners, foam shapes, glitter

These activities, suggested by Robin Sowl and Tamara Besser of the Sibshop at the Jewish Children's Bureau of Chicago, offer brothers and sisters opportunities to talk about what bugs them—and what they love—while constructing a bug. Frequently children are more open to talking about their feelings when engaged in an activity. For this activity, the paper plate (or two paper plates stapled together, plate side toward the middle) is the body of the bug. To prepare, cut out shapes and legs on construction paper. Have the participants write down something that bugs them on a leg or shape to attach to the plate. Questions can be, "What bugs you about school?" "What bugs you about relatives?" "What bugs you about your sibling?" "What bugs you about your parents?" "What bugs you about yourself?" Ask the participants to share what they have written as they attach the legs to their bugs. The Love Bug is the same activity, only the questions are about love. "What do you love about school?" "What do you love about your sibling?" "What do you love about your home?"

Variations: Don't limit yourself to the materials listed above—other materials (such as wallpaper remnants or fabric samples) can be used to decorate the bugs. Also, the two types of bugs can be combined into one bug; one side is the bothersome part of the bug and the other is the love bug.

GRAFFITI WALL

Materials: A long sheet of butcher paper, markers, and crayons

Graffiti Wall provides participants with a chance to express and discuss in a novel way a wide range of feelings they may have toward their brothers, sisters, and parents. To prepare, line a long wall (e.g., a hallway) with butcher paper and make vertical lines with a marker to create columns 2 feet wide. At the top of each column, print in large letters a word from the array of ambivalent feelings your participants may have for their brothers and sisters; for example, *proud, angry, left out, inspired, embarrassed, amazed,* and *confused.* Leave two columns blank. The number of columns you have will depend in part on the number of participants in your Sibshop. You should have at least one column for every two participants, with a minimum of eight columns.

In an area or room away from the wall, ask the participants to close their eyes and think of their brother or sister for a short while, perhaps 30–45 seconds. Then, with their eyes still closed, ask them to volunteer a feelings word that describes how they feel when they think about their sibling. After this, have them open their eyes. Explain to the group that most brothers and sisters have mixed feelings about their siblings, regardless of whether they have special needs or not. Tell the group that in Graffiti Wall they will have a chance to express this mixed bag of feelings in a new way. Hand the participants one felt-tip pen each (preferably each a different color) and lead them to the wall that you have prepared. Review the feelings listed on the wall, noting that these are feelings that brothers and sisters sometimes have about one another. Ask if they have any other feelings that should go into the two blank columns. Explain that they are to choose a column and in that column write about or illustrate a time when they had that feeling about their sibling with special needs. For participants who have poor writing skills, facilitators can help by serving as scribes. After the participants have finished one column, they are free to move to another column and contribute an additional story or picture. At the end, review the stories and pictures in each column with the group.

INSIDE/OUTSIDE BAGS OR MASKS

Materials for bags: Paper bags, glue, family and kid magazines, markers, scissors

Materials for masks: Poster board or paper plates, markers, scissors, elastic string

How we're feeling on the inside isn't always what we show on the outside. Inside/ Outside allows participants to represent artistically how they feel and what they choose to share with others.

Share with your participants an example—preferably a humorous example—of when you felt one way but acted another way. Perhaps you were really irritated by someone but had to smile anyway. Or perhaps you were embarrassed by something your child did but needed to pretend that nothing happened. Point out to the kids that most of us do that now and then, and for some people, much of their life is like that: The outside is different from the inside.

Tell them that with this activity, they'll be able to represent the inside/outside feelings they sometimes have. Although this can be about feelings the kids have about their siblings, it doesn't have to be. It can represent feelings they had at a certain time or how they feel all the time.

For the bag activity, set up a table with paper bags, kid and family magazines, glue, markers, and so forth. Have the kids rummage through magazines and cut out pictures that represent their feelings. Have them glue the "outside" feelings to the outside of the bag and have them either glue or place the "inside" feelings inside the bag.

For the mask version, have them draw their inside feelings on one side of the mask and their outside feelings on the other side. Cut out holes for the eyes and for string. Thread strings through the holes.

Have the kids share their artwork with the group. Ask them who they have to share their inside feelings with. It might be a parent, a favorite aunt or uncle, a friend, fellow Sibshoppers, a pet, or even a stuffed animal.

Adapted from Feelings Bag, contributed by Pat Walsh of the Sibshop at Shawnee Park Oral-Deaf Center School in Grand Rapids, Michigan.

SIBLING SLAM BOOK

Numerous Sibshop facilitators have used the questions posed in *The Sibling Slam Book: What It's Really Like to Have a Brother or Sister with Special Needs* (Meyer, 2005). In *The Sibling Slam Book*, 80 teenage brothers and sisters were asked to respond to 54 questions, and their responses are formatted in a casual style that suggests a composition notebook that was passed around the back of a classroom. Use these questions to have your Sibshoppers create their own slam book. Alternatively, cut them up fortune-cookie style, place the questions in a hat, and have the participants choose a question for the group to answer. Or, if you're really feeling brave, place the whole list on a dartboard and let a dart decide which question the group should answer!

- What should we know about you?

- What should we know about your sib?

- How many kids are in your family?

- Describe yourself to someone who can't see you.

- How would you describe your relationship with your sib?

- Do you like hanging out with your sib? What do you do?

- How do your friends describe you?

- What do you want people to know about your sib?

- Do you think your sib knows he or she has a disability? (If so, what does that mean to him or her?)

- Do you have any good stories about your sib?

- Is your outlook on life different from your friends' outlook on life? How?

- Do you think being a sib has affected your personality? How?

- What makes you proud of your sib?

- When you were younger, did you ever wish you had a disability so your parents would pay more attention to you?

- Do your friends get along with your sib? Do you tend to pick friends who are likely to get along with your sib?

- What do you tell your friends about your sib's disability?

- Do they ever ask questions?

- What is your pet peeve?

- What item must you have with you all the time?
- Can you imagine what it would be like if your sibling didn't have a disability?
- Does your sib ever frustrate you? How?
- What are some advantages—good parts—of having a sibling with a disability?
- What are some disadvantages—not so good parts—of having a sibling with special needs?
- Describe a perfect day.
- If you could change just one thing about your sib (or your sib's disability), what would it be?
- What do you see for your sibling's future? And what part do you think you'll play in that future?
- What annoys you the most about how people treat your sib?
- Do your parents include you in discussions about your sib? How do you feel about that?
- Has your sib ever embarrassed you?
- Do you know lots of other sibs and, if so, how do you know them?
- How is your sib treated by kids in your community?
- What career choices sound good right now?
- What is something you said you'd never do but did anyway?
- What is the hardest thing to do as a sibling of a child with special needs?
- What is the sweetest thing someone has done for (or said to) you?
- Is there something about your sib that just makes you smile?
- Is there anything about your sib that just pisses you off?
- What confuses you the most about the opposite sex?
- How do the people at your school/church/after-school group treat your sibling?
- What are some words or phrases you use the most?
- Has something ever happened to your sib that scared you?
- Do you ever feel invisible?
- If you could meet one person, dead or alive, who would it be?
- If you had a choice, would you get rid of all the disabilities in the world—or just the negative reactions to them?
- What was your most embarrassing moment?
- What's the best advice you've given or been given?
- Where do you see yourself in 10 years?
- What life lesson have you learned from being a sib?
- What is your happiest moment?

- If you could have just one day when your sibling didn't have a disability, what would you choose to do on that day?

- What's the toughest thing about being a sib of a child with a disability?

- What's the weirdest question you've ever been asked about your sib?

- If you had one wish for your brother or sister, what would it be?

- What's the one question we should have asked but didn't? (And what's the answer?)

- Do you have a favorite quote—or lyric?

OPEN DISCUSSIONS

Open group discussions may be used successfully with older siblings or with articulate younger participants who do not require the structure of a Dear Aunt Blabby or Time Capsule activity to talk about their lives. They may also be valuable for siblings who have participated in some of the above activities and are ready to participate in a more in-depth or personal discussion.

Open discussions follow a facilitated group discussion format. Although participants select the topics for discussion, the discussion is not without structure. Facilitators introduce the activity, establish a few ground rules, probe for topics of common interest or concern, and facilitate and close the discussion when appropriate.

Below is an example of how one facilitator introduced a discussion and established ground rules. He adapted his opening remarks from those given by Ken Moses at a 1982 conference offered for high school-age brothers and sisters:

> All of you are different from one another in hundreds of ways: what you like to eat, the way you look, the clothes you choose, and so on. But there is an important way that you are the same: You are all brothers and sisters of children with special needs.
>
> We've learned a lot about kids with special needs, but very little about their brothers and sisters. We don't know whether having a special sib is a good thing, a bad thing, or a little of both. Today, we'll have a chance to switch roles. In a way, you'll be the teacher and I'll be the student, although we'll all be learning from one another. We'll have a chance to learn what you think and how you feel about your special sib, your parents, your family, your friends, and yourself.
>
> There are a few rules. First, I'd like you to talk about yourself and how you feel rather than guess how others feel. Second, I'd like you to feel free to disagree with one another and me. If someone says something that doesn't ring true to you, speak up! Third, I'd like us to maintain confidentiality. That usually means not telling anyone outside of the group what was said inside the group. I'd like it to mean that we are kind to one another. That means not laughing when someone shares something personal. It also means that when we talk about what we say outside the group, we protect one another and do not use names.
>
> Now, I'd like you to introduce yourself, and tell us what brings you here today. If there is something you'd like the group to talk about, please mention it.

Going around the circle, siblings introduce themselves and share why they came. Facilitators will wish to acknowledge and accept all responses, including the inevitable, "My parents made me come." As participants introduce themselves, facilitators may ask a question or make a comment. Throughout the introductions, participants may need to be reminded that they can ask one another questions, make comments, or suggest topics for discussion.

When a sibling offers a problem or topic for discussion, the facilitator will want to find out if it is a concern that is shared by other participants. The facilitator may wish to "check in" with the other siblings and say, "I wonder if other brothers and sisters have ever experienced anything like this." This will not only give the facilitator an idea of how widespread the concern is, it will also make the participants reflect on their lives and think about their common experiences. The facilitator should list the topics the siblings suggest and note how many siblings indicate interest in each topic.

Look over the topics the siblings mention (we recommend that you write them down), and select a topic for discussion. The topic you choose will depend on the siblings' relative interest in the topic and its appropriateness for discussion. Some topics may not be appropriate—they may be too specific for general discussion. Some topics may be requests for specific information. Of course, you should not ignore these topics or questions, but rather try to address them individually.

To begin the discussion, ask the participant who suggested the chosen topic to share some further thoughts on the subject, and then open it up to the group for discussion. For instance, if the siblings want to talk about what to do when strangers stare at their sibling, the facilitator may wish to guide the discussion to elicit a wide range of problem-solving strategies for responding to people's stares. Below is an example of questions that can be used to facilitate a group discussion of effective strategies. Remember to use questions that begin with what, why, and how because those are most likely to elicit discussion.

Step 1. What is the problem?
Ask the person who brought up the topic to expand on it. For example: "Shannon, tell us some more about what happens when people stare at your brother."

Step 2. Who else has the problem?
You probably know from the siblings' introductions who else has experienced this problem. Present the concern to the group. For example: "Other people said that people sometimes stare at their sibs. I'm interested: Has that happened to the rest of you?"

Step 3. Why does the problem exist?
This can help the group explore the issues underlying the problem. For example: "Why do you think people stare at people who have disabilities? Why does this bother you?"

Step 4. What have you tried?
This will help draw out the array of strategies participants have used. "What do you do when people stare at your brother or sister?" The facilitator should acknowledge all responses but give special attention to those that are appropriate, creative, or workable.

Step 5. Has that worked?
An important follow-up question to Step 4. For example: "What happens when you do that or say that?"

Step 6. What are some other ways of solving this problem?

Drawing on what the group has learned in Step 3 (*Why does the problem exist?*) and the strategies that worked in Step 4 (*What have you tried?*), the group, under the facilitator's guidance, searches for additional creative solutions. For example, say, "A moment ago we said that people who stared at people with disabilities did so because they probably do not know anyone who has a disability. What are some other ways that we can help people get to know people with special needs so that they will not stare at them?" (A most creative solution to this problem was volunteered by a sibling whose mother says to staring strangers: "You seem to be interested in my daughter. Would you like to meet her?")

Remember that these are only guidelines for group problem solving; not all discussions will follow this outline exactly. Also, discussion may not always focus on problems siblings experience. Participants may wish to express their thoughts and opinions on a wide variety of subjects related to their experiences as siblings of a child with special needs.

CONCLUSION

Well run, Sibshops discussion activities are among the richest and most memorable experiences we can offer participants. During these activities, participants share knowing laughs, discuss the good times and the tough spots, and trade war stories and helpful strategies. When they learn that their age mates sometimes feel the same way they do, participants experience camaraderie, their feelings are validated, and they are less likely to feel alone with their concerns. These activities can be potent experiences for the people who lead them as well. The insight and wisdom expressed by these young participants often stay with facilitators for a long, long time.

Chapter 9

Sibshop Recreational and Food Activities

When we survey young participants about what they like best about Sibshops, the answer we invariably get is "the games and activities." Although Sibshops are intended to provide participants with peer support and education, we could not be more pleased with the participants' endorsement of our recreational and food events. The spirited games and activities—which account for more than half the time spent at a Sibshop —are an essential element of a successful program and are critical to accomplishing the model's first goal:

Goal 1: Sibshops will provide brothers and sisters of children with special needs an opportunity to meet other siblings in a relaxed, recreational setting.

We are unapologetically enthusiastic about having fun and feel that recreational events are key to providing peer support from a kid's-eye view. Recreational activities promote informal sharing and friendships among participants. The friendships begun during Sibshops frequently are continued outside the program, offering siblings ongoing sources of support that may last a lifetime. We recall watching several preteen girls playing in the gym at the close of a Sibshop held in a small New England city. The girls had just met that day but had become fast friends, having spent the previous 4 hours playing, cooking, and talking about their lives, families, and interests. Their parents, who had arrived to pick up their children, were struck by how well the girls were playing and how reluctant they were to leave. One parent noted, "You know, these girls will probably know each other as adults."

141

Recreational events also make Sibshops appealing to the young participants. We are never surprised to learn that a brother or sister is reluctant to attend a Sibshop for the first time. After all, a sibling might think, "Why should I give up a Saturday to hang out with a bunch of kids I don't know, just because they have a sibling with a disability?" A Sibshop's games and activities can encourage a participant to return to and benefit from the program's discussion and information activities. In short, recreation is essential to a Sibshop. The games, activities, and food projects reflect the model's emphasis on siblings' strengths and wellness. They are an indispensable component in a program that seeks to celebrate the many contributions made by brothers and sisters.

GAMES—NEW AND OTHERWISE

Many of the Sibshop recreational activities have been borrowed from various sources, most notably the New Games Foundation. If New Games are new to you, you are in for a treat. They are offbeat, fun, and sometimes silly games designed to appeal to a wide range of ages and abilities. (New Games, while ideal for school-age children, originally were developed by and for playful adults. Consequently, most of the activities we present will also work well with teenagers.) Some are competitive but most are not. In any event, playing, not winning, is what is fun and important. Most New Games require little equipment but a lot of energy.

In the next section, we provide capsule descriptions of some of our favorite games and activities. We have purposely selected activities that have minimal equipment needs. Some activities have been adapted with permission from *The New Games Book* (Flugelman, 1976), *More New Games!* (Flugelman, 1981), *The Incredible Indoor Games Book* (Gregson, 1982), and *The Outrageous Outdoor Games Book* (Gregson, 1984). Sadly, the *New Games* books are out of print. Used copies of these books, however, can be purchased for as little as a dollar on Amazon.com and other used-book resellers. These books are highly recommended; plan on purchasing as many as your program can afford. Besides providing you with enough Sibshop recreational activities so that you never need to repeat an activity (although you will want to!), the activities described in these books are also enjoyed by adults at picnics, retreats, and staff development events. (Other useful activity books are listed in Appendix B.)

Of course, you will want to customize and enrich these games with your own skills and ideas. If you have musical, artistic, or dramatic talents, be sure to share your gifts with the participants. The Sibshop model is sufficiently flexible to allow facilitators to express their own creativity.

PRESENTING SIBSHOP RECREATIONAL ACTIVITIES

As noted in Chapter 5, Sibshop facilitators will need diverse skills. On the one hand, presenting Sibshop discussion activities requires facilitators to model the thoughtfulness and reflection we desire from the young participants. On the other hand, Sibshop recreational activities call upon the facilitators to be exuberant, dramatic, and "on." The following are some general tips on how to make your games and activities successful:

• Before the Sibshop begins, decide who will "pitch" the activity. This person will be responsible for gathering materials (if any) and deciding what assistance he or she may need from the other facilitators. Will everyone do the activity together, or will we break into groups with a facilitator assigned to each group?

- Become familiar with the activity you will present. Sibshops are safe places to try a game or activity that is new to you and the group—and even to make mistakes. Do not, however, wait until a Sibshop has begun to read the directions for an activity. It will be difficult to inspire adventurous, imaginative play if you have to read the instructions to the group. As the Boy Scouts advise: Be prepared.

- When explaining the activity, place yourself at the edge—not the center—of the circle, so that everyone can see you. For large groups, have participants sit in a semicircle. They can watch you demonstrate the activity with a small group of volunteers before being dismissed to do the activity in smaller groups. Regardless, pitch the activity with gusto. Now's not the time to be tentative. If you pitch it with enthusiasm, they will love your activity!

- Explain the rules and the structure of the activity as simply and as clearly as possible. After you explain the activity, ask for questions but do not get involved with needlessly lengthy answers: Often, just playing the game will answer most questions.

- When explaining the activity, first describe it in a general way ("Who knows how to play Tag? Let's play Blob Tag—It's Tag with a twist!"). Demonstrate the game with volunteers as you explain the object of the game: "Let's pretend Sarah is It. She chases Jason and tags him." (Take Sarah's hand and tag Jason.) "Now they're both It!" (Join their hands.) "Holding hands, they chase Michael and tag him and then all three are It!" (Have one participant tag Michael.) "They keep tagging and the Blob keeps getting bigger and bigger until there is only one very fast person left! Are there any questions?"

- Present the activity in a style that encourages participation and playfulness. The New Games Foundation recommends inviting participants to play by saying, "Let's try. . ." instead of "You're going to. . . ."

- Encourage variations. Sibshop participants and their energetic facilitators can always come up with variations on games and activities. Think of your Sibshop as a games lab: Some of the ideas will work and some will not. Regardless, a Sibshop is an environment where playful invention and experimentation are indulged if not encouraged.

- Be certain to make all safety issues painfully clear! Make sure that all participants understand any warnings before proceeding with an activity. If necessary, ask them to repeat the warnings and say why they are being made. Most of the activities described below can be played in a gym or a large multipurpose room. Make sure that the environment is as free as possible of objects that might injure participants or facilitators as they zoom across the room in a spirited round of Tag-O-Rama.

- Be sensitive to mood and energy changes. Like a stand-up comedian who gauges laughter to determine when to go on to the next joke, assess the energy and interest remaining in an activity to determine when to move on to the next. Provide occasional low-energy activities to allow participants to catch their breath between the high-energy activities.

- Sometimes, you will be able to make a connection between the recreation activity you are presenting and some aspect of having a special need. An example would be Sightless Sculpture and artists who have disabilities. If you can make a connection, great—just don't overdo it.

Have fun! This isn't school! Model your ability to laugh at yourself and forgive yourself for making mistakes. One of the perks of facilitating a Sibshop is an opportunity to get in touch with your playful self. Your obvious enjoyment of the activities you present will set the tone for your young participants.

Below, in alphabetical order, are recreational activities that we have enjoyed. It is not an exhaustive list by any means. If you have a favorite that you would like to share with a wider audience, we hope you will let us know.

Airport

Good with younger participants—and a lively exercise in cooperation!

Energy Level: Medium

Environment: Indoors and large open space

Materials: Blindfolds (e.g., bandanas, inexpensive medical facemasks pulled over eyes instead of nose and mouth) and objects that can be used as safe obstacles such as pillows, chairs, coats, and shoes

To play, divide the group into pairs. One player will be the pilot; the other will be the air traffic controller. The players currently not the selected become the runway and form two lines about 10 feet apart, facing each other. Place items on the runway and then blindfold the pilot. (To make it more challenging with an older group, blindfold the pilot before placing the items.) The controller verbally guides the pilot with statements such as "Walk forward five steps, walk to the right, step to the side." The sideline players can give hints such as "Watch out," "Good job," or "You hit something." The pilot continues until he reaches the controller even if he touched an object. The game continues until all pairs have had a turn.

Altoids versus Wint-O-Greens!

Which is more powerful? Altoids—so strong they come in a steel box? Or Wint-O-Green Lifesavers—the only breath mint that "sparks in the dark"? Find out by using this highly dubious method!

Energy Level: Medium

Environment: Indoors

Materials: Altoids, Wint-O-Green Lifesavers, a ping-pong ball, rectangular table, and cardboard tube (wide enough to allow a ping-pong ball to pass through it)

To play, divide participants into two teams—the Altoids and the Wint-O-Greens. Distribute breath mints to team members—Altoids to the Altoid team and Wint-O-Greens to the Wint-O-Green team. Tell the participants that they will be a part of an "oh-so-serious" test to determine which breath mint is stronger. Have Altoids kneel on one side of the rectangular table and Wint-O-Greens on the other. Instruct them to eat their breath mint. Have the participants put their hands behind their backs and position their heads so that their chins are resting on the table. After everyone is in position, a facilitator, standing at the end of the table, rolls a ping-pong ball down the cardboard tube and onto the table surface. To win, members of one team must use their mint-fortified breath to blow the ping-pong ball off their opponents' side of the table. Play as many rounds as you wish!

Backlash

This makes for a great variation on the relay race, once partners can manage a few steps in their new form!

Energy Level: High

Environment: Gym or other open indoor or outdoor area

Materials: Balloons

To begin this relay-race variation, divide the participants into two (or more) teams, and then divide each team into pairs who are of similar height. Instruct the partners to stand back-to-back and link arms. Have facilitators place a balloon between the pairs' backs.

To begin the race, one pair from each team runs to the end of the gym and back in the balloon-in-the-middle, back-to-back, linked-arms position. The object—to keep the balloon between them—is not so hard while just standing, but running is something else! Players will likely try push-me/pull-you techniques until they realize that side-stepping is probably the best approach. Once back at the starting position, they unlink and wedge the balloon between the backs of the next pair, and the race continues.

There are at least two variations of Backlash. First, instead of wedging the balloon between their backs, each person can hold a balloon in his or her hands while running in the same linked, back-to-back position. When it comes time to transfer the balloons, the pair may not unlink arms. Second, for a truly wild version, try this variation with water balloons—outside, of course!

Source: The Outrageous Outdoor Games Book, p. 105

Balloon Birdseed Beanbags

Or should that be Birdseed Balloon Beanbags? Or maybe Balloon Birdseed Bags? Regardless, BBBs are multicolored lemon-shaped balls that are easy and fun to make and perfect for individual juggling, Group Juggling, or hacky sack.

Energy Level: Medium

Environment: Indoors, in a cleared, open area

Materials: See below

Blessed is the Sibshop that has "crafty" facilitators. All sorts of informal sharing occurs during the creation of crafts such as Balloon Birdseed Beanbags. Plan for stations for 2–4 kids. Each station will have

- A medium-sized bowlful of inexpensive birdseed or dry grain
- Balloons (9″–12″ round) of various colors. Each ball will require three balloons; consequently, if you wish to send your Sibshoppers home with a set of three balloons to juggle, you'll need nine balloons for each participant.
- Spoons, one per participant
- Scissors
- At least one funnel made from the cut-off top of a plastic soda bottle. Demonstrate making a BBB as follows:
  - Stretch balloon #1 over the mouth of the soda bottle funnel.
  - Spoon birdseed into the funnel until the balloon is filled up to its neck (smoosh down a bit if needed).
  - Using scissors, cut off most of the neck of balloon #1.
  - Select balloon #2, which should be a different color than balloon #1.
  - Cut off the neck of balloon #2.
  - Perhaps with the help of a partner, gently stretch the opening of balloon #2 over the opening of balloon #1. Your BBB should now be sealed.
  - Cut off the neck of balloon #3 (a different color from #1 and #2).
  - Take your scissors and make small slits into balloon #3.
  - Gently stretch the opening of balloon #3 over balloon #2 so that the opening of balloon #2 is sealed by balloon #3.
  - The color of balloon #2 will peek through the slits you made in balloon #3, resulting in a very cool effect!

Your BBB is ready to use!

Contributed by Sandy Ardnt of the Sibshops at Children's Hospital and Regional Medical Center, Seattle, Washington

Balloon Duo

This is another cooperative partner balloon race.

Energy Level: High

Environment: Field or gym

Materials: Balloons

To play, partners stand side by side and link arms. The leader gives each team one balloon. After the leader says, "Go," partners bat the balloon forward with their free arms, keeping it in the air while racing toward a finish line. If a balloon hits the ground, players may scoop it up but may not unlink arms.

Source: The Outrageous Outdoor Games Book, p. 106

Balloon Stomp

Does any Sibshop item offer more cheap thrills than balloons? Whether they're filled with water and juggled (see Group Juggling), used in place of a soccer ball (see Pushpin Soccer), or employed as faux muscles (see Muscle Beach Party), balloons are an indispensable Sibshop item. In this genteel game, they are stomped.

Energy Level: High

Environment: Indoors or outdoors

Materials: At least one large inflated balloon per player, with a yard of inexpensive yarn tied to the end

Use the yard of yarn to tie a balloon to the ankle of each player. On your signal, players stomp on the balloons of other participants while trying to protect their own balloon.

Beach Ball Bounce

Try this when weather turns your thoughts to the beach—and for many of us, that could be the middle of winter!

Energy Level: Medium

Environment: Indoors

Materials: One lightweight beach ball for each six players

To begin, divide the group into teams of equal numbers—six is a good amount. Have each team count off 1 through 6. To play, Player One hits the ball in the air, shouting "One!" Player Two continues, hitting the ball and shouting her number. The goal is to keep the ball in the air and to hit the ball in order. If a team drops the ball or hits it out of order, they begin the round over. Have teams keep track of how many "perfect" rounds (e.g., 1–6 with no drops). The winner is the team with the most perfect rounds within a predetermined time (e.g., 3 minutes).

Behavior Modification

Here is a crash course in shaping behavior.

Energy Level: Medium

Environment: Indoor

Materials: None

To play, ask two volunteers to leave the room. While they are gone, the rest of the group decides what physical position (not too difficult or detailed) they would like the volunteers to assume once they are back. The group also decides on how they will let the volunteers know whether they are getting close to the desired pose. Among the signals we have used are clapping loudly or softly, cheering or booing, or humming high or low. The volunteers then re-enter the room and attempt to replicate the pose.

Source: More New Games! p. 63

Blindfold Sort Out!

After a few exuberant activities, this low-energy yet appealing activity can be just the ticket!

Energy Level: Low

Environment: Indoors or outdoors

Materials: Blindfolds (e.g., bandanas, inexpensive medical facemasks pulled over eyes instead of nose and mouth)

To play, give each player a slip of paper with a unique number and then blindfold each participant. Shuffle the participants around, keeping them in a small group. Ask the group to put themselves into numerical order without using sight or sound. To finish, all players must be holding hands in a straight line in numerical order. Variations include sorting by alphabetical order, age order, tallest to smallest, and birthdays.

Blob Tag

A tag game that grows on you.

Energy Level: High

Environment: Field or gym

Materials: None

This is a great game in an open gym. One person is chosen to be It. When It tags someone, they both become It. Holding hands, they go after a third. The three, holding hands, go after a fourth, and so on until all players are It—except for one very fast-moving individual.

Source: The New Games Book, p. 107

Body Part Musical Chairs

A good activity to try with younger sibs

Energy Level: Medium

Environment: Indoors or outdoors

Materials: Chairs (e.g., folding chairs), recorded music, and an appropriate player

To start, have the participants sit in chairs in a big circle, with chairs facing out. Have music ready. When the music starts, remove one chair and have the players jog around the circle. When the music stops, the facilitator calls out a body part. Each person must then touch that body part to a chair—one person per chair. If a participant touches a chair before the body part is called, out she goes! And the one person who does not get a chair is out as well. Start simply: nose, hair, left elbow. As appropriate, make it more complicated: bare feet, someone else's left hand (they must grab one of the people who are already out, and so forth).

Body Surfing

This unique, if slightly goofy, form of surfing is as popular in Iowa as it is in Hawaii.

Energy Level: Medium

Environment: Grassy field or inside on mats

Materials: None

With the exception of the surfer, everyone lies face down, sardine-style, with a one-foot space between each person. The surfer gently lies down, arms extended, crossways over several bodies. Everyone simultaneously rolls in one direction to propel the surfer toward the end.

Source: More New Games! p. 133

Caterpillar

This "caterpillar" has more to do with heavy construction equipment (the kind that moves on large treads) than with future butterflies.

Energy Level: Medium

Environment: Grassy field or gym mats

Materials: None

Have the entire group lie face down and side by side. Pack everyone really close together, with any tiny people squeezed between two larger ones! Begin by having the person at one end roll over onto a neighbor and continue rolling down the whole line-up. When reaching the end, the roller lies on his or her tummy and the next person begins rolling from the other end. Before you know it, this human treadmill will have advanced its way across the gym or field.

Source: The New Games Book, p. 117

Centipede

A real wiggle

Energy Level: Medium

Environment: Open grassy area or gym

Materials: None

Divide the group into two teams of at least five similar-size players. (If your group has fewer than 10, don't worry—just stay as one team.) Instruct teams to line up behind each other at the starting line and sit down. Once seated, team members wrap their legs around the waist of the person in front of them, forming the body of a centipede. At "Go," players lift with their arms and wiggle the centipede across the field. If any centipede segments separate, they must reconnect en route. The winning centipede is the one who first makes it completely over the finish line with all segments connected.

Source: The Outrageous Outdoor Games Book, p. 97

Commons

A game wherein group members determine what they have in common—even if it is just a silly action

Energy Level: Medium

Environment: Indoor

Materials: None

Groups of three decide on three nonsensical actions that can be performed quickly, that is, thumb on nose with raspberry sound; a scary face with a lion's roar; or thumbs in ears, wiggling fingers, and a turkey gobble. Once each group has determined their sounds, players turn back to back. After a count of three, groups turn around and perform one of the three actions. If all members choose the same action, they "win," and play continues until all groups have won.

Source: More New Games! p. 25

Dangling Donut Eating Contest

As much fun to watch as it is to play, the Dangling Donut Eating Contest is sure to appeal to all Sibshop gourmands. Like many Sibshop games, this makes a great photo-op!

Energy Level: Low

Environment: Indoor hallway with beams or ceiling to which tape will stick; or outside, perhaps under monkey bars on a playground

Materials: Yarn, tape, broom (or drop cloth for the many crumbs), and a cake donut (powdered sugar is even better) for each player

Prepare for this activity by threading a piece of yarn through each donut, making sure that the yarn is long enough so that when taped to the ceiling (or tied to the monkey bars) the donut will dangle at the mouths of the players. To begin, line up the contestants, have them keep their hands behind their backs, and attach their donuts at proper height. At the "Go" signal, the participants race to see who indeed is the most capable dangling donut eater. There are sure to be crumbs, so have a broom or shakable drop cloth on hand. (If you are in a smaller area, this race can be done in heats.)

Source: The Outrageous Outdoor Games Book, p. 69

Dot's Dot

An opportunity to stretch the imagination, often with impressive results

Energy Level: Low/trickle-in

Environment: Tables and chairs

Materials: Sheets of blank paper, pencils, crayons. Optional: $\frac{1}{4}''$ circular color coding dots, available from office supply stores

Have the participants cover a sheet of paper with 20–25 randomly scattered dots. These papers are then collected and redistributed or simply traded with a neighbor. Have players concentrate on the dots to imagine a picture, and then connect the lines so that the picture emerges. If some are having difficulties, have participants turn the paper in different directions to imagine other possibilities.

Source: The Incredible Indoor Games Book, p. 91

Do You Want to Buy a Duck?

A game Groucho Marx would have loved

Energy Level: Low

Environment: Indoor

Materials: None

Do You Want to Buy a Duck? is a supremely silly circle game that kids love. If you're lucky, you will know someone who has played this game. If you've never played this, it's a good idea to practice by photocopying four copies of the diagram below. Round up three friends and read the diagram like it was a script—you'll catch on in no time! Although the script shows how the game is played with four people, there really isn't a limit on how many can play.

To begin, have the group sit in a circle, with facilitator A sitting to the left of facilitator B. Until the kids get the hang of the game, it is best to let the facilitators go first.

Round	Person A (facilitator A)	Person B (facilitator B)	Person C (participant)	Person D (participant)
1	Do you want to buy a duck?			
		A what?		
	A duck.			
		Does it quack?		
	Of course it quacks.			
2		Do you want to buy a duck?		
			A what?	
		A what?		
	A duck.			
		A duck.		
			Does it quack?	
		Does it quack?		
	Of course it quacks!			
		Of course it quacks!		

(continued)

(*continued*)

3			Do you want to buy a duck?	
				A what?
			A what?	
		A what?		
	A duck.			
		A duck.		
			A duck.	
				Does it quack?
			Does it quack?	
		Does it quack?		
	Of course it quacks!			
		Of course it quacks!		
			Of course it quacks!	
4				Do you want to buy a duck?
	And so on.			

Once you've mastered the basic game, spice it up by running two through the group at once, perhaps in opposite directions.

Fingerprint Pictures

It is amazing the amount of art that is available at one's fingertips!

Energy Level: Low/trickle-in

Environment: Tables and chairs

Materials: Paper, washable ink pads, thin markers or crayons, paper towels and a bar of soap for cleanup

Place a sheet of paper at each seat, and place enough ink pads and markers around so that materials are within easy reach of each artist. Once the participants' sleeves are rolled up, the finger inking can begin. Show the participants how to press their fingers and thumbs into the ink pad and then firmly onto the paper. Encourage them to experiment with different forms and different techniques such as rolling the fingertip or even printing the sides or heels of their hands.

Once the participants have finished making their fingerprints, have them wipe their hands with a paper towel and use markers to give their blotches some character.

Ask for some ideas to get imaginations rolling. For further inspiration, consult *Ed Emberley's Fingerprint Drawing Book* (2001), which is all about fingerprint illustrations. A super cleanup of hands will be necessary at the finish.

Fox and Chickens

Never underestimate the ferocity of a Mother Hen protecting her young!

Energy Level: High

Environment: Indoors, in a cleared, open area

Materials: None

To play, line up the group in a single file—except for one player. That player is the Fox! Have everyone in line hold the waist of the person in front. These are the Chicks, and the player at the head of the line is the Mother Hen.

At your cue, the Fox attempts to catch the last Chick in line. The Mother Hen flaps her wings and follows the Fox (with her Chicks following her) to prevent the Fox from catching the last Chick. When the last Chick in line is caught, this Chick falls in behind the Fox and holds the Fox's waist as he tries to get more Chicks. As more Chicks are caught, the Fox's line eventually gets longer than the Mother Hen's. The game continues until all Chicks are caught. For full effect, encourage clucking!

Hog Call

An activity as refined and subtle as its name suggests

Energy Level: High

Environment: Gym or other large room

Materials: Bandanas, if you wish to blindfold players. Alternatively, you can ask players to promise to keep their eyes closed during the playing of the game. More important, you will need slips of paper for the Red Team and the Blue Team. Each of the Red Team's slips of paper will have a word that somehow "goes with" the words found on the Blue Team's slips of paper. Consequently, if a member of the Red Team gets a slip of paper that says "bagel," someone on the Blue Team will get a slip of paper that says "cream cheese." Below are examples of things that go together to consider. When you create the slips of paper, you may wish to avoid confusion by writing the Red Team's slips in red, and the Blue Team's slips in blue.

Red Team	Blue Team
Batman	Robin
Peanut Butter	Jelly
Bacon	Eggs
Homer	Marge
Salt	Pepper
Bagel	Cream cheese
Ball	Glove
Bert	Ernie
Needle	Thread
Cookies	Milk
Nuts	Bolts
Lock	Key
Pen	Paper
Mickey	Minnie
Stars	Stripes
Bread	Butter
Salsa	Chips
Moon	Stars
Spaghetti	Meatballs
Hot chocolate	Marshmallows

To play, clear the room of all furniture, making a wide-open area that is free of obstacles. Divide the group into two teams of equal numbers and have each team go to opposing walls. Distribute the slips of paper carefully so that for every "Batman" you have a "Robin." It helps to stack the decks of slips in order. Consequently, if the order of the Red Team's deck is Batman, Peanut Butter, Bacon, the order of the Blue Team should be Robin, Jelly, Eggs. Dealing the deck from the top will assure that everyone has a match.

Explain to the group that a member of the other team has a slip of paper with a word that somehow goes with the word on the slip of paper they now have. Say, "For instance, if someone on the Red Team has Superman, someone on the Blue Team probably has Lois Lane." Further explain that to play the game, they must find their match with the other team by walking toward the middle of the room—with their eyes closed—and shouting whatever is on their slip of paper and listening for the word that goes with it. Once they find their match (by using only sound) players can open their eyes and go to the side of the room. Demonstrate with a fellow facilitator, using Superman and Lois Lane. There's one more catch, however, and this is what makes this game special: All players search for their matches simultaneously! Consequently, while

Salt is looking for Pepper, Bert is looking for Ernie, and Spaghetti is looking for Meat-balls. Hog Call is over when the last pair has been matched.

Source: The Outrageous Outdoor Games Book, p. 91

Hug Tag

Try out this new form of tag after you have warmed up with a round or two of Knots (see p. 111).

Energy Level: High

Environment: Field or gym

Materials: None

Use the same rules you use for Tag, only now a player is "safe" only when hugging another player! After playing for a bit, change the rules so that players are safe only when three people are hugging.

Source: The New Games Book, p. 115

Human Pinball

Everyone gets to be a flipper in this huge people-powered pinball machine.

Energy Level: Medium

Environment: Field or gym

Materials: One rubber gym ball

Set up this activity by having all participants (except one) stand in a circle, facing outward. Have the participants spread their legs as far apart as comfortable. Their feet should touch their neighbors' on both sides. Everyone bends down and swings their arms (now flippers) between their legs. (The upside-down view of everyone's backside will be good for a laugh.) The one non-flipper enters the circle as the target and the flippers try to hit him with the gym ball by knocking it back and forth across the circle. Whoever hits the target gets a point and becomes the new target. The target gets a point any time the flippers get wild and the ball escapes the confines of the pinball machine. Being a flipper can be quite exciting, but watch out for human head rushes!

Source: The New Games Book, p. 51

Human Spring

A counterpart game to Stand-Off (see p. 167). In this game, players cooperate to keep each other balanced upright.

Energy Level: Medium

Environment: Grassy area or indoor on mats

Materials: None

Two players stand with feet spread, facing each other at an arm's distance, holding their arms up in front, palms forward. Keeping their bodies as rigid as possible, partners gently lean forward and catch each other with their palms and rebound to a standing position. Too easy? Take a short step back and try again. This works best on a soft surface!

Source: More New Games! p. 17

Instant Replay

Try this decidedly silly name-learning game after a warm-up activity such as Knots, Group Juggling, or Human Bingo (see p. 111, p. 104, and p. 106, respectively).

Energy Level: Medium

Environment: Indoor

Materials: None

Standing in a circle, each group member announces his or her name while making an extravagant motion. For instance, Mike may hop into the circle on one foot (or turn circles with his hands raised, or slap his knees) and then shout his name. After Mike demonstrates, everyone else does an "instant replay." That is, they simultaneously perform the same motion and say, "Mike!" Going around the circle, encourage the participants to introduce themselves with dramatic gestures.

Source: More New Games! p. 71

Islands

Akin to Musical Chairs and contrary to Hug Tag (see p. 156), if you make contact in this game, you are out!

Energy Level: High

Environment: Field or gym

Materials: Paper plates (one for every three or four participants); recorded music (optional)

To play, scatter plates on the ground. Instruct the participants to begin wandering around the "islands." When the referee calls "Islands," everyone runs to touch a plate. Although more than one person can touch a plate, the last person to get to a plate is "out." In a departure from typical Sibshop activities, Islands does not promote contact—in fact, if any two people touch at all while scrambling for the plates, they are out! Continue to reduce the number of plates as the group grows smaller, until there are just a few people ready to pounce on a single island. A variation is to play music while the participants wander about the islands, stopping the music to signal that the land rush is on.

Source: The New Games Book, p. 127

Keep the Balloon in the Air

A good game with young Sibshoppers

Energy Level: Medium

Environment: Indoors, in a cleared, open area

Materials: Balloons

Give each child an inflated balloon. Tell the children that they can hit the balloons into the air but they can't let them touch the ground. The only additional rule is that the same person cannot touch the same balloon twice in a row. This encourages them to interact in creative ways, as well as engage in group problem solving.

Submitted by Tamara Besser, Jewish Children's Bureau of Chicago

The Lap Game

What is the one thing that disappears every time you stand up? Your lap, of course! In the Lap Game, participants attempt to sit on each other's laps—everyone, at the same time. Can it be done?

Energy Level: Medium

Environment: Indoor

Materials: None

Have all the participants stand shoulder to shoulder, elbow to elbow, and ankle to ankle in a tight circle. Each player then turns to the right and places his or her hands on the waist (or shoulders) of the players directly in front. When signaled by the leader, all players simultaneously guide the players in front of them to sit on their knees. If done correctly, all players are sitting in the laps (or, more correctly, on the knees) of the person behind them. If not done correctly, the players create a human—if ridiculous—representation of the domino theory. If all goes well and everyone has a lap to sit on, the group may try to lift their arms in the air and applaud themselves. Or, if players are feeling especially brave, they may try to walk in this seated position, with someone signaling "Right!" "Left!" and so on.

Source: The New Games Book, p. 171

Last Details

Try this one when the group needs a breather from some of the more raucous activities.

Energy Level: Low

Environment: Indoor

Materials: Optional: wearable props such as glasses, hats, scarves, gloves, buttons

Directions: Have the group divide into pairs. If you are using props (this can be done successfully without them), let each person select one or two at this time. Each person then faces his or her partner, carefully observing the other's details. When signaled by the leader, players turn their backs to each other, and, within a minute, rearrange six details. Both players face each other again and try to see if they can identify what has been changed.

Source: More New Games! p. 29

Last Kid Standing

Our favorite Sibshop activities require few materials, are easy to "pitch," and feature a healthy dose of barely contained chaos. Last Kid Standing meets these requirements handily! One warning: The materials required—spring-style clothespins—are living antiques and may be a challenge to find!

Energy Level: High

Environment: Indoors or outdoors

Materials: One clothespin for each player

To begin, give each participant a clothespin. With the help of friends, pin clothespins to the back of each player's shirt. To play, all players simultaneously attempt to remove the clothespins from the back of other players—while not allowing other players to remove theirs. Once a player's clothespin has been taken, he or she moves to the side. Continue until you have only one player left.

Lean-Two

A truly cooperative game where balancing the differences makes everyone a winner!

Energy Level: Medium

Environment: Open area, soft surface preferable

Materials: None

Have players stand in a circle and count off alternately by ones and twos and join hands. Keeping backs and legs as straight as possible, have all "ones" lean gently forward toward the center, and all "twos" lean backward toward the outside. This is a true act of cooperative counterbalance. Once balanced, have the group slowly reverse leaners: "twos" lean in and "ones" lean out. Once a comfortable balance has been attained, have everyone try stepping slowly to the right to move around in a circle.

Source: The Outrageous Outdoor Games Book, p. 61

Mime Rhyme

Mime rhyme: Perfect anytime

Energy Level: Medium

Environment: Indoor

Materials: None

One person selects a word (e.g., *rat*) and tells the group a word that rhymes with the word he or she has chosen (e.g., *mat*). The group then tries to guess the word by pantomiming words that rhyme. For instance, one at a time, individuals may try to act like a "cat" or a "bat"; or lie down in front of a door to impersonate a "mat"; or do their best beached-whale, just-finished-Thanksgiving-dinner routine to mime "fat"!

Source: More New Games! p. 83

Mouse Trap

Who is more cunning, the sneaky mice or the cat that is just pretending to sleep?

Energy Level: High

Environment: Open area

Materials: Minimum of 10 players

To begin, four or five players become The Dreaded Trap by standing in a circle with hands joined and raised in the air to create entrances and exits for the mice. One player is chosen to be the Fearsome Cat. The Cat, who pretends to sleep, faces away from the trap with eyes closed. Remaining players become the Cunning and Clever Mice who dart quietly in and out of the Trap past the sleepy Cat.

To capture the Mice, the Cat suddenly opens his or her eyes and yells, "Snap!" The players who are the Trap immediately bring their arms down, snaring the rascally rodents. Captured Mice now become part of the Trap. The game continues with the Trap becoming larger and larger until there is only one victorious Mouse.

Source: The Outrageous Outdoor Games Book, p. 54

Muscle Beach

This is a game sure to Pump You Up!

Energy Level: Medium

Environment: Indoors

Materials: For each group of five participants: one oversized sweatshirt (purchased, if needed, from a thrift store) and 10 balloons of assorted sizes. Handy to have: pictures of Arnold Schwarzenegger in his prime or Kevin Nealon and Dana Carvey as "Hans and Franz" (obtained from the Internet, perhaps)

To begin, have each group of five select a representative. The representatives come to the front of the room and are given oversized sweatshirts. You will acknowledge that these kids indeed look strong, but not nearly as strong as (whipping out your pictures) Ar-Nold or Hans and Franz. Tell them that's perfectly fine because you (and your fellow facilitators) are there to Pump Them Up!

Explain that their teammates will have 4 (or fewer—your choice) minutes and 10 balloons to blow up, tie, and stuff in the sweatshirt to make their teammate the most muscled dude or dudette there. Hand out the balloons and start the timer. Once the time is up, have facilitators (or kids) judge which balloon-enhanced kid is indeed "Most Buffalicious."

Adapted from Youth Ministry Games www.pastor2youth.com

Mutual Monsters

Step aside, Dr. Frankenstein; here come the real monster makers!

Energy Level: Low

Environment: Tables and chairs

Materials: A sheet of letter-size paper and pencil/crayons/markers for each person

Distribute paper and pencils and have the participants fold their papers in thirds. On the top third, everyone draws the head of a monster, person, animal, or creature. As they draw, have all the artists extend the neck of their creation a little past the first crease in the paper. When completed, have the participants fold back the top third so that it is hidden and pass their papers to neighbors. Now everyone draws a torso and arms in the middle section of the page connecting to the neck lines, but without looking at the head. This time, have them extend the waist a little past the second crease. Now fold the paper again and pass to a different neighbor. Everyone now draws legs and feet on the bottom third of the paper, without looking at the other sections. When all players are finished, the papers are unfolded and the creations are shared with the whole group.

Source: The Incredible Indoor Games Book, p. 94

Mummy

Hardly original but always fun, Mummy is another great crowd-pleasing activity for late October!

Energy Level: Medium

Environment: Indoors

Materials: Rolls of inexpensive white toilet paper, rolls of masking tape (optional)

To play, divide the group into teams and have the team decide who will be the mummy. Give each team two rolls of toilet paper and, optionally, a roll of tape. Tell your participants that the goal of the game is to wrap the mummy completely so that all that is showing are the mummy's eyes and nose—no clothing and no skin should show. Have teams race to see who will finish their mummy first; however, if you wish to make it a bit harder, you can tell them that they must wrap their mummy in one continuous strand of toilet paper. If their toilet paper breaks (and it will) they must connect the broken toilet paper with masking tape. Other variations include having non-playing players vote on their favorite mummy or having the fully-wrapped mummies compete in a race or competition of your invention.

Nose Toes

This game is sure to keep you on your toes, or is that nose?

Energy Level: Medium

Environment: Open space

Materials: None

To begin, everyone sits in a circle on the floor. The leader begins clapping in rhythm and the group joins in. Once the rhythm is established, the leader turns to a neighbor, points to his or her toes and says, "This is my nose." The neighbor repeats "This is my nose" and points to toes, and then adds another silly statement such as "This is my knee" while pointing to a thumb. The next person in the circle repeats "This is my knee" and points to a thumb, and then adds a new statement and gesture. This continues around the circle. NOTE: Each person repeats only the statement of the person before him or her—not the statements of all previous players.

Source: The Incredible Indoor Games Book, p. 69

Pass the Orange

This well-known neck-in-neck race is fun as a relay or as just a cooperative challenge once participants get to know one another.

Energy Level: Medium

Environment: Open space

Materials: Three to five oranges or grapefruits

To begin, line players up in two teams. Place an orange under the chin of each team's first player. The object is for the team to pass the orange, neck to neck, chin to chin, all the way down the line to the last player. Players should hold their hands behind their backs to resist the temptation to handle the orange during its tenuous transport.

Source: The Outrageous Outdoor Games Book, p. 90

Prui

Unlike the "Blob," in Blob Tag (see p. 148), which everyone wants to avoid becoming a part of, Prui (pronounced PROO-ee) is a gentle creature that everyone would like to join.

Energy Level: High

Environment: Field or gym

Materials: Blindfolds (optional)

To play, all players stand in a group with their eyes closed. The referee quietly selects someone to be Prui. Prui keeps eyes open but cannot talk. With eyes closed, everyone else begins milling around. When a player bumps into another player, he or she is to shake hands and ask, "Prui?" If the person replies, "Prui?" then the inquirer has not found Prui. If, however, the player finds someone, shakes hands, and this person does not reply, "Prui," then the player may suspect that the "true" Prui has been found. After checking again to be sure there is no response, the player joins hands with Prui and opens his or her eyes. Prui, still silent, grows as new players make the discovery and join hands. Participants can only shake Prui's hand at either end, so if they bump into joined hands, they must make their way to the end of the chain. When the last person joins Prui and opens his or her eyes, Prui breaks the vow of silence and lets out a victorious cheer!

Source: The New Games Book, p. 133

Psychic Shake

How can you find your comrades if you can't talk?

Energy Level: Low

Environment: Field or gym

Materials: None

Have all participants silently select a number—either one, two, or three. Once decided, people quietly circulate, giving each other handshakes of one, two, or three shakes. When players meet someone with the same number, they hold hands and search for others of their number. When all is done, for curiosity, see if there are three equal groups. Once you've tried it this way, ask your participants how the game could be changed. Instead of shaking hands, you might find yourself winking, hopping, stomping, or snapping your fingers!

Source: More New Games! p. 177

Pushpin Soccer

Caution: This game mixes kids and pushpins!

Energy Level: High

Environment: Gym

Materials: Inflated balloons (about two per player) 8 inches or larger (dollar stores can be a good source for inexpensive balloons), two pushpins (one red, one blue), two large rectangular tables

To prepare for this activity, clear the room and put two large rectangular tables at opposite ends of the room. These will be your goals. To begin, have players line up along a wall and arrange themselves according to height. Starting with the tallest player, have players count off "red," "blue," "red," "blue," and so on. This will assure two teams—a Red Team and Blue Team—of approximately equal heights. Have the teams meet at their goals. Explain that in Pushpin Soccer, they will compete with the other team for possession of the balloon. Their job is to use their hands to swat the balloon to their goal. To score, they must get their balloon across the goal (the table) so that their team's popper can pop the balloon with a pushpin. (At this point, select a person to be the teams' poppers.) Review—in great detail—the rule that will help ensure that the game is played safely: Players may never, ever place their hands over the table. Similarly, the popper may not reach his or her hands over the table for any reason. This makes the entire table area a "zone of safety" and keeps hands and pushpins apart. Adults stationed near each goal can monitor poppers' and players' adherence to safety rules.

Once warned, the poppers are handed their pushpins and a balloon is brought onto the court. It is tossed into the air and the game begins. Each team swats the balloon toward its popper, who pops the balloon. Players may swat the balloon with their hands only. For fun, try introducing more than one balloon at a time toward the end of the activity.

If the group has participants of greatly differing heights, consider alternating sets for taller and not-so-tall players.

Source: More New Games! p. 69

Red-Handed

Keep passing 'cause you wouldn't want to be caught red-handed!

Energy Level: Low

Environment: Open area

Materials: One small object (e.g., a marble)

With his or her eyes closed, one player stands in the middle of a circle of players who continuously circulate a small object such as a key or marble. Whether they have it or not, all players simultaneously pretend to be passing the object. When ready, the center player opens his or her eyes and has three guesses to determine which player has the marble. The player caught "red-handed" (or whoever has the marble after the third unsuccessful guess) becomes the new person in the center.

Source: The New Games Book, p. 71

Scrabble Scramble

Spelling tests should be so much fun!

Energy Level: Medium

Environment: Field or gym

Materials: 62 sheets of plain, inexpensive $8\frac{1}{2} \times 11$ white paper, wide felt-tip markers (one red, one blue), two large tables

To get ready, use the markers to make two sets of "alphabets"—one red, one blue. Each set will have one letter per page, drawn to fill the page. In addition to the usual 26 letters, each set will also have an extra A, E, I, O, and U. Consequently, the blue and the red sets will use 31 pieces of paper each.

Divide the group into two teams—a red team and a blue team. As older kids and adults will likely have a few advantages in this game, try to make sure that each team has a mix of young and not-so-young players. Place the sets of letters on the teams' tables and tell the participants the goal of Scrabble Scramble: to create a word or phrase on a topic you will give them using only the letters found on their table. Furthermore, tell them that there are three ways to score in Scrabble Scramble: One point is awarded to the team that "builds" their word first. "Building" a word means that the team has created a word and holds their word up—one alphabet sheet per player—for the other team to see. Another point is awarded for the team that builds the longest word or phrase. Finally, one point is given to a team that spells their word or phrase correctly! Consequently, a team may score up to three points per round and both teams can score a point for correct spelling.

Here are some Scrabble Scramble categories you may wish to try: "Anything Disney," "Anything [name of your state]," "Anything Summer," "Anything Food."

The team with the most points after a set number of rounds wins.

Source: The Outrageous Outdoor Games Book, p. 56

Scrabble Scramble

Team:	Team:
Round One ☐ Best time (1 point) ☐ Most letters (1 point) ☐ Correct spelling (1 point) ☐ Total:	Round One ☐ Best time (1 point) ☐ Most letters (1 point) ☐ Correct spelling (1 point) ☐ Total:
Round Two ☐ Best time (1 point) ☐ Most letters (1 point) ☐ Correct spelling (1 point) ☐ Total:	Round Two ☐ Best time (1 point) ☐ Most letters (1 point) ☐ Correct spelling (1 point) ☐ Total:
Round Three ☐ Best time (1 point) ☐ Most letters (1 point) ☐ Correct spelling (1 point) ☐ Total:	Round Three ☐ Best time (1 point) ☐ Most letters (1 point) ☐ Correct spelling (1 point) ☐ Total:

Sightless Sculpture

Can a person who no longer hears write music? Of course! Beethoven did. Can a person who no longer sees still make sculptures of her friends? Sure! Sightless Sculpture, a great low-energy activity, can also be an opportunity to talk about the intersection of disability and art.

Energy Level: Low

Environment: Inside

Materials: Bandanas, table

Place the table at one end of the room and have the participants sit on the floor facing the table. Ask the participants, "Do you think people who have disabilities can be artists?" They will surely answer in the affirmative, so ask them, "Who can give me an example of an artist—famous or not so famous—who had a disability?" You may hear about Van Gogh, Chuck Close, Beethoven, Stevie Wonder, Ray Charles, or a participant's talented sib. Then ask them, "Imagine this scenario: You're a sculptor. More than anything else in the world, you love to make sculptures. But something happened and you lost your vision. Could you continue to do what you so love to do?" Help the participants brainstorm how they would sculpt without being able to see. Then introduce the game by telling them that to play Sightless Sculpture, you'll need three participants. (It's best to have all-boy groups and all-girl groups.) To begin, one of the three participants will volunteer to be the Sightless Sculptor, another to be the Blob of Clay, and still another to be the Model (a.k.a. the Model Child). The Sculptor is blindfolded. The Model then assumes any position she can maintain for up to 5 minutes. The model can stand, kneel, sit, lean on the table—whatever! The Sculptor then uses her hands to determine the Model's position and manipulates the Blob of Clay to create an identical statue. Leaders may need to help the Sculptor locate the Model and the Blob of Clay. (It is best when they are close to the Sculptor, and the table can be a good point of reference for all players.) When the Sculptor feels that the creation is complete, she opens her eyes to assess her work. Should you wish, this activity can be done in groups of three or with three people at a time in front of a group.

Source: More New Games! p. 77

Snowball Fight

This simple game is loved by Sibshoppers of all ages at Children's Hospital and Regional Medical Center in Seattle.

Energy Level: Medium

Environment: Indoors

Materials: Masking tape and 8½ × 11 paper (rescued from recycling is fine!), one piece per player

To get ready, divide the room in half by making a dividing line on the floor with masking tape. Divide the participants into two equal groups and have the groups stand on either side of the masking tape line. Distribute one piece of paper per participant. Have them crumple their piece of paper into a "snowball."

To play, have teams throw snowballs found on their side of the masking tape to their opponent's side as quickly as they can and as far as they can. During play, teams may not put any parts of their bodies over the masking tape lines—only snowballs.

At a time known only to you (and a minute is about right), shout "Stop!" Play should come to a screeching halt. Have each team collect all the snowballs on their side and compare the two piles. The team with the fewest snowballs wins.

Repeat as desired!

Contributed by Sandy Ardnt of the Sibshops at Children's Hospital and Regional Medical Center, Seattle, Washington

Stand-Off

Be careful how you throw your weight around in this game. It is easy to lose your balance!

Energy Level: Medium

Environment: Open area

Materials: None

Each player stands with feet together, one arm length away from his or her partner. To begin, players make palm-to-palm contact and attempt to unbalance their partners by moving their hands and shifting their weight. Points are given when a partner moves a foot, loses balance, or makes contact with any part of the body other than palms. No points are given if both partners lose balance.

Source: The New Games Book, p. 35

Stand Up!

Included below are variations on this Sibshop classic. Can you and your participants think of others?

Energy Level: Medium

Environment: Outdoors or soft surface

Materials: None

To begin, have pairs of equal height sit back to back, bend their knees, put their feet flat on the ground, and then reach back and lock elbows. On the count of three, everyone yells, "Stand Up!" and players, digging their heels into the ground, push back. If done right, the pair will pop up into a standing position. Can this be done with three or even four people? How about three people facing one another, feet to feet, and holding hands?

Source: The New Games Book, p. 65

Tag-O-Rama

Also known as Dodge Tag, this is a simple but exciting version of an old standby.

Energy Level: High

Environment: Field or gym

Materials: None

To begin, have the group divide into pairs. Each pair decides who will be "It" first. Then the group is spread out across the field or gym. At the signal "Go," all players begin their individual games of Tag, dodging other players caught up in their own games.

Source: The Outrageous Outdoor Games Book, p. 121

That's a Wrap!

A simple game that brings kids together!

Energy Level: Medium

Environment: Indoors

Materials: Items to make two simple but identical obstacle courses using traffic cones, ropes, chairs, tables, or whatever is available

To begin, divide the group into two teams. Have each team line up, holding hands. Have the person on the far right turn to the left and continue curling until each group is a tight spiral. Once wound up, have each team complete the obstacle course. Should any player lose his or her grip, the team must stop, line up, and rewind before continuing. (If the course proves too easy, try a challenge mode; for example, if a team starts to laugh at any point, they must start over!)

Source: Games to Keep Kids Moving

Trains, Planes, and Automobiles

No, this has nothing to do with the Steve Martin and John Candy movie! It's a fast-moving variation of Musical Chairs. It's fun, fast-paced, and, like many good Sibshop activities, there are different ways to play it.

Energy Level: Medium

Environment: Indoors

Materials: Chairs (e.g., folding chairs), wide tape that you can write on, and a wide-tipped marker (e.g., a Sharpie)

To prepare, arrange chairs in a circle with seats facing out. You'll need one chair per person, minus one—like Musical Chairs! Tape the strips of tape to the seat or back of each chair. On the strips of tape, print in large letters a different mode of transportation: bus, plane, pogo stick, monorail, bicycle, and so forth. You'll need one strip for each chair. Finally, prepare a large sheet of paper with the modes of transportation used printed in large type. Have your Sibshoppers—except for one—sit in the chairs. The Sibshopper who doesn't sit in a chair is It.

To play, It picks two types of transportation (in this example bus and plane) from the large-type list. Then the players with "bus" and "plane" on their chairs must switch chairs without allowing It to sit in one of the (recently vacated!) chairs. If It successfully gets to a chair, then the person left standing becomes the new It. After you try this with two modes of transportation—and two kids changing chairs—try three modes of transportation and three kids changing chairs. And so on!

Triangle Tag

A geometric twist on tag. Also an excellent demonstration of how exhausting running around in circles can be!

Energy Level: High

Environment: Field or gym

Materials: Bandanas or wristbands (one per group of four)

To play, groups of three players hold hands to make a triangle. One wears a wristband or a bandana around the wrist to identify him or her as the "target." A fourth player attempts to tag the target while the triangle maneuvers around to protect the target. There is really only one other rule: The "tagger" cannot reach over the arms of triangle members to reach the target.

Source: More New Games! p. 43

Tug of War

Simple as can be, and great fun for Sibshop participants of all sizes

Energy Level: Medium

Environment: Field or gym

Materials: Stout rope

Tug of War needs little explanation: Divide into two teams, grab a rope, and pull! However, do try some variations, including having players wait 10 feet away and, on signal, run to the rope and commence pulling; or stretching the rope over a sprinkler or small, filled plastic swimming pool.

Source: The New Games Book, p. 153

Ultimate Nerf

Somewhat like football—but much more fun

Energy Level: High

Environment: Field or gym

Materials: Nerf football or Frisbee

Ultimate Nerf starts with one team "kicking off" to the other by tossing a Nerf ball, Frisbee, or whatever. Members of the receiving team may run anywhere on the field—except for the person with the ball, who may not move his or her feet until the ball is thrown to a teammate. Members of the opposite team must stand one arm length away from the person who has the ball. If a passed ball is dropped, thrown out of bounds, or intercepted, the other team immediately takes possession and the direction of the play shifts.

Source: More New Games! p. 53

Undercover Leader

Wherein leaders exert a very subtle leadership style

Energy Level: Low

Environment: Open space

Materials: None

To begin, have players sit in a circle on the floor. Choose one person to be "It" and have this person leave the room. Choose another player in the circle to be the Undercover Leader. During the game, the Leader starts various body movements, such as head nodding, foot tapping, elbow scratching, or chicken wings, and the rest of the group follows his lead. Throughout the game, it is important that players not look directly at the Leader for movement changes, or they might give away the Leader's cover! Once a movement has started, the person who is It is invited back into the room. It watches closely to determine who the Leader is. The Leader, meanwhile, continues to change the movements. When It discovers the Leader's identity, two other players are chosen to become It and the new Undercover Leader, and the play resumes.

Source: The Incredible Indoor Games Book, p. 53

Vampire

Perfect for that late-October Sibshop

Energy Level: Medium

Environment: Field or gym

Materials: None

To begin, have all players close their eyes and begin shuffling around. The referee, who must assure that the players do not bump into inanimate objects, also secretly appoints one of the players to be the Vampire. The Vampire must also keep his or her eyes closed. When humans bump into humans, nothing happens; but when a player bumps into the Vampire, the ghoul grabs the prey by the arms and lets out a blood-curdling scream. The victim now becomes a Vampire as well, and, keeping his or her eyes closed, seeks other humans on which to feast. Lest everyone become vampires too quickly, here's a catch: Any two vampires who try to feast on each other are automatically returned to human status!

Source: The New Games Book, p. 123

Whispers!

Not all Sibshop games are boisterous—just most of them! Whispers is a great, slightly quieter game for young Sibshoppers.

Energy Level: Medium

Environment: Indoors

Materials: Slips of papers with instructions such as "Tell the next person your name and age," "Tell the next person what your favorite color is and why."

To play, divide the group into two teams and have each team stand in a line. The person at the front of the line reads the instruction on the slip of paper out loud and whispers her answer to the second person in line and so on down the line. The last person in line yells out the final message and runs to the front of the line collecting a new question and starting the process again.

Wind in the Willow

Create a proper mood for this quiet, gentle game by having players make low wind-blowing sounds.

Energy Level: Low

Environment: Grassy area or inside

Materials: None

To begin, have a small circle of players (about eight or so) stand shoulder to shoulder with hands held at shoulder height, palms forward. To maintain balance during this activity, one foot should be behind the other. A volunteer "willow" stands in the middle of the circle with eyes closed, arms crossed at the chest, keeping his or her body as straight as possible. Circle members support the willow as it gently sways back and forth in the "wind."

Source: More New Games! p. 67

SAMPLE SIBSHOP FOOD ACTIVITIES

Food activities are among the most rewarding Sibshop activities. When we make and eat food together, we are nourished, we express our creativity, and we derive enjoyment from eating the kid-friendly meal we have prepared together. As we cook and eat, we also laugh, tell bad jokes, learn about our likes and dislikes, and talk about our schools, friends, and families. The sharing and informal support that occurs during the breaking of bread should never be underestimated! If you have never organized a group-cooking activity, the following are a few thoughts to keep in mind:

1. Be prepared. Locate and set up your materials before your participants arrive. If you are not familiar with the kitchen, plan on visiting it well before your Sibshop to take an inventory of the tools you need (and prepare a list of tools you will need to bring) and to be sure that necessary equipment (e.g., ovens) work. Even a simple cooking activity such as Super Nachos (a good first-time activity) can be difficult if an important ingredient or tool is forgotten.

2. Keep it simple—especially the first few times. If you cannot remember back that far, kids can be picky eaters. We know that more than 50% of Sibshop participants think that tomatoes (much less green peppers, pineapple, black olives, and so forth) are just "too weird" to go on nachos. Ditto for mushrooms in pasta sauce. That does not mean that you cannot have some on hand for adults and kids who like them, but do not assume that everyone will want them.

3. Identify as many jobs as possible. We have found that participants would rather be doing something than watching. They frequently display enthusiasm for even the less glamorous chores like pot scrubbing, which has amazed us and shocked their parents. As you plan your food activity, consider the number of hands you will want to keep busy. If space permits, consider breaking the kitchen into stations, each responsible for a specific chore. When shopping, purchase food that can be readied by your young participants: Buy blocks of cheese for grating rather than pre-grated cheese or canned cheese sauce.

4. Think about how much time you will need for the project. Select or adapt projects to accommodate the time you have available.

To get you started, we have listed some food activities that we and others have enjoyed. Share the foods you love with your young participants, whether it is egg rolls, stir fries, giant chocolate chip cookies, tacos, Belgian waffles, or fruit kabobs!

Super Nachos

The jobs here are grating cheese; chopping tomatoes, green peppers, olives, and maybe onions; spreading the mixture on tortilla chips; and assembling the dish before running it under the broiler. Good with sour cream, beans, and, of course, salsa. Also a good project when time is limited.

Pizza

For this perennial favorite, try using small pizza rounds and let the young chefs customize their pizzas with a variety of toppings.

Sibshop Subshop

A 6-foot-long submarine sandwich roll sold at some bakeries can add an extra dollop of fun to this activity. You can, of course, pile almost anything on a sub, but we think the sprinkling of Italian dressing is what puts it "over the top." Subs can be a good choice when kitchen space and equipment are minimal.

Homemade Pasta

If you have a pasta machine and know how to use it and your sauce is already made, a group of siblings can turn flour and eggs into homemade linguine or fettuccine in less than an hour. It cooks in seconds. Don't forget the candles, the Italian bread, and maybe a Frank Sinatra CD!

Homemade Ice Cream

A time-honored method of channeling youthful excess energy is to crank an ice cream freezer. If you can find an old-fashioned, people-powered ice cream freezer, by all means use it. Making ice cream is as educational as it is rewarding. We are always surprised at the number of children who have never had or made homemade ice cream before. Sometimes we will churn the ice cream early in the program, pack it in ice to harden, and enjoy it at the end of the Sibshop when participants serve it to their parents, their brothers and sisters, and themselves!

CONCLUSION

Please remember that recreational and food activities are indispensable in creating an appealing, memorable, and sometimes magical Sibshop. As noted at the beginning of this chapter, recreational and food activities provide participants with informal opportunities for support and help keep the program's focus on the participants' many strengths. Select, plan, and present these activities with the same care and attention that you would give to other activities. The energy, joy, and imagination that you and your colleagues bring to these activities will be reflected in the faces of the children you are there to serve. Have fun—and they will too!

Chapter 10

Information Activities, Guest Speakers, and Special Events

As noted in Chapter 4, numerous authors, researchers, and siblings have noted that brothers and sisters have a lifelong need for information on the specifics and implications of their sibling's disability or illness. As with many sibling issues, this need for information is similar to parents' need for information. Compared with parents, however, brothers and sisters usually have far fewer opportunities to acquire this information.

Because of their changing needs as they mature, brothers and sisters will need to have their sibling's condition and the implications of the condition reinterpreted as they grow. This need is best addressed when parents and service providers are aware of the concerns of the brothers and sisters and regularly share information with them throughout their lives. (If you have not done so already, read Chapter 3 for implications for parents and service providers.) Activities for parents and service providers, such as workshops and sibling panels (see Chapter 11), can be an important step in creating readily available, natural sources of information for brothers and sisters as they grow.

WRITTEN SOURCES OF INFORMATION

When available, written information can help brothers and sisters as well. A few agencies (e.g., the Epilepsy Foundation of America) have prepared materials for children, including some specifically for brothers and sisters. Books such as *Living with a Brother or Sister with Special Needs* (Meyer & Vadasy, 1996) or those listed in Appendix B can provide siblings with information on disabilities, therapies, future concerns, and even emotions they may experience. If children cannot read these books on their own, parents can read them to their children—a practice that can be a wonderful means of keeping the lines of communication open.

SIBSHOPS AS INFORMATION SOURCES

In addition to providing recreation and discussion, Sibshops can also be places to learn as noted in the fourth Sibshop goal:

 Goal 4: Sibshops will provide siblings with an opportunity to learn more about the implications of the special needs of their brothers and sisters.

There are, however, limits to the type and amount of information that can be conveyed at a Sibshop. Sibshops for brothers and sisters of children with a specific condition (e.g., autism, hearing impairment, cancer) can be a valuable opportunity to convey information about the nature of a sibling's special needs. These Sibshops are generally held as a part of a state, national, or regional conference. Except perhaps in large urban communities, it can be challenging, if not impossible, to attract sufficient numbers of siblings of people with a specific condition to make a viable local program. Consequently, most community-based Sibshops are for brothers and sisters of children with various disabilities or illnesses, which can make an in-depth or ongoing discussion about any one disability or illness impractical. Despite these limitations, Sibshops can be a fine place for participants to gain information about topics of common interest, such as those described below.

Services for People with Special Needs

Many participants will have brothers and sisters who receive services from a wide range of professionals, including adapted physical education teachers, audiologists, interpreters, mobility teachers, nurses, occupational and physical therapists, physicians, psychologists, recreational therapists, respite care providers, social workers, and special education teachers. Often, however, brothers and sisters have only a vague idea of what these service providers do with their siblings on a daily basis. Consider inviting a therapist or teacher to your next Sibshop as a guest speaker. Ask the guest to briefly describe what he or she does with kids with special needs and, if at all possible, demonstrate using the "tools of the trade" such as adaptive spoons, augmentative communication devices, or therapy balls. Be sure to leave ample time for questions and listen carefully to the questions because they will help you determine the participants' knowledge of disabilities, illnesses, and services and can help you plan future informational activities.

Information About Disabilities

Often, siblings are interested in learning more about many disabilities, even disabilities other than those that their brothers and sisters have. If your participants seem to have such an interest, consider inviting guest speakers who can provide an overview of a disability and answer the participants' questions. Many disability-related organizations provide community education, often delivered by people who have the disability themselves.

Learning about different disabilities can be helpful in at least two ways. First, it provides participants with a fresh, broadened perspective as they listen and compare and contrast their siblings' disabilities with the one presented. Second, as guests speak, common themes (e.g., self-advocacy, inclusion) frequently emerge, providing siblings with a growing understanding of issues facing all people with disabilities.

Technology for People with Disabilities

Today's children are fascinated by computers and their various applications. Throughout the United States, there are many examples of how computers and other technologies are making life better for people with disabilities. If you are not aware of a local expert on computers for people with special needs, search the Internet for "assistive technology state office" and then state-by-state lists such as the one currently found on the web site of the National Assistive Technology Technical Assistance Partnership.

VSA Arts

Most states have VSA Arts (formerly Very Special Arts) organizations. For those unfamiliar with VSA Arts, it is a cultural and educational organization dedicated to providing opportunities in the arts for, by, and with people who have disabilities, and it sponsors a wide range of events. Like Sibshops, VSA Arts celebrates strengths and diversity. Plan on inviting a representative from your state's VSA Arts organization to be a guest artist at your Sibshop. Also, consider contacting VSA Arts to see how your Sibshop could take part in your state's next VSA Arts Festival. To locate state or national affiliates, simply search the Internet for "VSA Arts affiliates."

Kids on the Block

Many communities have Kids on the Block puppet troupes that feature puppets with and without disabilities and chronic health conditions. Sibshop participants are likely to enjoy Kids on the Block's programs, which provide information about a wide range of special needs using accessible, interactive, and frequently humorous short plays. Participants may especially like the programs "Paper Airplanes," "Michael Darling," and "Oh, Brother." All three scripts address sibling concerns. Because many siblings have a greater knowledge of disabilities than their age peers, these productions allow participants to "show off" what they know about special needs as they interact with the puppets. Most Kids on the Block programs are created for third- through sixth-grade audiences, similar to Sibshop's intended age range. You can learn more about Kids on the Block troupes, including contact information for local troupes, on their web pages.

Future Issues

As the research literature suggests, brothers and sisters often have unasked questions about the future. Questions that could be addressed during a Sibshop may include "What will happen to my brother and sister when we grow up?" and "Will my sibling live with me someday?" Survey your group to determine which issues are of greatest interest.

To lead an informational discussion on the suggested topics, the Sibshop facilitator will need to be aware of the range of housing and vocational opportunities available for adults with disabilities, or will need to invite others who are familiar with the range of services in the community to participate. You may also wish to invite as a guest speaker an adult with a disability who can talk about where he or she lives, works, and plays. If you need help finding appropriate resources or speakers on adult services, a good place to start will be your local chapter of The Arc. Alternatively, you may wish to sponsor a field trip to supported employment sites and meet adults with disabilities who are working and living in the community.

Parents of Children with Special Needs

Perhaps because of parents' desire to protect their typically developing children, many brothers and sisters have never heard parents candidly discuss the impact their child's disability can have on them and their families and the unique concerns and rewards parents experience. Brothers and sisters who have an opportunity to hear parents discuss their families' situations can gain insights into the workings of their own parents and families.

When inviting two or three parents to share their families' stories and answer participants' questions, for confidentiality reasons make sure that the parents you invite have more than one child and are not parents of Sibshop participants. It will also help if these presenters have previously spoken to groups about their children and families.

Topics the parents could briefly address are the family's reaction to the child's diagnosis; the special joys and concerns they have regarding their child and family; and the effect that the child with special needs has had on his or her family, especially brothers and sisters. We have found that children often find it easier to talk to other children's parents, so leave plenty of time for questions.

Older Siblings

Listening to the experiences of adult brothers and sisters can be instructive and validating for Sibshop participants. Hearing adults talk about growing up as a sibling of a person with special needs will encourage your participants to talk about their lives and will stimulate conversation among the entire group. To prepare your Sibshop participants, announce the panel at the beginning of the program and encourage the participants to think of questions for the panel. To help prepare the panel, you may wish to send panelists guidelines and questions prior to the Sibshop. A sample letter is shown in Figure 10.1.

When a project seemed to be finished, Walt Disney always encouraged his staff to look at it one more time and "plus it." In other words, how can we make this good

Dear Panelist, ...

Thanks for agreeing to be on our adult sibling panel at our upcoming Sibshop. As I mentioned on the phone, you and the other panelists will have a chance to informally discuss with our 8- to 13-year-old Sibshop participants your experiences growing up with a brother or sister who has special needs. We will ask you to share information about

• **Yourself.** We'll want to know what you do, whether you have a family of your own, where you grew up and went to school, and anything else you wish to share.

• **Your brother or sister with special needs.** We'll want to know what kind of disability your sibling has, how old your sibling is, where he or she went to school, what your sibling currently does during the day, where he or she lives, and so on.

• **Your family.** We'll be interested in how many children there are in the family you grew up in. If you're older than your sibling, we'll want to know how old you were when you learned that your sibling had special needs. If you are younger than your sibling, we'll want to know how much younger and if you remember when you realized that your older brother or sister had special needs.

• **What it was like when you were a kid.** Did the special needs of your brother or sister cause any problems with your parents, friends, schoolmates, or even strangers? Did you come up with solutions to these problems? Growing up, did you have any questions or secret worries about your sibling's special needs? Were there good things that happened to you or your family as a result of having a brother or sister with special needs? Does your family have funny, treasured stories about life with your brother or sister?

A desired outcome of the panel will be the discussion with the younger siblings. Frequently, upon hearing "testimony" of the panelists, younger siblings will describe similar experiences that they've had.

Thanks again for being a part of our program!

Sincerely,

Erica Lewis

....

Figure 10.1. Sample letter to panel participants. (For the reader's use, this material may be reproduced.)

experience even better? You will want to "plus" your Sibshop frequently to be sure that it stays fresh and exciting for participants.

Special guests can help keep a Sibshop lively and especially rewarding to attend. As with many Sibshop activities, you are limited only by your imagination when choosing a special guest. Examples of special guests you can invite to help ensure that your Sibshops are truly memorable events include chefs who can show participants how to make a special dish or dessert, clog or tap dancers who are willing to perform and teach a step or two, jugglers who share the basics of their craft, folk singers who can create songs based on participants' suggestions, actors adept at improvisational theater, gymnasts, martial arts instructors, or even a local football hero who would enjoy playing touch football with admiring participants.

As you plan your Sibshop, please don't forget informational activities and guest speakers. After all, we promote Sibshops as opportunities to provide brothers and sisters with peer support *and information* with a recreational context. Experience has taught us that arranging for informational activities is not difficult and that the rewards are great. Your young participants will be eager to learn!

Chapter 11

Workshops on Sibling Issues for Parents and Service Providers

One of the most gratifying aspects of providing training on the Sibshops model has been parents' and professionals' keen interest in sibling issues. Parents, who witness the sibling experience on a daily basis, tell us that they appreciate an opportunity to discuss and learn about sibling relationships in other families. Teachers, administrators, social workers, physicians, and therapists who realize that a child's disability has an impact on all family members tell us that they welcome opportunities to expand their understanding of issues for brothers and sisters. In this chapter we describe how to present three different types of workshops on sibling issues: a panel of siblings, a workshop for parents and service providers, and an informal meeting for parents of Sibshop participants. All three are designed to address the fifth Sibshop goal:

Goal 5: Sibshops will provide parents and other professionals with opportunities to learn more about the concerns and opportunities frequently experienced by brothers and sisters of people with special needs.

Because some parents and professionals prefer to read a book or a newsletter or watch a videotape than attend workshops, we list alternative resources at the end of the chapter.

SIBLING PANELS

Panels of brothers and sisters of people with special needs can be a potent, valuable method of educating parents and professionals about issues facing siblings. Panelists frequently remark that they, too, leave with an expanded understanding of the sibling experience as a result of listening to the other panelists.

Panel Guidelines

Sibling panels are relatively easy to run, considering the value of the information exchanged. Following are guidelines to help ensure that a sibling panel is as productive as possible:

1. *Begin early.* As soon as you decide to host a sibling panel, begin to recruit five to seven panelists, using the selection guidelines discussed below. Finding appropriate panelists who are available on the dates you select may take longer than you think. Decide upon location, time (allowing at least 90 minutes), and how you will publicize the event to parents and professionals.

2. *Publicize the event.* As noted in Chapter 10, sibling panels are wonderful learning opportunities. Publicizing the panel will ensure that this opportunity is offered to as many parents and professionals as possible. A good turnout will also ensure a rich dialogue between panel and audience.

3. *Seek balance.* Ideally, your sibling panel will be balanced with respect to

   • Disability or illness type. Unless the purpose of the panel is to discuss the concerns of siblings with a specific disability or illness, attempt to have several disabilities and/or illnesses represented.

   • Age relative to the sibling with the disability. Attempt to balance the panel by inviting brothers and sisters who are older, younger, and very close in age to their siblings with special needs. As you can easily imagine, the experiences of a brother who is 10 years older than a sibling with cerebral palsy will be very different from the experiences of a brother who is 1 year younger than a sibling with cerebral palsy.

   • Gender. Brothers and sisters often have different experiences, especially with regard to caregiving expectations and their involvement with the sibling as an adult. Seek to have equal representation of males and females on the panel.

4. *Invite primarily adult siblings.* Sibling panels benefit from the reflection provided by young adult and older adult brothers and sisters. Although school-age siblings are often more readily available than adult siblings and can comment on issues they currently face, they lack the perspective of older siblings and occasionally suffer from stage fright. If you do include young siblings, invite no more than two panelists between the ages of 8 and 15.

5. *Don't invite parents.* If possible, ask the panelists' parents not to attend the session. This will help ensure that panelists feel free to talk about their lives and their families.

Two weeks prior to the sibling panel, send each panelist a Sibling Panel Workshop Sheet (see Figure 11.1) outlining questions they may be asked during the program. This "advanced organizer" will reduce the panelists' anxiety and help them prepare their thoughts on the topic prior to the panel. In the event that they forget to bring these sheets along, make additional copies to give to the panelists before the program begins.

SIBLING PANEL WORKSHOP SHEET

Greetings!

Thank you for agreeing to be a member of our sibling panel. During the panel you will have a chance to discuss what life is like for a brother or sister of a person with special needs—the good parts, the not-so-good parts, and everything in between.

Parents, professionals, and others who have attended sibling panel discussions usually say that they left knowing a lot more about sibling issues than they did before. Panelists have usually learned a lot too.

During the panel discussion, you may be asked to share information on

- Yourself (e.g., where you live, your work or school status, your interests)
- Your brother or sister with special needs (e.g., age, work or school status, interests)
- Your family (e.g., total number of children)
- How you learned about your sibling's illness or disability and how it was explained to you
- Whether your sibling's disability or illness ever caused special problems for you (with friends, at school, at home)
- Whether your sibling's disability or illness ever resulted in unusual opportunities
- What comes to mind when you think about your and your sibling's future
- Stories or anecdotes about your sibling, your family, or yourself that you would like to share

We'll leave plenty of time for members of the audience to ask questions. This is often the most informative part of the workshop. At the very end, I may ask

- In retrospect, what do you think your parents did especially well in helping your family accept and adjust to your sibling's special needs?
- What things do you wish they had done differently?
- What advice would you give to a young brother or sister of a child with special needs? To parents?
- What message would you give to service providers who work with families of people with special needs?

Thanks for your thoughts on this important topic!

Figure 11.1. Sibling panel workshop sheet.

Hosting the Panel

To prepare, arrange chairs behind a rectangular table. If the group is large, arrange for tabletop microphones. Make sure that extra copies of the Sibling Panel Workshop Sheet and water are available. Have a box of tissues nearby but out of sight.

First, welcome the panelists and the audience and read Sibshops Goal 5 aloud:

 Goal 5: Sibshops will provide parents and other professionals with an opportunity to learn about the unique joys, concerns, and issues experienced by brothers and sisters of people with special needs.

If time permits and the audience is small, ask audience members to introduce themselves briefly and say what brought them to a sibling panel. Following introductions, let the audience know that they will have an opportunity to ask panel members questions, seek advice from them, and share family experiences.

Then ask the panelists to introduce themselves and share with the audience information suggested in the first item of the workshop sheet. You may then ask them to respond to subsequent items on the workshop sheet. After asking the panel a few introductory questions, be sure to offer the audience a chance to ask additional questions or make comments. Questions and discussion among parents and panel members will be the most valuable portion of the workshop, so be sure to allow ample time for this. As parents' concerns surface, you may wish to encourage panel members and other parents to share how their families handled a similar situation.

Conclude the program by selecting closing questions from the workshop sheet. (What do you think your parents did especially well? What do you wish they had done differently? What advice would you give to a young brother or sister of a child with special needs? To parents? What message would you give to service providers who work with families of people with special needs?)

At the very end, be sure to thank the panel members. The questions posed for the panel members will yield valuable insights. Questions also will require panelists to examine and comment on a lifetime of experiences with their siblings, families, and friends that were sometimes happy, sometimes sad, and frequently challenging—no easy task.

A WORKSHOP ON SIBLING ISSUES

During this $1\frac{1}{2}$ to 2-hour workshop, parent and service provider participants work together to define and discuss sibling concerns, opportunities, and strategies. Discussions are based on participants' observations and experiences. Rather than using an imported "expert" on sibling issues, this workshop utilizes the group's collective expertise.

At the beginning of the workshop, ask the participants to introduce themselves briefly and (if appropriate) their families and share with the group what brings them to a workshop on sibling issues. Following introductions, acknowledge that for siblings, as for their parents, having a family member with a disability is usually an ambivalent experience. As do their parents, siblings may have unique concerns (e.g., need for information about the disability, guilt, resentment) but they may also have unique opportunities (e.g., increased empathy, a special pride, a singular sense of humor).

Suggest to the participants that they, as parents and providers who work with families, are as capable as anyone of defining the concerns and opportunities that their typically developing children experience. In short, the collective expertise and wisdom of the group is considerable. Tell them that by sharing and discussing their insights with the rest of the group, everyone can leave with an expanded understanding of the sibling experience.

Prior to the meeting, prepare a four-sided worksheet (two pages, printed front to back, stapled), such as the one shown in Figure 11.2. Distribute the pages to the participants and provide pens or pencils. Ask each participant to pair off with another participant (and introduce themselves if they have not met) and take 10 minutes to discuss page 1. At the end of this time, ask a representative from each pair to share

Sibshop Issue Worksheet

**PAGE 1
(one full page):**

BROTHERS AND
SISTERS OF
CHILDREN WITH
SPECIAL NEEDS

UNUSUAL
CONCERNS

The goal of this workshop is to define and discuss the unusual opportunities and concerns experienced by brothers and sisters. By sharing your observations and experiences, you can help all workshop participants gain a broader understanding of the joys, concerns, and challenges that are a part of being a sibling of a child with special needs.

With your partner, please take a few minutes to discuss any concerns that you feel brothers and sisters of children with special needs may experience. Please briefly note the concerns you discuss below:

**PAGE 2
(one full page):**

STRATEGIES:
CONCERNS

Next, please discuss with your partner ways that parents and other professionals can minimize the concerns of siblings of children with special needs. Please briefly list your strategies below:

**PAGE 3
(one full page):**

UNUSUAL
OPPORTUNITIES

Please discuss benefits or unusual opportunities that brothers and sisters may experience as a result of growing up with a sibling who has special needs. Please briefly note these benefits or opportunities below:

**PAGE 4
(one full page):**

STRATEGIES:
OPPORTUNITIES

Finally, please discuss how we as parents and service providers can maximize opportunities experienced by brothers and sisters of children with special needs. Please note these strategies below:

Figure 11.2. Sibling issues worksheet (prepared as a four-sided worksheet, two sheets of paper printed front to back, and stapled).

with the larger group the concerns they have observed or identified. Record the general headings on a chalkboard or, preferably, large sheets of paper.

Next, ask each participant to pair off with a different partner and discuss page 2, strategies to decrease concerns. After 10 minutes, have the participants report back to the group. Continue with pages 3 and 4. By the end of the session, the participants will have generated a wide range of issues and have had an opportunity to discuss these issues individually with four different participants, as well as with the larger group.

Let the participants know that you (or a participant volunteer) will transcribe the concerns, opportunities, and strategies from the sheets or chalkboard and send each participant a copy.

INFORMAL DISCUSSIONS FOR PARENTS OF SIBSHOP PARTICIPANTS

If you hold your Sibshops as a series of meetings, we suggest that you plan one meeting with a concurrent gathering for parents of participants. This meeting for parents, ideally held midway through the series, need not be as long as the Sibshop itself—usually 2 hours will suffice. During the meeting, you may wish to utilize the workshop formats described above, or simply have an open-ended discussion with the participants' parents. To begin, ask parents to introduce themselves, describe their families, and share their reasons for enrolling their children in a Sibshop. This will usually be enough to initiate a lively discussion. Your job is to facilitate conversation and to listen.

This discussion is also an excellent opportunity to seek parents' feedback on the Sibshop. Ask parents what comments their children have made about the program and what suggestions they have to make it better. It is also a good time to discuss the direction of the program and to seek parents' counsel on how to make Sibshops as responsive and available to families as possible.

This is not, however, a time to share with parents the details of their children's conversations during your Sibshops. Despite some parents' desire to know what their children are saying, the information and opinions shared during Sibshops should be treated as confidential. There is an important exception: If a participant shares information that in your best judgment parents need to know, it is your responsibility to meet privately with the participant, share your concerns, and discuss strategies for telling his or her parents. Sometimes participants will elect to tell their parents themselves; other times they will appreciate your offer to talk to the parents; and still other times they will want your company as you both discuss your concern with the parents.

OTHER RESOURCES FOR PARENTS AND SERVICE PROVIDERS

Not all parents will be able to (or wish to) attend workshops. Many parents will prefer to learn about sibling issues through written materials or other media. The following are publications you may wish to recommend and have in your library to refer to parents:

- *Being the Other One: Growing Up with a Brother or Sister Who Has Special Needs* by Kate Strohm (2002)

- *Brothers & Sisters: A Special Part of Exceptional Families* (paperback) by Peggy Gallagher, Thomas H. Powell, and Cheryl Rhodes (2006)

- *Living with a Brother or Sister with Special Needs: A Book for Sibs* by Donald J. Meyer and Patricia F. Vadasy (1996)

- *Riding the Bus with My Sister: A True Life Journey* by Rachel Simon (2003)

- *Special Siblings: Growing Up with Someone with a Disability* by Mary McHugh (2002)

- *The Ride Together: A Brother and Sister's Memoir of Autism in the Family* by Judy Karasik and Paul Karasik (2004)

- *The Sibling Slam Book: What It's Really Like to Have A Brother Or Sister with Special Needs* by Donald J. Meyer (Editor) (2005)

- *Views from Our Shoes: Growing Up with a Brother or Sister with Special Needs* by Donald J. Meyer (Editor) and Cary Pillo (Illustrator) (1997)

- *Without Apology,* a documentary film by Susan Hamovitch (2005)

References

Abramovitch, R., Stanhope, L., Pepler, D., & Carter, C. (1987). The influence of Down's syndrome on sibling interaction. *Journal of Child Psychology and Psychiatry, 28*(6), 865–879.

Antonovsky, A. (1993). The implications of salutogenesis: An outsider's view. In A.P. Turnbull, J.M. Patterson, S.K. Behr, D.L. Murphy, J.G. Marquis, & M.J. Blue-Banning (Eds.), *Cognitive coping, families, & disability* (pp. 111–122). Baltimore: Paul H. Brookes Publishing Co.

Bank, S.P., & Kahn, M.D. (1982). *The sibling bond.* New York: Basic Books.

Bendor, S.J. (1990). Anxiety and isolation in siblings of pediatric cancer patients: The need for prevention. *Social Work in Health Care, 14,* 17–35.

Binkard, B., Goldberg, M., & Goldberg, R.E. (Eds.). (1987). *Brothers and sisters talk with PACER.* Minneapolis, MN: PACER Center.

Brodzinsky, D.M., Schechter, D., & Brodzinsky, A.B. (1986). Children's knowledge of adoption: Developmental changes and implications for adjustment. In R.D. Ashmore & D.M. Brodzinsky (Eds.), *Thinking about the family: Views of parents and children* (pp. 205–232). Hillsdale, NJ: Lawrence Erlbaum Associates.

Burslem, A. (1991). Never a dull moment! *Mencap News: The Journal of the Society for Mentally Handicapped Children and Adults, 19*(11), 12–13.

Cairns, N., Clark, G., Smith, S., & Lansky, S. (1979). Malignancy. *Journal of Pediatrics, 95*(3), 484–487.

Callahan, C.R. (1990). *Since Owen.* Baltimore: The Johns Hopkins University Press.

Cleveland, D.W., & Miller, N. (1977). Attitudes and life commitments of older siblings of mentally retarded adults: An exploratory study. *Mental Retardation, 15*(3), 38–41.

Cobb, M. (1991). A senior essay. *Outlook, the newsletter of the Down Syndrome Association of Charlotte, NC, 5*(6) 6, 3.

Coleman, S.V. (1990). The sibling of the retarded child: Self-concept, deficit compensation motivation, and perceived parental behavior (Doctoral dissertation, California School of Professional Psychology, San Diego, 1990). *Dissertation Abstracts International, 51*(10-B), 5023. (University Microfilms No. 01147421-AAD9I-07868).

Collins, K. (Producer), & Emmerling, D.P. (Director). (1991). *The rest of the family* [Videotape]. Landover, MD: Epilepsy Foundation of America.

Cramer, S., Erzkus, A., Mayweather, K., Pope, K., Roeder, J., & Tone, T. (1997). Connecting with siblings. *Teaching Exceptional Children,* Sept/Oct., 46–51.

Cuskelly, M., Chant, D., & Hayes, A. (1998). Behaviour problems in the siblings of children with Down syndrome: Associations with family responsibilities and parental stress. *International Journal of Disability, Development and Education, 45,* 195–311.

de Vinck, C. (1985, April 10). Power of the powerless. *The Wall Street Journal,* p. 28.

de Vinck, C. (2002). Power of the powerless: *A brother's legacy of love.* Grand Rapids, MI: Zondervan Publishing House.

Devencenzi, J., & Pendergast, S. (1988). *Belonging.* San Luis Obispo, CA: Belonging Publishing Co.

Dickens, R. (1991). *Notes for siblings/adult children.* (Available from National Alliance for the Mentally Ill, 2101 Wilson Blvd. Suite 302, Arlington, VA 22201).

Dieden, Bob. (1995). *Games to keep kids moving.* New York: Parker Publishing Company.

Doherty, J. (1992). A sibling remembers. *Candlelighters Childhood Cancer Foundation Newsletter, 16*(2), 4–6.

Drotar, D., & Crawford, P. (1985). Psychological adaptation of siblings of chronically ill children: Research and practice implications. *Developmental and Behavioral Pediatrics, 6,* 355–362.

Dudish, M.P. (1991). My sister Ellen. . ., my daughter Tara. *Sibling Information Network Newsletter, 7*(3), 1–3.

Duvall, E.M. (1962). *Family development.* Philadelphia: J.B. Lippincott.

Dyson, L.L. (1989). Adjustment of siblings of handicapped children: A comparison. *Journal of Pediatric Psychology, 14*(2), 215–229.

Dyson, L.L. (1996). The experiences of families of children with learning disabilities: Parental stress, family functioning, and sibling self-concept. *Journal of Learning Disabilities, 29,* 280–286.

Dyson, L.L., & Fewell, R. (1989). The self-concept of siblings of handicapped children: A comparison. *Journal of Early Intervention, 13*(3), 230–238.

Eisenberg, L., Baker, B.L., & Blacher, J. (1998). Siblings of children with mental retardation living at home or in residential placement. *Journal of Child Psychology and Psychiatry, 39,* 355–363.

Ellis, A. (1992). *Siblings: The "forgotten child" in childhood cancer.* Unpublished manuscript.

Emberly, E. (1977). *Ed Emberly's great thumbprint drawing book.* Boston: Little, Brown.

Emberly, E. (2001). *Ed Emberly's fingerprint drawing book.* New York: Little, Brown Young.

Faber, A., & Mazlish, E. (1999). *How to talk so kids will listen and listen so kids will talk.* New York: Collins.

Farber, B. (1960). Family organization and crisis: Maintenance of integration in families with a severely mentally retarded child. *Monographs of the Society for Research in Child Development, 25*(1, Serial No. 75).

Faux, S.A. (1985). Parental child-rearing practices as perceived by the siblings and mothers of chronically impaired children. In K. King, E. Prodrick, & B. Bauer, (Eds.), *Proceeding: 10th National Research Conference: Nursing Research, Science for Quality Care* (pp. 308–314). Toronto, Canada: University of Toronto Press.

Faux, S.A. (1991). Sibling relationships in families of congenitally impaired children. *Journal of Pediatric Nursing, 6,* 175, 184.

Faux, S.A. (1993). Siblings of children with chronic physical and cognitive disabilities. *Journal of Pediatric Nursing, 8,* 305–317.

Featherstone, H. (1980). *A difference in the family: Life with a disabled child.* New York: Basic Books.

Ferrari, M. (1984). Chronic illness: Psychosocial effects on siblings. 1: Chronically ill boys. *Journal of Child Psychology and Psychiatry, 25,* 459–476.

Feshbach, N., Feshbach, S., Fauvre, M., & Ballard-Campbell, M. (1983). *Learning to care.* Glenview, IL: Scott, Foresman.

Fink, L. (1984, November 6). Looking at the role played by siblings of the retarded. *Newsday,* pp. 6–9.

Fish, T. (Producer). (1993). *The next step* [Videotape]. (Available from Publications Office, Nisonger Center UAP, 434 McCampbell Hall, The Ohio State University, 1581 Dodd Dr., Columbus, OH, 43210.)

Fish, T., & Fitzgerald, G.M. (1980, November). *A transdisciplinary approach to working with adolescent siblings of the mentally retarded: A group experience.* Paper presented to Social Work with Groups Symposium, Arlington, TX. (Available from T. Fish, The Nisonger Center, The Ohio State University, 1580 Canon Drive, Columbus, OH, 43210.)

Flugelman, A. (Ed.). (1976). *The new games book.* Garden City, NY: Doubleday.

Flugelman, A. (Ed.). (1981). *More new games!* Garden City, NY: Doubleday.

Fowle, C. (1973). The effect of a severely mentally retarded child on his family. *American Journal of Mental Deficiency, 73,* 468–473.

Gamble, W.C., & McHale, S.M. (1989). Coping with stress in sibling relationships: A comparison of children with disabled and nondisabled siblings. *Journal of Applied Developmental Psychology, 10,* 353–373.

Gath, A. (1974). Sibling reactions to mental handicap: A comparison of the brothers and sisters of mongol children. *Journal of Child Psychology and Psychiatry, 15,* 187–198.

Gerdel, P. (1986). Who are these researchers and why are they saying such terrible things about me? In M. Hanson & A. Turnbull (Eds.), *The family support network series.* University of Idaho: Research in Family Involvement Practices Monographs, No. 3.

Glasberg, B.A. (2000). The development of siblings' understanding of autism spectrum disorders. *Journal of Autism and Developmental Disorders, 30,* 143–156.

Gorelick, J. (1996, July 8–13). *A strong sibling network: Forgotten children no more.* Presentation to the 10th World Congress of the International Association for the Scientific Studies of Intellectual Disabilities, Helsinki, Finland.

Gregson, B. (1982). *The incredible indoor games book.* Belmont, CA: Fearon Teacher Aids.

Gregson, B. (1984). *The outrageous outdoor games book.* Belmont, CA: Fearon Teacher Aids.

Grossman, F. (1972). *Brothers and sisters of retarded children: An exploratory study.* Syracuse, NY: Syracuse University Press.

Gruszka, M.A. (1988). *Family functioning and sibling adjustment in families with a handicapped child.* Unpublished doctoral dissertation. Kingston: University of Rhode Island.

Hannah, M.E., & Midlarsky, E. (1999). Competence and adjustment of siblings of children with mental retardation. *American Journal on Mental Retardation, 104,* 22–37.

Hanson, M. (1985). *Straight from the heart.* (Available from the Saskatchewan Association for the Mentally Retarded, 331 Louise St., Saskatoon, Saskatchewan, S7J 3L1 Canada.)

Harkleroad, D. (1992). Growing up with Raymond. *Parents and Friends Together for People with Deaf-Blindness News, 1*(5), 5.

Harland, P., & Cuskelly, M. (2000). The responsibilities of adult siblings of adults with dual sensory impairments. *International Journal of Disability, Development, and Education, 47*(3), 295–307.

Harvey, D.H.P., & Greenway, A.P. (1984). The self-concept of physically handicapped children and their nonhandicapped siblings: An empirical investigation. *Journal of Child Psychology and Psychiatry, 25,* 273–284.

Helsel, E., Helsel, B., Helsel, B., & Helsel, M. (1978). The Helsels' story of Robin. In A.P. Turnbull & H.R. Turnbull (Eds.), *Parents speak out: Views from the other side of the two way mirror* (pp. 99–114). Columbus, OH: Charles E. Merrill.

Herndon, L. (1992, November 15). A special brother. *Seattle Times,* p. 2.

Iles, P. (1979). Children with cancer: Healthy siblings' perceptions during the illness experience. *Cancer Nursing, 2,* 371–377.

Itzkowitz, J. (1990). Siblings' perceptions of their needs for programs, services, and support: A national study. *Sibling Information Network Newsletter, 7*(1), 1–4.

"Jennifer." (1990). Mailbag: A column for siblings to speak out. *Sibpage: A Newsletter for and by Brothers and Sisters of Children with Special Needs, 2*(4), 2.

Johnson, A.B. (2005). *Sibshops: A follow-up of participants of a sibling support program.* Unpublished master's thesis. University of Washington, Seattle.

Johnson, A.B., & Sandall, S. *Sibshops: A follow-up of participants of a sibling support program.* Manuscript in preparation.

Kazak, A.E., & Clarke, M.W. (1986). Stress in families with myelomeningocele. *Developmental Medicine and Child Neurology, 28,* 220–228.

Koch-Hattem, A. (1986). Siblings' experience of pediatric cancer: Interviews with children. *Health and Social Work, 10,* 107–117.

Konczal, D., & Petetski, L. (1983). *We all come in different packages: Activities to increase handicap awareness.* Santa Barbara, CA: The Learning Works.

Konstam, V., Drainoni, M., Mitchell, G., Houser, R., Reddington, D., & Eaton, D. (1993). Career choices and values of siblings of individuals with developmental disabilities. *The School Counselor, 40,* 287–292.

Koocher, G.P., & O'Malley, J.E. (1981). *The Damocles syndrome: Psychological consequences of surviving childhood cancer.* New York: McGraw-Hill.

Krauss, M., Seltzer, M., Gordon, R., & Friedman, D. (1996). Binding ties: The role of adult siblings of persons with mental retardation. *Mental Retardation, 34*(2), 83–92.

Landy, L. (1988). *Child support through small group counseling.* Mount Dora, FL: KIDSRIGHTS.

Leder, J.M. (1991). *Brothers and sisters: How they shape our lives.* New York: St. Martin's Press.

Leonard, B. (1992). Siblings of children with chronically ill children: A question of vulnerability versus resilience. *Pediatric Annals, 20*(9), 501–506.

Liska, V.D. (1996, July 8–13). *The Siblings: A lifelong journal of care.* Presentation to the 10th World Congress of the International Association for the Scientific Studies of Intellectual Disabilities, Helsinki, Finland.

Lobato, D.J. (1990). *Brothers, sisters, and special needs: Information and activities for helping young siblings of children with chronic illnesses and developmental disabilities.* Baltimore: Paul H. Brookes Publishing Co.

Lobato, D., Barbour, L., Hall, L.J., & Miller, C.T. (1987). Psychosocial characteristics of preschool siblings of handicapped and nonhandicapped children. *Journal of Abnormal Child Psychology, 15,* 329–338.

Lynn, M.R. (1989). Siblings' responses in illness situations. *Journal of Pediatric Nursing, 4,* 127–129.

McConachie, H. (1982). Fathers of mentally handicapped children. In N. Beal & J. McGuire (Eds.), *Fathers: Psychological perspectives* (pp. 144–173). London: Junction.

McCullough, M.E. (1981). Parent and sibling definitions of situations regarding transgenerational shift in the care of a handicapped child (Doctoral dissertation, University of Minnesota, 1981). *Dissertation Abstracts International, 42*(1-B), 161. (University Microfilms No. 8115012)

McHale, S.M., Sloan, J.L., & Simeonsson, R.J. (1986). Sibling relationships of children with autistic, mentally retarded, and nonhandicapped brothers and sisters. *Journal of Autism and Developmental Disorders, 16,* 399–413.

McKeever, P. (1983). Siblings of chronically ill children: A literature review with implications for research and practice. *American Journal of Orthopsychiatry, 53*(2), 209–218.

Meyer, D.J. (1986). Fathers of handicapped children. In R. Fewell & P. Vadasy (Eds.), *Families of handicapped children* (pp. 35–73). Austin, TX: PRO-ED.

Meyer, D.J., (Ed.) (2005). *The sibling slam book: What it's really like to have a brother or sister with special needs.* Bethesda, MD: Woodbine House.

Meyer, D.J., & Erickson, E.L. (1992). [*Survey of Seattle-area adult siblings of people with disabilities*]. Unpublished raw data.

Meyer, D.J., & Erickson, E.L. (1993, Winter, p. 6). *The National Association of Sibling Programs Newsletter.*

Meyer, D.J., & Vadasy, P.F., (1996). *Living with a brother or sister with special needs: A book for sibs.* Seattle: University of Washington Press.

Meyer, D.J., Vadasy, P.F., Fewell, R.R., & Schell, G. (1985). *The Fathers program: How to organize a program for fathers and their handicapped children.* Seattle: University of Washington Press.

Miller, S.G. (1974). An exploratory study of sibling relationships in families with retarded children (Doctoral dissertation, Columbia University, 1974). *Dissertation Abstracts International, 35*(6-B), 2994–2995. (University Microfilms No. 74-26m 606)

Morrow, J. (1992). Terry Cunningham: A brother who sticks up for his siblings. *Parents and Friends Together for People with Deaf-Blindness News, 1*(5), 2.

Moses, K. (1982). Brothers and sisters of special children. *Interactions* (pp. 20–25). Madison, WI: Harry A. Waisman Center on Mental Retardation.

Murphy, A.T. (1979). Members of the family: Sisters and brothers of handicapped children. *Volta Review, 81*(5), 352–362.

Murphy, A.T (1981). *Special children, special parents.* Englewood Cliffs, NJ: Prentice-Hall.

Murray, G., & Jampolsky, G.G. (Eds.). (1982). *Straight from the siblings: Another look at the rainbow.* Berkeley, CA: Celestial Arts.

Nester, J. (1989, March). Adult sibling panel notes. *Down Syndrome Association of New Jersey, Inc.* [newsletter], p. 4.

1988 award winning summer programs. (1989, March). *Exceptional Parent,* 16–26.

Orsmond, G.I., & Seltzer, M.M. (2000). Brothers and sisters of adults with mental retardation: The gendered nature of the sibling relationship. *American Journal of Mental Retardation, 105,* 486–508.

Parfit, J. (1975). Siblings of handicapped children. *Special Education: Forward Trends, 2*(1), 19–21.

Piers, E. (1984). *The Piers Harris Children's Self-Concept*

Scale (Rev. ed.). Los Angeles: Western Psychological Services.

Podeanu-Czehotsky, I. (1975). Is it only the child's guilt? Some aspects of family life of cerebral palsied children. *Rehabilitation Literature, 36*, 308–311.

Powell, T.H., & Gallagher, P.A. (1993). *Brothers & sisters: A special part of exceptional families* (2nd ed.). Baltimore: Paul H. Brookes Publishing Co.

Pruchno, R.A., Patrick, J.H., & Burant, C.J. (1996). Aging mothers and their children with chronic disabilities: Perception of sibling involvement and effects on well-being. *Family Relations, 45*, 318–326.

Remsberg, B. (1989). *What it means to have a handicapped brother or sister.* Unpublished manuscript.

Rinehart, J. (1992, May). My sister's hand. *Children's Health Issues, 1*(1), 10–11.

Royal, D. (1991). *The other child.* Unpublished manuscript.

Schild, S. (1976). Counseling with parents of retarded children living at home. In F.J. Turner (Ed.), *Differential diagnosis and treatment in social work* (2nd ed., pp. 476–482). New York: Free Press.

Schorr-Ribera, H. (1992). Caring for siblings during diagnosis and treatment. *Candlelighters Childhood Cancer Foundation Newsletter, 16*(2), 1–3.

Seligman, M. (1979). *Strategies for helping parents of exceptional children.* New York: Free Press.

Seligman, M. (1983). Sources of psychological disturbance among siblings of handicapped children. *Personnel and Guidance Journal, 67*, 529–531.

Seligman, M. (1991). Siblings of disabled brothers and sisters. In M. Seligman (Ed.), *The family with a handicapped child* (2nd ed., pp. 181–198). Boston: Allyn & Bacon.

Seltzer, G.B., Begun, A., Seltzer, M., & Krauss, M.W. (1991). Adults with mental retardation and their aging mothers: Impact on siblings. *Family Relations, 40*(3), 3310–3317.

Seltzer, M.M., Greenberg, J.S., Krauss, M.W., Gordon, R.M., & Judge, K. (1997). Siblings of adults with mental retardation or mental illness: Effects on lifestyle and psychological well-being. *Family Relations, 46*(4), 395–405.

Seltzer, M.M., & Krauss, M.W. (2002). *Adolescents and adults with autism: Reflections from adult siblings who have a brother or sister with an autism spectrum disorder.* Retrieved July 15, 2003, from http://www.uic.edu/orgs/rrtcamr/autismreport3.htm

Shanley, S. (1991). My brother Peter. *Sibling Information Network Newsletter, 7*(4),1–2.

Simeonsson, R.J., & McHale, S.M. (1981). Review: Research on handicapped children: Sibling relationships. *Child: Care, Health and Development, 7*, 153–171.

Skrtic, T., Summers, J.A., Brotherson, M.J., & Turnbull, A., (1983). Severely handicapped children and their brothers and sisters. In J. Blacher (Ed.), *Severely handicapped young children and their families: Research in review* (pp. 215–246). New York: Academic Press.

Sloper, P., & White, D. (1996). Risk factors in the adjustment of siblings of children with cancer. *Journal of Child Psychology and Psychiatry, 37*, 597–607.

Sourkes, B. (1990). Siblings count too. *Candlelighters Childhood Cancer Foundation Newsletter, 12*(3), 2, 6.

Sourkes, B.M. (1980). Siblings of the pediatric cancer patient. In J. Kellerman (Ed.), *Psychological aspects of childhood cancer* (pp. 47–69). Springfield, IL: Charles C. Thomas.

Spinetta, J. (1981). The sibling of the child with cancer. In J. Spinetta & P. Deasy-Spinetta (Eds.), *Living with childhood cancer* (pp. 133–142). St. Louis: C.V. Mosby.

Stoneman, Z., & Brody, G.H. (1993). Sibling relations in the family context. In Z. Stoneman & P.W. Berman (Eds.), *The effects of mental retardation, disability, and illness on sibling relationships* (pp. 3–30). Baltimore: Paul H. Brookes Publishing Co.

Stoneman, Z., Brody, G.H., Davis, C.H., & Crapps, J.M. (1987). Mentally retarded children and their older same-sex siblings: Naturalistic in-home observations. *American Journal on Mental Retardation, 92*, 290–298.

Stoneman, Z., Brody, G.H., Davis, C.H., & Crapps, J.M. (1988). Child care responsibilities, peer relations, and sibling conflict: Older siblings of mentally retarded children. *American Journal on Mental Retardation, 93*, 174–183.

Stoneman, Z., Brody, G.H., Davis, C.H., & Crapps, J.M. (1989). Role relations between mentally retarded children and their older siblings: Observations in three in-home contexts. *Research in Developmental Disabilities, 10*, 61–76.

Stoneman, Z., Brody, G.H., Davis, C.H., Crapps, J.M., & Malone, D.M. (1991). Ascribed role relations between children with mental retardation and their younger siblings. *American Journal on Mental Retardation, 95*, 527–536.

Summers, A. (2004, Winter). Siblings. *Connections: A Newsletter for Fathers and Families of Children with Special Needs, 8*(2), 7–8.

Thibodeau, S.M. (1988). Sibling response to chronic illness: The role of the clinical nurse specialist. *Issues in Comprehensive Pediatric Nursing, 11*, 17–28.

Torrey, E.F. (1992, July). Sibling issues. *Siblings of People with Mental Illness.* Conference sponsored by Washington Alliance for the Mentally Ill, Seattle.

Tritt, S., & Esses, L. (1988). Psychosocial adaptation of siblings of children with chronic medical illnesses. *American Journal of Orthopsychiatry, 58*(2), 211–220.

Turnbull, A.P., & Turnbull, H.R. (1993). Participatory research on cognitive coping: From concepts to research planning. In A.R. Turnbull, J.M. Patterson, S.K. Behr, D.L. Murphy, J.G. Marquis, & M.J. Blue-Banning (Eds.), *Cognitive coping, families, & disability* (pp. 1–14). Baltimore: Paul H. Brookes Publishing Co.

Unruh, S. (1992). Serena. *Parents and Friends Together for People with Deaf-Blindness News, 1*(5), 1.

Usdane, S., & Melmed, R. (1988). *Facilitator's manual, Siblings exchange program.* Phoenix, AZ: Phoenix Children's Hospital.

Watson, J. (1991). The Queen. *Down Syndrome News, 15*(8), 108.

Westra, M. (1992). An open letter to my parents. *Sibling Information Network Newsletter, 8*(1), 4.

Wikler, L. (1981). Chronic stresses of families of mentally retarded children. *Family Relations, 30,* 281–288.

Williams, P.D. (1997). Siblings and pediatric chronic illness: A review of the literature. *International Journal of Nursing Studies, 34,* 312–323.

Ylven, R., Bjorck-Akesson, E., & Grandlund, M. (2006, December). Functioning in Families with Children with a Disability. *Journal of Policy and Practice in Intellectual Disabilities, 3*(4), 253–270.

Zatlow, G. (1981, Winter). A sister's lament. *Our Home Newsletter and Annual Report, 5,* 1–2.

Zatlow, G. (Producer). (1987). *The other children—Brothers and sisters of the developmentally disabled* (Videotape). (Available from Special Citizens' Futures Unlimited, Inc., United Charities Building, 105 East 22nd Street, New York, NY 10010.)

Zatlow, G. (1992, Fall). Just a sister. *Momentum,* pp. 13–16.

Appendix A

The Sibshop Standards of Practice

A simple web search for "Sibshop" or even "Sib Shops" results in literally thousands of hits. In addition to the wonderful community-based Sibshops[SM] that are being run in almost every state and in countries from Japan to Ireland, Sibshops are increasingly being offered as part of state and national conferences and as an adjunct to parent support groups throughout the United States and elsewhere.

Although I am truly pleased that there is such interest in the model, we need to protect young sibs by making sure that when parents send their children to a Sibshop, they are sending them to a program that is true to the spirit and goals of the model.

To this end, I have worked with long-time Sibshop facilitators in drafting Standards of Practice for programs wishing to become registered Sibshops and to use the service marked and trademarked Sibshop name, a "sound-alike" name (e.g., "Sib Shop"), or the Sibshop logo. I am grateful to the members of the Sibshop Standards of Practice Committee for helping me with this important project.

Please make copies of the Standards of Practice for each adult facilitator of your Sibshop program and extra copies for any staff members who may join your program. Please also review the Standards with the other Sibshop facilitators and administrators. Then register your Sibshop online as discussed at the end of this document. If you have questions along the way, please do not hesitate to write or call.

Thank you, in advance, for taking the time to work through this document, and thanks for understanding the need for high standards in our efforts to provide brothers and sisters with peer support and information.

One final note: As a Sibshop facilitator or administrator, you likely offer Sibshops in addition to your other responsibilities. Still, you and your colleagues find time in your busy schedules and lives because you care deeply about brothers and sisters and their concerns. Local providers like you—who are making a difference in the

---

Sibshop and Sibshops are service marks and trademarks owned by Donald J. Meyer on behalf of the Sibling Support Project.

lives of sibs on a daily basis—are my heroes. I can't thank you enough for what you are doing for the brothers and sisters in your community. Please let me know how I can support your important work.

All the best,

Don Meyer
Sibling Support Project
6512 23rd Avenue NW
#213
Seattle, WA 98117
206-297-6368
donmeyer@siblingsupport.org

Sibling Support Project
www.siblingsupport.org

Sibshop and Sibshops are service marks and trademarks owned by Donald J. Meyer on behalf of the Sibling Support Project.

Sibshop Standards of Practice

1. What Sibshops Are—and Are Not

On the very first page of *Sibshops: Workshops for Siblings of Children with Special Needs, Revised Edition (Sibshops)*, Sibshops are described this way:

> For the adults who plan them and the agencies that sponsor them, Sibshops are best described as opportunities for brothers and sisters of children with special health, mental health, and developmental needs to obtain peer support and education within a recreational context. They often reflect an agency's commitment to the well-being of the family member most likely to have the longest-lasting relationship with the person with special needs.
>
> For the young people who attend them and the energetic people who run them, however, Sibshops are best described as *events*. Sibshops are lively, pedal-to-the-metal celebrations of the many contributions made by brothers and sisters of kids with special needs. Sibshops acknowledge that being the brother or sister of a person with special needs is for some a good thing, for others a not-so-good thing, and for many something in between. They reflect a belief that brothers and sisters have much to offer one another—if they are given a chance. The Sibshop model intersperses information and discussion activities with new games (designed to be unique, offbeat, and appealing to a wide ability range), cooking and art activities, and special guests. Well run, Sibshops are as fun and rewarding for the people who host them as they are for the participants.
>
> Sibshops seek to provide siblings with opportunities for peer support. Because Sibshops are designed for school-age children, peer support is provided within a lively, recreational context that emphasizes a kids'-eye view.
>
> Sibshops are *not* therapy, group or otherwise, although their effect may be therapeutic for some children. Sibshops acknowledge that most brothers and sisters of people with special needs, like their parents, are doing well, despite the challenges of an illness or disability. Consequently, although Sibshop facilitators always keep an eye open for participants who may need additional services, the Sibshop model takes a wellness approach.

Sibshops should never be confused with child care. Sometimes agencies wish to offer Sibshops concurrently with parent support meetings. Although this "two-ring" approach is acceptable, agencies will need to add a "third ring": child care for the children who have special needs *and* for the typically developing siblings who are either not in the target age range or simply do not wish to be a part of your Sibshop.

Sibshops, therefore,

- Should be decidedly fun to attend
- Should provide peer support and information within a recreational context
- May be therapeutic to attend but are not therapy—group or otherwise
- Should utilize an approach that emphasizes wellness
- Should never be considered child care

2. Endorsing the Goals of Sibshops

As described on pages 3 and 4 of *Sibshops*, the following are Sibshop goals:

Goal 1: Sibshops will provide brothers and sisters of children with special needs an opportunity to meet other siblings in a relaxed, recreational setting.

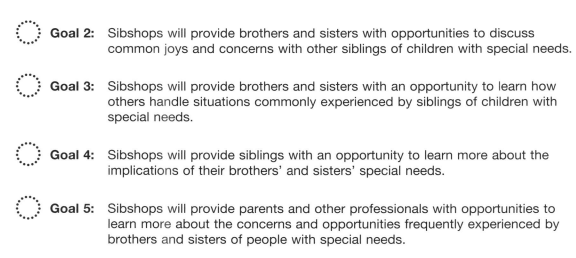

Goal 2: Sibshops will provide brothers and sisters with opportunities to discuss common joys and concerns with other siblings of children with special needs.

Goal 3: Sibshops will provide brothers and sisters with an opportunity to learn how others handle situations commonly experienced by siblings of children with special needs.

Goal 4: Sibshops will provide siblings with an opportunity to learn more about the implications of their brothers' and sisters' special needs.

Goal 5: Sibshops will provide parents and other professionals with opportunities to learn more about the concerns and opportunities frequently experienced by brothers and sisters of people with special needs.

These goals will drive the activities of your Sibshop. Although most Sibshops do an excellent job with Goals 1–3, Goals 4 and 5 are sometimes overlooked—but shouldn't be.

Brothers and sisters will have a lifelong and ever-changing need for information about their sibs' disabilities and the services they receive. As a peer support *and* education model, Sibshops are a marvelous opportunity to provide participants with kid-friendly information about a wide range of topics, from guest speakers to tours and discussions.

If we hope that parents will attend to the needs of their typically developing children, we will need to inform them of sibs' lifelong concerns. If we wish to create systemic change ensuring that sibs are on agencies' radar screens and in their working definition of "family," it will require that we educate our colleagues and advocate for sibs' concerns.

3.   Referring Children When Sibshops Are Not the Right Approach

Most, but not all, siblings of children with special needs will be well served by Sibshops' lively mix of fun, peer support, and information. For some children, however, Sibshops may not be the right approach. These children may not be comfortable in groups or they may prefer to get peer support and information in other ways (e.g., listservs, books, informal opportunities). Other children will have needs that go beyond what a Sibshop can reasonably provide. As mentioned in the above description of Sibshops, facilitators should keep an eye open for participants who may need additional services. Your Sibshop team of facilitators and appropriate administrators should know—in advance of a problematic situation—people and agencies in your community who might be able to help a child (and family) not being well served by your Sibshop effort.

4.   Reporting Worrisome Information and Behavior to Parents and Appropriate Agencies

To the extent possible, Sibshops attempt to give participants a safe place where they can openly discuss the good and not-so-good aspects of life with a sibling who has special needs. To ensure that they can speak freely, facilitators, as a rule, will not specifically divulge to parents what participants discuss during a Sibshop. (Facilitators,

---

Sibshop and Sibshops are service marks and trademarks owned by Donald J. Meyer on behalf of the Sibling Support Project.

however, are encouraged to discuss the *general* topics that participants discussed during parent meetings.)

On rare occasions, however, children may reveal information that will need to be shared with parents or, in extreme cases, with appropriate agencies. Before such contact is made with either parents or agencies, the concern should be discussed with the entire Sibshop team. Your Sibshop's team should be aware—in advance of a problem—of your state's rules regarding mandated reporting.

5. Making Sibshops Available for Families Who Cannot Afford to Pay

It is reasonable to ask parents to pay a fee for their children to attend a Sibshop. Most Sibshops cost far less than child care would for the same amount of time. Fees can help offset costs associated with running a Sibshop. Perhaps most important, fees help ensure that parents bring their children to the Sibshop that facilitators have worked so hard to make rewarding.

A significant effort should be made, however, to ensure that Sibshops are available to families who cannot afford the set fee. On the registration forms of many Sibshops is a statement similar to the following: "A limited number of Sibshop scholarships are available on a first-come, first-served basis. Check here if you'd like your child considered for a Sibshop scholarship." On the same form, parents who do not have money issues can be given an opportunity to contribute to the Sibshops scholarship fund.

6. Family Involvement in Sibshops

Ideally, at least one of your Sibshop's facilitators will be an adult sibling for the reasons mentioned on page 74 of *Sibshops.* If this is not possible, seek a parent who can offer advice, provide a family perspective, and help you spread the word about your program. Good word of mouth among families is critical to drawing children to your Sibshop. Family involvement—as well as Goal 5 of the Sibshop curriculum—will also be achieved by hosting at least one meeting per year for the parents of the children who attend your Sibshop. These meetings may be held concurrently with your Sibshop and can be informal discussions of why parents enrolled their children in Sibshops, Sibshop goals and activities, and general topics.

7. Involving Sibs in the Selection of Sibshop Activities

The brothers and sisters who attend your Sibshop should be given some say about Sibshop activities. This is especially true for Teen Sibshops. Seek their feedback about activities they liked and disliked and ideas they have for recreation, discussion, and informational activities. The Sibshop curriculum is not so regimented that it can't accommodate bright ideas from the young people who attend them!

8. Evaluation

At least once per year, your Sibshop should plan on "checking in" with both the young siblings who attend your Sibshop and their parents. Use or adapt the evaluation forms found on pages 99–102 of *Sibshops.* These evaluations are easy to administer and will provide your team with valuable feedback.

9. Seek Appropriate Facilitators

Based on years of conducting programs for siblings, we believe that Sibshop facilitators should share some varied core skills. As described in detail on pages 75–78 of *Sibshops,* it is strongly desired that Sibshop facilitators

---

Sibshop and Sibshops are service marks and trademarks owned by Donald J. Meyer on behalf of the Sibling Support Project.

- Have a working knowledge of the unique concerns and opportunities experienced by brothers and sisters of children with special needs

- Have personal or professional experience with people who have special needs and their families

- Be familiar with active listening principles

- Have experience leading groups, preferably groups of children

- Convey a sense of joy, wonder, and play

- Be available to meet at the times and dates identified by the planning committee

- Be somewhat physically fit

- Appreciate that the Sibshop participants, not the facilitators, are the experts on living with a brother or sister with special needs

Review pages 74–77 with members of your team to make sure that your team of facilitators embodies these qualifications. In certain instances, allowances can be made for one team member lacking a particular skill if it is compensated by another team member who possesses that skill. For instance, your Sibshop may have a team member who is gifted at leading group discussions but has a physical disability that makes it impossible for her to pitch lively recreational activities. Her difficulty might be compensated by a team member who may not be especially good at leading group discussions but is highly skilled at leading recreational activities.

10. Training

All Sibshop facilitators are strongly encouraged to attend a 2-day Sibshop training offered by the Sibling Support Project. It is the best way to get up to speed on sibling issues and learn what Sibshops are all about.

These trainings are best when hosted in the community where the new Sibshop is to be created. As training includes a Demonstration Sibshop, these 2-day events are a great way to kick off a local Sibshop and to educate parents, service providers, and future Sibshop facilitators about siblings' lifelong concerns.

When hosting a training is not possible, you may attend a Sibshop training offered elsewhere as an alternative. To learn where Sibshop trainings are being held, consult the Sibling Support Project's online training calendar at www.siblingsupport.org or contact the Sibling Support Project directly.

If hosting or attending a training is impossible, a third alternative would be to 1) commit to reading the Sibshop curriculum in its entirety and 2) arrange to visit an established, ongoing Sibshop run by a facilitator who *has* attended training offered by the Sibling Support Project. Facilitators trained this way are, in effect, "second-generation" trainees. To avoid a photocopy-of-a-photocopy-of-a-photocopy phenomenon, Sibshops run by second-generation trainees may not be used to train new Sibshop facilitators.

Although attending training by the Sibling Support Project is preferred, local Sibshop facilitators who have attended training by the Sibling Support Project may train new staff at their own agencies and may train individuals who visit their agency as described in the previous paragraph.

As discussed in Standard 2 (Endorsing the Goals of Sibshops), community-based Sibshop facilitators are encouraged to conduct awareness-level workshops on Sibs-

---

Sibshop and Sibshops are service marks and trademarks owned by Donald J. Meyer on behalf of the Sibling Support Project.

hops. They may not, however, train others on how to run a Sibshop model at regional, state, or national venues without the specific, prior permission of the Sibling Support Project.

11. Membership in SibGroup

SibGroup is the Sibling Support Project's no-cost listserv for those running Sibshops and similar sibling programs. It is an excellent forum to meet others running Sibshops and to share ideas, challenges, and stories of your successes. It is also the easiest way for the Sibling Support Project to communicate with Sibshops across the world. *To be a registered Sibshop, the contact person for your Sibshop must subscribe to the Sib-Group listserv.* Other Sibshop facilitators are encouraged to be members as well. To subscribe, simply visit www.siblingsupport.org

12. Enriching the Sibshop Curriculum

Each week, Sibshop facilitators come up with novel activities that are not in the pages of *Sibshops.* To encourage sharing the wealth and enriching the Sibshop curriculum, each Sibshop program should submit at least one, and preferably three, activities to the SibGroup listserv each year in the format found in the Sibshop curriculum. These may be recreational (e.g., new games, crafts, art and cooking projects), discussion, or information activities. Sharing will give all Sibshops a rich array of activities from which to choose. Contributors will always be acknowledged!

13. Appropriate Use of Sibshop Name and Logo

Registered Sibshops may use the Sibshop name and the Sibshop logo, but the name and logo must be used correctly. Please note that it is "Sibshop" and never "SibShop" or "Sib Shop." The Sibshop curriculum is copyrighted and the Sibshop logo is trademarked. Consequently, the Sibshop logo may not be altered in any way without the permission of the Sibling Support Project.

14. Registering Your Sibshop

To use the Sibshop name and logo, your program must be a registered Sibshop. Luckily, registration is easy and quick, and now can be completed online. Please note: All Sibshops must complete a one-time online registration.

During the online registration, you will:

- Indicate that you have completed the necessary requirements to become a registered Sibshop

- Indicate that you agree with the Standards

- Provide us with contact information about your Sibshop program

Once you register online, we will post key contact information about your Sibshop on our web site's online directory. This information will assist the hundreds of parents who visit the Project's web pages seeking a local Sibshop for their children. *Please note: It will be your responsibility to make sure that the contact information we have for you is current.* Following registration, you will be provided with instructions on how to update the information we have about your program.

To register online, please visit: www.siblingsupport.org. Fill out the online registration form, indicate that you agree with the Standards of Practice, and submit your application for approval by the Sibling Support Project.

Sibshop and Sibshops are service marks and trademarks owned by Donald J. Meyer on behalf of the Sibling Support Project.

Books for Young Readers on Sibling and Disability Issues

Following is a list of books for young readers that have been suggested by Sibshop providers and reviewed favorably by readers on Amazon.com. Information on ordering these and other sibling-related books may be found at www.siblingsupport.org

- *A Real Christmas This Year* by Karen Lynn Williams (1995)
- *Andy and His Yellow Frisbee* by Mary Thompson (1996)
- *Are You Alone on Purpose?* by Nancy Werlin (2007)
- *Autism Through a Sister's Eyes* by Eve B. Band, Emily Hecht, Gary B. Mesibov, and Sue Lynn Cotton (2001)
- *Ben, King of the River* by David Gifaldi and Layne Johnson (2001)
- *Big Brother Dustin* by Alden R. Carter, Dan Young, and Carol S. Carter (1997)
- *Brothers and Sisters* by Laura Dwight (2005)
- *Eddie Enough!* by Debbie Zimmett and Charlotte Murray Fremaux (2001)
- *Everybody Is Different: A Book for Young People Who Have Brothers or Sisters with Autism* by Fiona Bleach (2002)
- *I Have a Sister—My Sister Is Deaf* by Jeanne Whitehouse Peterson and Deborah Kogan Ray (1984)
- *Ian's Walk: A Story About Autism* by Laurie Lears and Karen Ritz (2003)
- *I'm the Big Sister Now* by Michelle Emmert and Gail Owens (1989)
- *Invincible* by Sally Rosenberg Romansky and Margot J. Ott (2006)
- *Joey and Sam* by Illana Katz, Edward, M.D. Ritvo, and Franz Borowitz (1993)
- *Lee, the Rabbit with Epilepsy* by Deborah M. Moss and Carol Schwartz (1989)

- *Living with a Brother or Sister with Special Needs: A Book for Sibs* by Donald J. Meyer and Patricia F. Vadasy (1996)

- *Los Hermanos de Personas con Discapacidad: una Asignatura Pendiente* by Blanca Nunez and Luis Rodriguez (2004)

- *My Brother Sammy* by Becky Edwards and Jill Newton (2000)

- *My Brother, Matthew* by Mary Thompson (1992)

- *My Brother's a World-Class Pain: A Sibling's Guide to ADHD-Hyperactivity* by Michael Gordon (1992)

- *My Extra Special Brother* by Carly Heyman and Stephanie Conley (2003)

- *My Friend with Autism: A Coloring Book for Peers and Siblings* by Beverly Bishop and Craig Bishop (2003)

- *My Sister Annie* by Bill Dodds (1997)

- *Our Brother Has Down's Syndrome* by Irene McNeil, Shelley Cairo, and Jasmine Cairo (1988)

- *Power of the Powerless: A Brother's Legacy of Love* by Christopher De Vinck (2002)

- *Princess Pooh* by Kathleen M. Muldoon and Linda Shute (1989)

- *Qué le Pasa a Este Niño? Guia Para Conocer a los Ninos con Discapacidad* by Angels Ponce (2005)

- *Rolling Along with Goldilocks and the Three Bears* by Cindy Meyers and Carol Morgan (1999)

- *Sara's Secret* by Suzanne Wanous and Shelly O. Haas (1995)

- *The Best Worst Brother* by Stephanie Stuve-Bodeen (2005)

- *The Sibling Slam Book: What It's Really Like to Have a Brother or Sister with Special Needs* by Don Meyer (2005)

- *The Summer of the Swans* by Betsy Byars (1981)

- *Tru Confessions* by Janet Tashjian (1999)

- *Views from Our Shoes: Growing Up with a Brother or Sister with Special Needs* by Donald J. Meyer (1997)

- *Way to Go, Alex!* by Robin Pulver and Elizabeth Wolf (1999)

- *Welcome Home, Jellybean* by Marlene Fanta Shyer (1988)

- *We'll Paint the Octopus Red* by Stephanie Stuve-Bodeen and Pam Devito (1998)

- *What About Me?* by Colby F. Rodowsky (1989)

- *What's Wrong with Timmy?* by Maria Shriver and Sandra Speidel (2001)

Appendix C

A Brief Description of the Sibshop Model

For more information on how to start a registered Sibshop, contact the Sibling Support Project. Phone: 206-297-6368; e-mail: donmeyer@siblingsupport.org; web site: www.siblingsupport.org

What are Sibshops? For the adults who plan them and the agencies that sponsor them, Sibshops are best described as opportunities for brothers and sisters of children with special health and developmental needs to obtain peer support and education within a recreational context. They reflect an agency's commitment to the well-being of the family member most likely to have the longest-lasting relationship with the person with special needs.

However, for the young people who attend them and the energetic people who run them, Sibshops are best described as *events*. Sibshops are lively, pedal-to-the-metal celebrations of the many contributions made by brothers and sisters of kids with special needs. Sibshops acknowledge that being the brother or sister of a person with special needs is for some a good thing, for others a not-so-good thing, and for many, something in between. They reflect a belief that brothers and sisters have much to offer one another—if they are given a chance. The Sibshop model intersperses information and discussion activities with new games (designed to be unique, off-beat, and appealing to a wide ability range), cooking activities, and special guests who may teach participants mime, how to juggle, or, in the case of one guest artist who has cerebral palsy, how to paint by holding a toothbrush in your mouth. Sibshops are as fun and rewarding for the people who host them as they are for the participants.

Sibshops seek to provide siblings with opportunities for peer support. Because Sibshops are designed (primarily) for school-age children, peer support is provided within a lively, recreational context that emphasizes a kids'-eye view. Sibshops are not therapy, group or otherwise, although their effect may be therapeutic for some children. Sibshops acknowledge that most brothers and sisters of people with special needs, like their parents, are doing well, despite the challenges of an illness or disability. Consequently, although Sibshop facilitators always keep an eye open for participants who may need additional services, the Sibshop model takes a wellness approach.

Who attends Sibshops? Originally developed for 8- to 13-year-old siblings of children with developmental disabilities, the Sibshops model is easily adapted for slightly younger and older children. It has been adapted for brothers and sisters of children with other special needs, including cancer, hearing impairments, epilepsy, emotional disturbances, and HIV-positive status. Sibshops have also been adapted for use with children who have lost a family member. Children who attend Sibshops come from diverse backgrounds including suburban communities (e.g., Bellevue, Washington; Springfield, Massachusetts; Tallahassee, Florida), urban communities (e.g., Detroit, Michigan; Washington, D.C.), rural communities (e.g., Wyoming, Iowa), and communities with unique cultural heritages (e.g., Alaska, New Mexico, Hawaii, South Central Los Angeles).

Who sponsors Sibshops? Any agency serving families of children with special needs can sponsor a Sibshop, provided the agency can financially support and properly staff the program and can attract sufficient numbers of participants. We strongly recommend that agencies work together to cosponsor a local Sibshop. This important topic is further discussed in Chapter 5 of *Sibshops*. We have found that Sibshops are well within the reach and abilities of most communities. They are not expensive to run and logistically are no more difficult to coordinate than other community-based programs for children such as Scouts or Camp Fire.

Who runs Sibshops? We believe that Sibshops are best facilitated by a team of service providers (e.g., social workers, special education teachers and professors, psychologists, nurses) and adult siblings of people with special needs. At the very least, the team of facilitators will need to 1) be knowledgeable about the disability or illness represented, 2) possess a sense of humor and play, 3) enjoy the company of children, and 4) respect the young participants' expertise on the topic of life with a brother or sister with special needs. Qualifications for Sibshop facilitators are further discussed in Chapter 5 of *Sibshops*.

What is the optimal number of participants for a Sibshop? Sibshops have been held for as few as 5 children and as many as 45. Around a dozen children, with at least two facilitators, is a comfortable number.

When are Sibshops offered? Usually Sibshops are offered on Saturdays—often from 10 A.M. until 2 P.M. This allows ample time for games, discussion, and information activities and for making and eating lunch. Of course, Saturdays from 10 until 2 will not be ideal for all families or communities. Each community will need to determine the best day and length of time for its Sibshop, as further discussed in Chapter 5.

How often are Sibshops held? Depending on the needs and resources of the community, Sibshops may be offered as frequently as weekly (as with a $1\frac{1}{2}$ hour after-school program) or as infrequently as yearly (as with an all-day Sibshop that is a part of an annual conference for families from around the state or nation). Generally, Sibshops are presented monthly or bimonthly.

Sibshops may be offered in a series (e.g., five Sibshops, meeting once a month,

---

Sibshop and Sibshops are service marks and trademarks owned by Donald J. Meyer on behalf of the Sibling Support Project.

with one registration). Offering Sibshops in a series can provide a stable group that can form an identity during the months they are together. It can be difficult, however, for some participants and families to commit to a series of dates due to interference with other activities. Sibshops may also be offered as stand-alone events (e.g., bimonthly meetings with separate registrations). The stand-alone events offer families flexibility, but participants will vary somewhat from Sibshop to Sibshop.

What are the goals of the Sibshop model?

All Sibshop activities proceed from the following goals.:

Goal 1: Sibshops will provide brothers and sisters of children with special needs an opportunity to meet other siblings in a relaxed, recreational setting.

Goal 2: Sibshops will provide brothers and sisters with opportunities to discuss common joys and concerns with other siblings of children with special needs.

Goal 3: Sibshops will provide siblings with an opportunity to learn how others handle situations commonly experienced by siblings of children with special needs.

Goal 4: Sibshops will provide siblings with an opportunity to learn more about the implications of the special needs of their brothers and sisters.

Goal 5: Sibshops will provide parents and other professionals with opportunities to learn more about the concerns and opportunities frequently experienced by brothers and sisters of people with special needs.

SAMPLE SIBSHOP SCHEDULE

10:00 A.M. Trickle-In Activity: Facetags!

10:20 A.M. Introductory/Peer Support Activity: Strengths & Weaknesses

10:45 A.M. Recreational Activity: Knots

10:50 A.M. Recreational Activity: Lap Game

11:00 A.M. Recreational Activity: Stand Up!

11:10 A.M. Recreational Activity: Group Juggling

11:30 A.M. Recreational Activity: Triangle tag

11:40 A.M. Recreational Activity: Sightless Sculpture

11:50 A.M. Lunch prep

12:00 Noon Lunch: Super Nachos!

12:20 P.M. Lunch cleanup

12:30 P.M. Peer Support Activity: Dear Aunt Blabby

12:55 P.M. Recreational Activity: Pushpin Soccer

1:15 P.M. Recreational Activity: Hog Call

1:30 P.M. Peer Support Activity: Sound Off

1:55 P.M. Closure

What Siblings Would Like Parents and Service Providers to Know

In the United States, there are more than six million people who have special health, developmental, and mental health concerns. Most of these people have typically developing brothers and sisters. Brothers and sisters are too important to ignore, if for only the following reasons:

- These brothers and sisters will be in the lives of family members with special needs longer than anyone else. Brothers and sisters will be there after parents are gone and special education services are a distant memory. If these brothers and sisters are provided with support and information, they can help their siblings live dignified lives from childhood to their senior years.

- Throughout their lives, brothers and sisters share many of the concerns that parents of children with special needs experience, including isolation, a need for information, guilt, concerns about the future, and caregiving demands. Brothers and sisters also face issues that are uniquely theirs, including resentment, peer issues, embarrassment, and pressure to achieve.

Despite the important and lifelong roles they will play in the lives of their siblings who have special needs, even the most family-friendly agencies often overlook brothers and sisters. Brothers and sisters, often left in the literal and figurative waiting rooms of service delivery systems, deserve better. True family-centered care and services will be achieved when siblings are actively included in agencies' functional definition of "family."

Sibshop and Sibshops are service marks and trademarks owned by Donald J. Meyer on behalf of the Sibling Support Project.

The Sibling Support Project facilitated a discussion on SibNet, its listserv for adult siblings of people with disabilities, regarding the considerations that siblings want from parents, other family members, and service providers. Following are themes discussed by SibNet members and recommendations from the Sibling Support Project:

1. *The Right to One's Own Life*

Throughout their lives, brothers and sisters may play many different roles in the lives of their siblings with special needs. Regardless of the contributions they may make, the basic right of siblings to their *own* lives must always be remembered. Parents and service providers should not make assumptions about responsibilities that typically developing siblings may assume without a frank and open discussion. "Nothing about us without us"—a phrase popular with self-advocates who have disabilities—applies to siblings as well. Self-determination, after all, is for everyone—including brothers and sisters.

2. *Acknowledging Siblings' Concerns*

Like parents, brothers and sisters will experience a wide array of often ambivalent emotions regarding the effect their siblings' special needs has on them and the family as a whole. These feelings should be both expected and acknowledged by parents and other family members and service providers. Because most siblings will have the longest-lasting relationship with the family member who has a disability, these concerns will change over time. Parents and providers would be wise to learn more about siblings' lifelong and ever-changing concerns.

3. *Expectations for Typically Developing Siblings*

Families need to set high expectations for all of their children. Some typically developing brothers and sisters, however, react to their siblings' disability by setting unrealistically high expectations for themselves, and some feel that they must somehow compensate for their siblings' special needs. Parents can help their typically developing children by conveying clear expectations and unconditional support.

4. *Expect Typical Behavior from Typically Developing Siblings*

Although difficult for parents to watch, teasing, name calling, arguing, and other forms of conflict are common among most brothers and sisters--even when one has special needs. Although parents may be appalled at siblings' harshness toward one another, much of this conflict can be a beneficial part of normal social development. A child with Down syndrome who grows up with siblings with whom he sometimes fights will likely be better prepared to face life in the community as an adult than a child with Down syndrome who grows up as an only child. Regardless of how adaptive or developmentally appropriate it might be, however, typical sibling conflict is more likely to result in feelings of guilt when one sibling has special health or developmental needs. When conflict arises, the message sent to many brothers and sisters is, "Leave your sibling alone. You are bigger, you are stronger, you should know better. It is your job to compromise." Typically developing siblings deserve a life where they, like other children, sometimes misbehave, get angry, and fight with their siblings.

5. *Expectations for the Family Member with Special Needs*

When families have high expectations for their children with special needs, everyone will benefit. As adults, typically developing brothers and sisters will likely play impor-

---

Sibshop and Sibshops are service marks and trademarks owned by Donald J. Meyer on behalf of the Sibling Support Project.

tant roles in the lives of their siblings with disabilities. Parents can help siblings now by assisting their children with special needs acquire skills that will allow them to be as independent as possible as adults. To the extent possible, parents should have the same expectations for the child with special needs regarding chores and personal responsibility as they do for their typically developing children. Not only will similar expectations foster independence, they will also minimize the resentment expressed by siblings when there are two sets of rules—one for them and another for their sibs who have special needs.

6. *The Right to a Safe Environment*

Some siblings live with brothers and sisters who have challenging behaviors. Other siblings assume responsibilities for themselves and their siblings that go beyond their age level and place all parties in vulnerable situations. Siblings deserve to have their own personal safety given as much importance as the family member with special needs.

7. *Opportunities to Meet Peers*

For most parents, the thought of "going it alone"—raising a child with special needs without the benefit of knowing another parent in a similar situation—would be unthinkable. Yet, this routinely happens to brothers and sisters. Sibshops, listservs such as SibNet and SibKids, and similar efforts offer siblings the common-sense support and validation that parents get from Parent-to-Parent programs and similar programs. Brothers and sisters—like parents—like to know that they are not alone with their unique joys and concerns.

8. *Opportunities to Obtain Information*

Throughout their lives, brothers and sisters have an ever-changing need for information about their sibling's disability—and its treatment and implications. Parents *and* service providers have an obligation to proactively provide siblings with helpful information. Any agency that represents a specific disability or illness and prepares materials for parents and other adults should prepare materials for siblings and young readers as well.

9. *Siblings' Concerns About the Future*

Early in life, many brothers and sisters worry about what obligations they will have toward their sibling in the days to come. Parents can reassure their typically developing children by making plans for the future of their children with special needs, listening to their typically developing children's suggestions as they make these plans, considering backup plans, and realizing that their typically developing children's availability may change over time. When brothers and sisters are brought "into the loop" and given the message early that they have their parents' blessing to pursue their own dreams, their future involvement with their sibling who has a disability will be a choice instead of an obligation. For their own good and for the good of their siblings with disabilities, brothers and sisters should be afforded the right to their own lives. This includes having a say in whether and how they will be involved in the lives of their siblings with disabilities as adults and the level, type, and duration of that involvement.

10. *Including Both Sons and Daughters*

Just as daughters are usually the family members who care for aging parents, adult sisters are usually the family members who look after the family member with special needs when parents no longer can. Serious exploration of sharing responsibilities among siblings—including brothers—should be considered.

11. Communication

Although good communication between parents and children is always important, it is especially important in families where there is a child who has special needs. An evening course in active listening can help improve communication among all family members, and books such as *How to Talk So Kids Will Listen and Listen So Kids Will Talk* (2004) and *Siblings without Rivalry* (1999) (both by Adele Faber and Elaine Mazlish) provide helpful tips on communicating with children.

12. One-on-One Time with Parents

Children need to know from their parents' deeds and words that their parents care about them as individuals. When parents carve time out of a busy schedule to grab a bite at a local burger joint or window shop at the mall with their typically developing children, it conveys a message that parents are there for them as well and provides an excellent opportunity to talk about a wide range of topics.

13. Celebrate Every Child's Achievements and Milestones

Over the years, we've met siblings whose parents did not attend their high school graduation—even when their children were valedictorians—because the parents were unable to leave their child with special needs. We've also met siblings whose wedding plans were dictated by the needs of their sibling with a disability. One child's special needs should not overshadow another's achievements and milestones. Families who seek respite resources and creative solutions and strive for flexibility can help ensure that the accomplishments of all family members are celebrated.

14. Parents' Perspective Is More Important than the Actual Disability

Parents would be wise to remember that the parents' interpretation of their child's disability will be a greater influence on the adaptation of their typically developing sibling than the actual disability itself. When parents seek support, information, and respite for themselves, they model resilience and healthy attitudes and behaviors for their typically developing children.

15. Include Siblings in the Definition of "Family"

Many educational, health care, and social service agencies profess a desire to offer family-centered services but continue to overlook the family members who will have the longest-lasting relationship with the person who has the special needs—the sisters and brothers. When brothers and sisters receive the considerations and services they deserve, agencies can claim to offer "family-centered"—instead of "parent-centered"—services.

16. Actively Reach Out to Brothers and Sisters

Parents and agency personnel should consider inviting (but not requiring) brothers and sisters to attend informational, individualized education program (IEP), individualized family service plans (IFSP), and transition planning meetings and clinic visits. Siblings frequently have legitimate questions that can be answered by service providers. Brothers and sisters also have informed opinions and perspectives and can make positive contributions to the child's team.

Sibshop and Sibshops are service marks and trademarks owned by Donald J. Meyer on behalf of the Sibling Support Project.

17. Learn More About Life as a Sibling

Anyone interested in families ought to be interested in siblings and their concerns. Parents and providers can learn more about life as a sib by facilitating a Sibshop, hosting a sibling panel, or reading books by and about brothers and sisters. Guidelines for conducting a sibling panel are available from the Sibling Support Project and in the Sibshop curriculum. Visit the Sibling Support Project's web site for a bibliography of sibling-related books.

18. Create Local Programs Specifically for Brothers and Sisters

If your community has a Parent-to-Parent program or a similar parent support effort, a fair question to ask is: Why isn't there a similar effort for the brothers and sisters? Like their parents, brothers and sisters benefit from talking with others who "get it." Sibshops and other programs for preschool, school-age, teen, and adult siblings are growing in number. The Sibling Support Project, which maintains a database of more than 200 Sibshops and other sibling programs, provides training and technical assistance on how to create local programs for siblings.

19. Include Brothers and Sisters on Advisory Boards and in Policies Regarding Families

Reserving board seats for siblings will give the board a unique, important perspective and reflect the agency's concern for the well-being of brothers and sisters. Developing policies based on the important roles played by brothers and sisters will help ensure that their concerns and contributions are part of the agency's commitment to families.

20. Fund Services for Brothers and Sisters

No classmate in an inclusive classroom will have a greater impact on the social development of a child with a disability than brothers and sisters will. They will be their siblings' lifelong "typically developing role models." As noted earlier, brothers and sisters will likely be in the lives of their siblings with disabilities longer than anyone else—longer than their parents and certainly longer than any service provider. For most brothers and sisters, their future and the future of their siblings with special needs are inexorably entwined. Despite this, there is little funding to support projects that will help brothers and sisters get the information, skills, and support they will need throughout their lives. Governmental agencies would be wise to invest in the family members who will take a personal interest in the well-being of people with disabilities and advocate for them when their parents no longer can. As one sister wrote: "We will become caregivers for our siblings when our parents no longer can. Anyone interested in the welfare of people with disabilities ought to be interested in us."

About the Sibling Support Project

The Sibling Support Project, believing that disabilities, illness, and mental health issues affect the lives of *all* family members, seeks to increase the peer support and information opportunities for brothers and sisters of people with special needs and to increase parents' and providers' understanding of sibling issues.

Sibshop and Sibshops are service marks and trademarks owned by Donald J. Meyer on behalf of the Sibling Support Project.

Our mission is accomplished by training local service providers on how to create Sibshops (lively community-based programs for school-age brothers and sisters); hosting workshops, listservs, and web sites for young and adult siblings; and increasing parents' and providers' awareness of siblings' unique, lifelong, and ever-changing concerns through workshops, web sites, and written materials.

Based in Seattle since 1990, the Sibling Support Project is the only national effort dedicated to the interests of more than six million brothers and sisters of people with special health, mental health, and developmental needs.

For more information about Sibshops, sibling issues, and our workshops, listservs and publications, contact:

Sibling Support Project
Don Meyer
6512 23rd Avenue NW #213
Seattle, WA 98117
206-297-6368
donmeyer@siblingsupport.org

Sibling Support Project

Sibshop and Sibshops are service marks and trademarks owned by Donald J. Meyer on behalf of the Sibling Support Project.

Sibshops: Workshops for Siblings of Children with Special Needs, Revised Edition, by Don Meyer and Patricia Vadasy. Copyright © 2008. Paul H. Brookes Publishing Co. All rights reserved.

Appendix

SIBSHOP REGISTRATION FORM!

Announcing Children's Sibshops for the Upcoming School Year!

Register Soon!
Spaces Limited!

Last year's Sibshop season was another huge success! Almost one hundred brothers and sisters from around Western Washington attended the two Sibshops coordinated by the Sibling Support Project at Children's Hospital and Regional Medical Center. And we're looking forward to an even better year during the next school year.

As usual, we will have two "flavors" of Sibshops: one for brothers and sisters of children with special developmental and learning needs[1] and another for brothers and sisters of children with special health needs[2].

Please share these registration materials with families you know (and feel free to make copies).

Sibshops for Sibs of Kids with Special Developmental and Learning Needs

Sibshop's "home" is still at Children's Hospital where we're able to use the hospital's facilities and visit with hospital staff. The kids especially enjoy raiding the Sound Café for lunch!

Similar to previous years, we will have Sibshops for 6–9-year-old and 10–13-year-old sibs on alternating months, and we'll meet from 9:30 A.M.–12:30 P.M. We're excited

to have two Sibshop veteran facilitators return this year. Shana Hornstein (a special education teacher in a Seattle public school and the sister of a young man with autism) and Kari Nelson (a child life specialist at Children's). Assisting them will be several veteran volunteers.

Sibshops for Sibs of Kids with Special Health Needs

Our Sibshops for kids with sibs who have special health needs is in full gear and ready for another great season! On alternating months, we will have Sibshops for 6–9-year-old and 10–13-year-old brothers and sisters. We will meet from 2 P.M. to 5 P.M. at the Sound Café at Children's Hospital. We are fortunate to have a wonderful team of facilitators: Kiko Van Zandt (a nurse clinician at Children's), Melissa Christiansen (a child life specialist at Harborview), and Bill Blackburn (former therapeutic recreation specialist at Harborview). Once again, they will be assisted by teen brothers and sisters of people with special health needs.

Our Sibshops are made possible by Voohris Edwards Endowment for Sibling Support, the William A. and Betty Anne Nyberg Endowment for Sibling Support, the King County Family Support Expansion/Discovery Trust Program, registration fees, and your generous financial support.

[1] Including, but not limited to: Autism, Down Syndrome, ADD/ADHD and developmental delays
[2] Including, but not limited to: diabetes, cancer, cystic fibrosis, muscular dystrophy and heart, kidney, liver, gastrointestinal or lung disease.

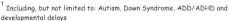

Sibshop and Sibshops are service marks and trademarks owned by Donald J. Meyer on behalf of the Sibling Support Project.

How to register your child for Sibshops!

First, pick which type of Sibshop you wish your child to attend. You will enroll your child in the Sibshop for sibs of children with special health needs **OR** the Sibshop for sibs of children with special developmental needs. If you are uncertain of which Sibshop is best for your child, call (206) 987-3285.

Second, select the dates for the Sibshop you wish your child to attend on the enclosed registration sheet. **Please note: Sibshops are more like a club than a class! Don't worry if your child cannot attend every Sibshop during the upcoming school year. Also, parents who learn about Sibshops during the school year are encouraged to register their children for the remaining dates.**

Third, clip and save the dates you've chosen. *Unlike previous years, we may not be providing "reminder calls"!*

Fourth, fill out the enclosed Sibshop information form and sign the release. Send the information form, registration form, and payment for Sibshops to:

Sibshops
CHRMC-MS-2C1
4800 Sand Point Way NE
Seattle, WA 98105

A limited number of scholarships are available. If you would like a scholarship for your child, please indicate so on the registration form.

Although we make every attempt to accommodate everyone who wishes to register, we do have a limited number of spaces for each Sibshop. Registration will be handled on a first-come, first-serve basis. If you have any questions about the Sibshops registration process, please call us at (206) 987-3285.

In case you are not familiar with Sibshops, below are two frequently asked questions:

What are Sibshops?

When a child becomes ill, the entire family is affected. Sibshops provide support and guidance to siblings of children with special medical or developmental needs.

Siblings are encouraged to share the challenges and celebrate the joys with brothers and sisters in similar situations.

Sibshops are lively, action packed, 3-hour workshops that celebrate the many contributions made by brothers and sisters of kids with special needs. Sibshops acknowledge that being the brother or sister of a person with special needs is for some a good thing, for others a not-so-good thing, and for many, something in between. They reflect a belief that brothers and sisters have much to offer one another—if they are given a chance. The Sibshop model mixes information and discussion activities with new games (designed to be unique, off-beat, and appealing to a wide ability range), and special guests. *There are currently more than 200 Sibshops across the United States, Canada, and elsewhere.*

Who runs Sibshops?

Sibshops are run by a team of people who have professional and, in some cases, a personal understanding of the impact a child's illness or disability can have on family members. Equally important, they all have great kid skills! Both Sibshops often have "junior facilitators" who are sibs in their later teen years. Cathy Harrison, a Child Life Specialist, coordinates both Sibshop teams.

Sibshop and Sibshops are service marks and trademarks owned by Donald J. Meyer on behalf of the Sibling Support Project.

REGISTRATION FORM

For use any time during the school year!

Children's Sibshops for brothers and sisters of children with special developmental and learning needs* Sound Café, Children's Hospital and Regional Medical Center from 9:30 a.m. to 12:30 p.m.	
<u>For Brothers and Sisters ages 6 to 9</u>	<u>For Brothers and Sisters ages 10 to 13</u>
Please check the dates you would like your child to attend: ☐ October 18 ☐ December 13 ☐ February 21 ☐ April 17 ☐ June 5 Cost per Sibshop: $12 (includes lunch)	Please check the dates you would like your child to attend: ☐ September 6 ☐ November 15 ☐ January 10 ☐ March 13 ☐ May 8 Cost per Sibshop: $12 (includes lunch)

*Including, but not limited to: Autism, Down syndrome, ADD/ADHD, and developmental delays

Child's name:_____

Child's age: _____

Home Phone number: (_____)_____

Total amount enclosed: $_____. Please make checks or money orders payable to *Children's Sibshop. Registration fees are nonrefundable.*

I would like to request scholarship assistance. __Yes __No Amount requested $_____

I would like to make a donation to help sponsor a Sibshop participant __Yes __No
                                            Donation amount $_____ enclosed

===========================Clip and Save the Dates!===========================

<u>Sibshops for Brothers and Sisters ages 6 to 9</u>	<u>Sibshops for Brothers and Sisters ages 10 to 13</u>
We've registered for the following dates: ☐ October 18 ☐ December 13 ☐ February 21 ☐ April 17 ☐ June 5 Cost per Sibshop: $12 (includes lunch)	We've registered for the following dates: ☐ September 6 ☐ November 15 ☐ January 10 ☐ March 13 ☐ May 8 Cost per Sibshop: $12 (includes lunch)

What: Children's Sibshops for brothers and sisters of children with special developmental and learning needs
Where: Sound Café, Children's Hospital and Regional Medical Center. Driving directions: (206) 987-2226
When: 9:30 a.m.-12:30 p.m.
Regrets: If you can't make a Sibshop that you have registered for, please call (206) 987-3285.
Parking: Please park on the 5th level of the Whale Garage to access the Sound Café.

REGISTRATION FORM

For use any time during the school year!

Children's Sibshops for brothers and sisters of children with special health concerns*	
Sound Café, Children's Hospital and Regional Medical Center from 2-5 p.m.	
<u>For Brothers and Sisters ages 6 to 9</u>	<u>For Brothers and Sisters ages 10 to 13</u>
Please check the dates you would like your child to attend: ☐ October 18 ☐ December 13 ☐ February 21 ☐ April 17 ☐ June 5 Cost per Sibshop: $15 (includes snack)	**Please check the dates you would like your child to attend:** ☐ September 6 ☐ November 15 ☐ January 10 ☐ March 13 ☐ May 8 Cost per Sibshop: $15 (includes snack)

* including, but not limited to: diabetes, cancer, cystic fibrosis, muscular dystrophy, and heart, kidney, liver, gastrointestinal or lung disease.

Child's name:_____

Child's age: _____

Home Phone number: (_____)_____

Total amount enclosed: $_____. Please make checks or money orders payable to Children's Sibshop. Registration fees are nonrefundable.

I would like to request scholarship assistance. __Yes __No Amount requested $_____

I would like to make a donation to help sponsor a Sibshop participant. __Yes __No
Donation amount $_____ enclosed

=========================Clip and Save the Dates!=============================

Sibshops for Brothers and Sisters ages 6 to 9	Sibshops for Brothers and Sisters ages 10 to 13
We've registered for the following dates: ☐ October 18 ☐ December 13 ☐ February 21 ☐ April 17 ☐ June 5 Cost per Sibshop: $15 (includes snack)	We've registered for the following dates: ☐ September 6 ☐ November 15 ☐ January 10 ☐ March 13 ☐ May 8 Cost per Sibshop: $15 (includes snack)

<u>What:</u>	Children's Sibshops for brothers and sisters of children with special health concerns.
<u>Where:</u>	Sound Café, Children's Hospital and Regional Medical Center. Driving directions: (206) 987-2226
<u>When:</u>	2-5 p.m.
<u>Regrets:</u>	If you can't make a Sibshop that you have registered for, please call (206) 987-3285.
<u>Parking:</u>	Please park on the 5th level of the Whale Garage to access the Sound Café.

SIBSHOP INFORMATION FORM

(This information form must be completed for *all* who wish to participate in Sibshops during the upcoming school year, *even those who have participated in prior years.*)

❑ **I am enrolling my child for the Sibshop for brothers and sisters of children with** *special developmental and learning needs.*

❑ **I am enrolling my child for the Sibshop for brothers and sisters of children with** *special health needs.*

(PLEASE PRINT!)

Date:_____

Child's name:_____

Birth date:_____ Age:_____ Gender:_____

Has your child ever attended a Seattle Sibshop before: ❑ Yes ❑ No
If yes, where? _____

School:_____ Grade:_____

Parent(s) Name(s):_____

Home address_____

City:_____ State:_____ Zip:_____

Home phone: (_____)_____
Alternate phone:(_____)_____

Name of brother or sister with special needs:_____
Birth date:_____ Age:_____ Gender: _____
School:_____
Name or description of disability or health concern:_____

_____

What kind of related special education services (e.g., speech, occupational or physical therapy, counseling, etc.) does this child receive:

_____

_____

_____

Other Siblings:

Name	Age	Gender

What do you hope your child will gain from our Sibshop? Are there any particular topics you would like addressed?

_____

_____

Does your enrolled child have any special needs, food allergies, or other health restrictions of their own that we should know about?

_____

_____

Please provide any other information that you feel would make Sibshops a more enjoyable and educational experience for your child:

_____

_____

Would you like your name placed on a list to be distributed to siblings and their families?__Yes__No

Would you like your phone number included?__Yes__No

Comments:

_____

I hereby give my child permission to participate in Sibshops. I also agree to hold Children's harmless for any and all liability incurred as a result of my child's participation. Further, I grant full permission to use any photographs, videotapes, recordings or any other record of this program for the purpose of education and promotion of Sibshops. If my child is enrolled in Sibshops for brothers and sisters of children with developmental or learning needs, I understand that King County Division of Developmental Disabilities Discovery Trust/Family Support Expansion Grant provides partial funding for this program. I give permission for Children's to release the name, birth date, and diagnosis of the child with special needs to King County as part of the documentation for this funding.

_____   Date: _____

Signature of Parent or Guardian

_____

Please return with Registration form and payment to:
Sibshops
CHRMC—MS-2C1
4800 Sand Point Way NE
Seattle, WA 98105

Additional registration forms and information are available by calling (206) 987-3285.
Registration forms are also available online at
www.seattlechildrens.org/parents/special/sibshops.html

Visit the Sibling Support Project web site at www.siblingsupport.org
On the web page, you can join SibKids, a no-cost listserv for sibs of
kids with special needs and meet brothers and sisters from around the
world!

Sibshop and Sibshops are service marks and trademarks owned by Donald J. Meyer on behalf of the Sibling Support Project.

Dear Aunt Blabby Letters

The first collection of letters to Dear Aunt Blabby is from brothers and sisters of children who have developmental disabilities. The second collection, starting on page 233, is from siblings of children who have cancer or other chronic illnesses. No matter which type of sibling group you are working with, be sure to read all the letters. You will likely find letters you can easily adapt for the participants you serve.

Dear Aunt Blabby,

Sometimes I feel like the invisible man. My brother has Down syndrome. He has a lot of needs that seem to take up all my parents' time. It seems like the only time my parents pay attention to me is when I get into trouble. How do I let them know that they have two kids instead of one?

(signed)
The Invisible Man

Dear Aunt Blabby,

Maybe you can help me with my problem. My big sister has a disability. Sometimes, my friends ask me what's the matter with her and how she got that way. Once my teacher even asked. I never know how to explain it. Any suggestions?

(signed)
Speechless

Dear Aunt Blabby,

Boy, am I mad! For the fifth time tonight my sister has bugged me while I'm trying to do my homework. She is always bugging me! Especially when my friends come over. Help!

(signed)
Fuming

Dear Aunt Blabby,

I have a problem. My brother Michael has a disability. I hate to admit it, but sometimes he embarrasses me. Don't get me wrong—in a lot of ways Mike is a great guy. He can really do a lot for himself, even with all of his special needs. My problem is that I get embarrassed when he acts up in church or has a temper tantrum at the shopping mall. What can I do?

(signed)
Embarrassed

Dear Aunt Blabby,

I hope you can help. My brother has a lot of problems, and I have a lot of questions! My mom never really told me what happened to Josh. I feel funny asking her. Can you give me some tips on how to ask my mom about what happened to Josh?

(signed)
Need to Know

Dear Aunt Blabby,

Maybe you can help me. I really like my sister. She has a lot of special needs, but I love her a lot. My problem is that I get bored just going for walks and watching TV with her. What else can I do with her that will be fun for both of us?

(signed)
Curious

Dear Aunt Blabby,

I have a problem that maybe you can help me with. Just because my brother has a disability and I don't, my parents expect me to be a "Superkid." They expect me to get perfect grades in school. Does that seem fair to you? What can I do?

(signed)
I'm No Superkid

Dear Aunt Blabby,

I'm really worried. If I don't get an A in history, I won't get in the honor society. My parents have so many problems with my sister. I'd really like to make them happy with my schoolwork. Do you think they will be disappointed if I don't get in the honor society?

(signed)
Worried

Dear Aunt Blabby,

Is it O.K. to tease your sister? I mean, I tease my other brothers and sisters, but when I tease my "special" sister, my grandma yells at me. I'm not doing it to be mean or anything—it's just teasing. Is it O.K. or not?

(signed)
To Tease or Not to Tease

Dear Aunt Blabby,

I don't know what to do. My little brother Mark has lots of problems learning. In September, Mark started going to my school. Some kids at my school make fun of the special education kids. I even heard them call my brother names and laugh at things he does. Aunt Blabby, what should I do?

(signed)
Perplexed

Dear Aunt Blabby,

I'm not sure what I should do. I have a new friend, Tom. We have a lot of fun together. We like the same sports and video games. My problem is that when Tom is joking around, he will say things like "cut it out, you retard!" I hate it when he says that because my baby sister, Jamie, has Down syndrome. How can I get him to stop using that word?

(signed)
Still Want to Be Friends

Dear Aunt Blabby,

My brother uses a wheelchair. When we go to the mall, people are always looking at him. I never know what to do. Sometimes people look at him and smile. But sometimes people just stare. Do I stare back at them or just pretend I don't see them? What can I do?

(signed)
Tired of Rude People

Dear Aunt Blabby,

My little sister is deaf. Our whole family is learning sign language. It is fun to be able to talk in a secret language! But I feel funny about using signs when I'm with my family in the mall or something. Sometimes kids make fun of us. They will flap their hands or make weird noises. Even adults stare at us sometimes and use words that are wrong like "deaf and dumb." Mom tells me I have to be polite to adults. How can I tell them to use the right words without sounding rude?

(signed)
Kid Teacher

Dear Aunt Blabby,

I am beginning to feel like Cinderella. My parents make me take care of my little brothers and sisters, especially my little sister who has autism. Also, I spend every Saturday helping my mom clean the house. I never get to do anything! Does that seem fair to you?

(signed)
Where's My Fairy Godmother?

Dear Aunt Blabby,

My sister is driving me nuts. Melissa is 4 years old and has Down syndrome and everybody thinks she's so cute. Wherever we go, it's Melissa this and Melissa that. It's like I'm not even there! What can I do?

(signed)
Look at Me Too!

Dear Aunt Blabby,

My brother Jason has a hard time at school. My dad says he has a learning disability. School is pretty easy for me, except for last week when I really bombed out on a math test. Do you think that I might have a learning disability, too?

(signed)
Worried

Dear Aunt Blabby,

My brother gets away with murder. He never has to do anything around the house just because he has a disability. I know he can do things. It's just that my parents won't make him.

(signed)
Ripped Off

Dear Aunt Blabby,

I feel kind of bad. Next month I will turn 16 and my mom says that I can take driver's ed. My sister is 18 and has a disability. My mom says she won't ever be able to drive. Should I feel bad that I can do things that my sister can't?

(signed)
Confused

Dear Aunt Blabby,

Lately, I've been thinking about the future. Our family lives in Ohio, but I think it would be neat to live in California someday. When I grow up, will I have to stay in Ohio to take care of my brother who has a disability?

(signed)
California Dreamin'

Dear Aunt Blabby,

Help! No one seems to understand! When I tell my friends about my little sister, they don't understand what a neat kid she is and all the things she can do. All they see is her wheelchair and floppy arms. Am I the only one with this problem? What can I do?

(signed)
I Like My Sister!

Dear Aunt Blabby,

I wish I knew someone who has a sister with problems like Amy's. I have friends, but they don't understand what it is like when your little sister has seizures and gets sick and goes to the hospital all the time. My friends don't understand the good stuff either. I was really proud when Amy (who is 6) finally learned to go the bathroom by herself! Are there other kids who know what it's like to have a sister like Amy?

(signed)
Who Knows?

Dear Aunt Blabby,

I wish I was like my friend Jenny. She has a big sister and they do lots of things together. They borrow each other's clothes, put on plays, yell at each other, and laugh a lot too. My sister, Melinda, has lots of problems. I love her, but we're not like Jenny and her sister at all. I wish we were.

(signed)
Only Sort of a Sister

Dear Aunt Blabby,

I have an older brother and sister with special needs. My parents and teachers expect me to do everything right. They call me "the lucky normal one." I know my parents have lots of problems, so I want to make them happy. But sometimes I feel under so much pressure! Do other kids feel this way?

(signed)
Not So Lucky

Dear Aunt Blabby,

When my sister does not cooperate in school, the teachers come to me to get some help. I feel sorry that my sister is having such a hard time, but can't they deal with it? How can I get the teachers to stop coming to me?

(signed)
Not My Job!

Dear Aunt Blabby,

My mother dresses my brother like a nerd. I want him to look cool like a normal kid. What can I do?

(signed)
Joe Cool

Dear Aunt Blabby,

My brother has Down syndrome. When our family goes to the mall, he is very friendly with people. Even if he doesn't know someone, he will give them a hug! He's 10 years old and it's sort of embarrassing. What can I do and not hurt my brother's feelings?

(signed)
Sensitive

Dear Aunt Blabby,

I always have to babysit for my sister. She has problems and my parents say I am the only one they can trust. I want to get a job after school but I'll feel bad if I leave them empty-handed. What should I do?

(signed)
Penniless

Dear Aunt Blabby,

My brother always wants to play with my friends and me. He can't hit the ball. He can't catch the ball. He doesn't understand the rules. My friends get mad. This is more than I can take!

(signed)
Caught Between

Dear Aunt Blabby,

I just started a new school. My mom said that I can invite two friends to spend the day at my house on Saturday. I'm really excited about them coming over. I'm also a little worried about Tonya. Tonya has a lot of special problems, and my new friends don't know a thing about her. When should I tell them about Tonya? Before they come over? Or should I wait until they get to the house? What should I say?

(signed)
Anxious

Dear Aunt Blabby,

I got in trouble at school and almost got suspended because I punched a kid who was staring at my sister. He stared and said something to his friends, and then they all laughed and pointed at her. I admit, she looks different, but she is my sister and I love her. What should I do?

(signed)
Jake the Rake

Dear Aunt Blabby,

My sister has epilepsy. Last week, at my birthday party, my sister had a seizure in front of my friends. Yesterday, when my friends came over to play, my sister ran upstairs to her room, locked her door, and started to cry. How can I make her feel O.K.?

(signed)
The Pits

Dear Aunt Blabby,

I have a younger brother who has Down syndrome. He is not at school yet. Sometimes I see my school friends teasing other kids with Down syndrome. I feel like I should make them stop, but I want them to like me. What should I do?

(signed)
Soon It Will Be My Brother

Dear Aunt Blabby,

My brother has Down syndrome. When we are together, people ask me questions for him. How can I get people to ask him—not me?

(signed)
He's Got Answers

Dear Aunt Blabby,

I have a terrible secret. When my mom was pregnant with Jamie, I had this huge temper tantrum. My mom got real mad at me. Later that day, she went to the hospital and had Jamie. Now Jamie has all these problems. Dear Aunt Blabby, I think Jamie's problems are all my fault!

(signed)
Guilty

Dear Aunt Blabby,

  I have this problem. Yesterday, two people I know were talking about my brother and making fun of the noises he makes. They didn't see me, but I didn't stop them or stick up for my own brother! I feel bad and don't understand why I didn't stick up for him.

(signed)
Torn-Up Inside

Dear Aunt Blabby,

  My sister doesn't get asked to friends' houses or birthday parties like I do. She gets mad at me or Mom when I get to do something she can't. What should I do?

(signed)
Need a Life of My Own

Dear Aunt Blabby,

  My sister always complains to me about her spina bifida. She then upsets me by saying, "Why do you think God made me different?" I really don't know what to answer.

(signed)
Feeling Guilty

Dear Aunt Blabby,

  When I was little, I used to tell my parents that I wanted my sister Jenna to live with me when we grew up. Aunt Blabby, now I think I don't want her to always live with me. Is that O.K.? Where would she live? By the way, I love my sister a lot!

(signed)
Don't Know

Dear Aunt Blabby,

  My brother is always getting into my room and totally trashing it. My mom doesn't make him clean it up. She says he can't clean it the way it is supposed to be cleaned. Mom says she doesn't have time to do it by herself. What do I do with him? And what do I do about my room?

(signed)
Miss Compulsively Neat

Dear Aunt Blabby,

  My older brother Andrew has epilepsy. His seizures started when he was 10. I'm going to be 10 soon. Do you think I'll have seizures like my brother?

(signed)
A Little Worried

Dear Aunt Blabby,

You would think that the only kid that mattered in our family is Evan, my brother with Down syndrome. Whatever our family does, we do for Evan. On our vacations we go to these Down syndrome meetings. At dinner it's always Down syndrome this, Down syndrome that. My parents are always at some meeting about Evan or Down syndrome. Evan is an O.K. brother, I guess, but I'm sick of everything always being for him.

(signed)
Too Much

Dear Aunt Blabby,

My summer is ruined!! I was looking forward to sleeping in every morning and having fun and goofing off. My brother, who has autism, still has to go to school all summer. My mom makes me go with her when she drops him off. We have to get up at 7:00 A.M. and drive for an hour! Mom says I'm not old enough to stay by myself. There goes my time off. What can I do?

(signed)
Tired of Traveling

Dear Aunt Blabby,

I'm 11 years old and my brother is 14. My brother has lots of seizures even though he takes his medication. My parents don't want to leave him alone at home so we never get to go anywhere like the mall, the movies, or out to dinner. Mom can't find anyone to babysit for my brother because everybody is afraid of his seizures. Why do I have to suffer and not have any fun like all my friends?

(signed)
Feeling Trapped

Dear Aunt Blabby,

My sister has something called ADHD. My mom says sugar makes her jump around. Just because she can't have sugar, we have no candy, pop, or cookies in our house. Mom says if I have it then she will want it too. That's not fair!

(signed)
Sweet Tooth

Dear Aunt Blabby,

This will sound weird, but I wish my brother had Down syndrome. Some of the kids at our Sibshop talk about how cool their sibs are even if they have Downs. My brother has ADHD and is a pain. All the time! It is hard to find anything positive to say about him.

(signed)
Jealous

Dear Aunt Blabby,

I have a younger brother who has a disability. We go to the same school. Whenever I want to go to a school basketball or football game with my friends, my parents make me take my brother with me. Aunt Blabby, I love my brother, but I don't think this is fair. Does that seem right to you?

(signed)
This Sister Needs Help

Dear Aunt Blabby,

My sister who has Down syndrome never gets punished like me. My mom is unfair and gives in to her moods and stubbornness too much. What can I do?

(signed)
Miss Treated

Dear Aunt Blabby,

Sometimes I feel like I'm chained to my younger brother. He always wants to go where I go and play with my friends. My brother has cerebral palsy, uses a wheelchair, and can be a real pain. Why won't my mom let me go by myself?

(signed)
Chained

Dear Aunt Blabby,

I'm really frustrated. My sister is always kicking. I know it is part of her disability because she is really hyper. But what can I do? She just gets me so angry!!! Help!!!

(signed)
Frustrated! GRRR!

Dear Aunt Blabby,

I'm confused. My sister has many behavior problems. I love my little sister and I'd like to play with her, but I'm afraid of her because she sometimes hurts me. She bites me and punches me. My mom says I shouldn't hit her back and I should play with her. What should I do?

(signed)
Want to Play

Dear Aunt Blabby,

My brother, who has autism, sometimes hits kids when we are at the playground. These kids get mad and want to hit him back. What should I do?

(signed)
All Mixed Up

Dear Aunt Blabby,

My brother has mental retardation. Sometimes, he gets very angry and throws things. Now that he is bigger, I am afraid he might hurt me or someone else. What should I do?

(signed)
Tired of Ducking

Dear Aunt Blabby,

My sister has autism. She wakes me up all night and breaks all my toys, and I can't even have friends over because she's so mean to them. What can I do?

(signed)
What's the Limit?

Dear Aunt Blabby,

Sometimes I can't understand my friends. They complain when their little brothers or sisters bug them. I don't see what the big deal is. They should try living with my sister Mary. Mary has autism! Then they wouldn't complain! Know what I mean?

(signed)
Life Is Not So Bad

Dear Aunt Blabby,

Most people probably wouldn't think that Michael could teach you much—he has so many problems and can't even talk. But he has really taught me a lot about caring and love and stuff like that. Do you think that is weird?

(signed)
Learned a Lot

Dear Aunt Blabby,

Sometimes kids look at Lisa and say, "Is that your sister?" "Who is she?" They think that because Lisa looks different that she is different on the inside. But she is just like us inside. She doesn't want to be stared at and laughed at or ignored. Am I the only one who feels this way?

(signed)
Cut It Out!

Dear Aunt Blabby,

My friends say my brother can't do very much, but you should see what he did at Special Olympics! Wow! I didn't know he could run so fast! It may sound funny to some people but I am really proud of what my brother can do!

(signed)
One Proud Brother

Dear Aunt Blabby,

To tell the truth, my brother Mark is a butt most of the time, but I hate it when kids pick on him because of his disability. Sometimes I have to defend him. Am I the only one?

(signed)
Somebody Has to Stick Up for Him!

The following Dear Aunt Blabby letters are for siblings of children who have cancer or other chronic illnesses.

Dear Aunt Blabby,

I'm 14 years old, and I have an 8-year-old sister with medical troubles. I'm always expected to "understand" and "know better" and "act like an adult" and "think of what your sister's been through." I'm just 14! Does that seem fair to you?

(signed)
Give Me a Break

Dear Aunt Blabby,

Kids at my school know that my sister has cancer. Most of them are pretty nice about it, except for the jerks who ask, "Is your sister going to die?" Aunt Blabby, what can I say to them?

(signed)
They're So Rude!

Dear Aunt Blabby,

It seems like everything has changed since Jennie got leukemia. My friends won't even come to my house anymore. They say they don't want to catch her leukemia and die. What can I do?

(signed)
Home Alone

Dear Aunt Blabby,

Michael, my little brother, has a brain tumor. He needs to spend a lot of time in the hospital. When he does, I have to stay over at my aunt's house. I'm sick of staying there. None of my cousins are even my age. Any suggestions?

(signed)
I Wanna Go Home

Dear Aunt Blabby,

My brother has cancer and is on these drugs. They are supposed to help him, but they made him lose most of his hair and now he's really fat. People stare at him when they see him. I know I shouldn't be embarrassed about how he looks, but I am. What can I do?

(signed)
Embarrassed

Dear Aunt Blabby,

I am sick of my sister being sick. I know she has cancer, and I know cancer is serious, but I am tired of it. We can't go on a vacation because my sister might get sick. I can't bring friends over because they might make her sick. Everything is for her. What about me?

(signed)
Sick of It!

Dear Aunt Blabby,

I know this sounds weird, but sometimes I wish I had cancer too. You should see all the stuff people give my brother! He gets Nintendo systems, videos, expensive drawing sets, you name it. Every once in a while they'll give me and my sister a little something, but nothing like the stuff our brother gets.

(signed)
It's Not Fair

Dear Aunt Blabby,

My sister has cancer and it's really hard on all of us, especially my mom and dad. I try not to bother them with my troubles. They have enough problems with Michelle. I'm glad I can write to you when I have a problem, but I'd rather talk to my parents.

(signed)
Don't Know Where to Go

Dear Aunt Blabby,

Since we learned that my brother has a tumor, I worry all of the time. I worry that my brother might die in the middle of the night. I worry that the doctors or my parents are keeping secrets from me about David. It is getting hard to do schoolwork! Aunt Blabby, what should I do?

(signed)
Really Worried

Dear Aunt Blabby,

My sister has cancer and I think I have cancer too. A year ago, her legs hurt a lot and we took her to the hospital. That is when we found out that she has cancer. When I woke up this morning, my legs hurt. Can you catch cancer?

(signed)
Scared Stiff

Index

Page numbers followed by *f* indicate figures; those followed by *t* indicate tables.